CHRIST THE LIGHT

CHRIST THE LIGHT

THE THEOLOGY OF LIGHT AND ILLUMINATION IN THOMAS AQUINAS

DAVID L. WHIDDEN III

Fortress Press
Minneapolis

CHRIST THE LIGHT
The Theology of Light and Illumination in Thomas Aquinas

Cover design: Alisha Lofgren

Library of Congress Cataloging-in-Publication Data
Print ISBN: 978-1-4514-7013-0
eBook ISBN: 978-1-4514-7232-5

The paper used in this publication meets the minimum requirements of American National Standard for Information Sciences — Permanence of Paper for Printed Library Materials, ANSI Z329.48-1984.

Manufactured in the U.S.A.

This book was produced using PressBooks.com, and PDF rendering was done by PrinceXML.

For Alicia
and
all those who follow in the light of Christ

CONTENTS

List of Abbreviations

Ad Rom.	*Expositio super Epistolam ad Romanos*
CEG	*Contra errores Graecorum*
DA	*Sententia libri De anima*
De Caelo	*In libros De Caelo et Mundo*
De Causis	*Super librum De causis*
De Hebd.	*Expositio Libri Boetii De Ebdomadibus*
De Sensu	*Sententia libri De sensu et sensate*
De Trin.	*Super Boetium De Trinitate*
DDN	*Super librum Dionysii De divinis nominibus*
DM	*Quaestiones disputatae de malo*
DP	*Quaestiones disputatae de potentia*
DV	*Quaestiones disputatae de veritate*
In Col.	*Super ad Colossenses*
In I Cor.	*Super I ad Corinthios*
In II Cor.	*Super II ad Corinthios*
In Eph.	*Super ad Ephesios*
In Gal.	*Super ad Galatas*
In Heb.	*Super ad Hebraeos*
In Iob	*Expositio super Iob ad litteram*
In Ioh.	*Lectura super evangelium S. Ioannis*
In Psalmos	*Postilla super Psalmos*
In I Tim.	*Super I ad Timotheum*
Lectura romana	*Lectura romana in primum Sententiarum Petri Lombardi*
Meta.	*Sententia super Metaphysicam*
PA	*Sententia superi Posteriora Analytica*
Phys.	*Commentaria in octo libros Physicorum Aristotelis*
PL	*Patrologia Latina* (Migne)
Quodl.	*Quaestiones de quodlibet I–XII*
SCG	*Summa contra Gentiles*
Sent.	*Scriptum super libros Sententiarum*
ST	*Summa Theologiae*

For a list of editions and translations, see the bibliography. All translations will be taken from the English versions listed in the bibliography unless marked otherwise.

Acknowledgements

This book had its material origin in my doctoral dissertation, completed at Southern Methodist University under the direction of Bruce Marshall. At the same time, its origin extends further than the dissertation, as I had been thinking about Christ the light since my undergraduate days, in one form or another. When I was a master's student, William Abraham shared with me an article connecting the theology of light in Gregory Palamas with that of Jonathan Edwards; it was in this article that I first began to realize that light had an important history in Christian doctrine, a history that needed to be investigated and recovered for contemporary theology, which was the project I outlined as I applied for doctoral programs. In the SMU doctoral program, Robin Lovin was kind enough to spend a great deal of time helping me read some of the important philosophical and source material regarding light, but it was a providential encounter with Bruce Marshall one summer that inspired me to take his seminar on Aquinas, where I began to explore the theme of light in Aquinas and came to realize that I was in largely unexplored territory. I am grateful to all three of these scholars and teachers for patiently guiding me through this journey and for their willingness to let me pursue the project by following my own vision, so that I could develop my own scholarly voice. I am also grateful to Mark Johnson, of Marquette, whose feedback after my dissertation defense helped me frame this work in a way that I hope is helpful. If there are any errors in this book, they are my responsibility and are not a reflection of the quality of the teaching or learning provided by these scholars.

I am also grateful for the institutional support that made this book possible. Much of the research for this book was conducted at Bridwell Library at SMU, where the excellent staff made every effort to make sure that I had all of the resources necessary to complete my research. Upon arrival at my first academic position at Our Lady of the Lake College in Baton Rouge, the library staff there has also been fully supportive of my research and has tracked down numerous obscure articles and books for me. Our Lady of the Lake also generously provided a course reduction, which greatly aided my efforts to complete this project. I also benefited greatly from a grant from the Wabash Center for Teaching and Learning in Religion and Theology, which provided support that allowed me to spend a large part of a summer focused only on this book.

Likewise, I am grateful to the many people at Fortress Press who have worked to make this book possible.

But the greatest debt of gratitude I owe is to my wife, Alicia, who provided the light, love, and friendship that made this work possible. There are not enough words to describe what her love and support means to me, so I will not try, but rather leave the whole work as a testament to her and to what Christ has done through her in my life. This book is dedicated to her and to all others who follow in the light of Christ.

Introduction

Christ the Light

Every year, Christians around the world gather to mark the Easter Vigil, the liturgical expression of Christ's death and resurrection. In Catholic parishes the liturgy begins with the *Lucernarium*, a liturgical exploration of light. The liturgy begins with the people in the dark, holding unlit candles. A priest then lights a fire, blesses it, takes the paschal candle, and inscribes a cross on it. Once the priest has prepared the candle, he lights it from the fire and says, "May the light of Christ rising in glory dispel the darkness of our hearts and minds."[1] The priest and deacons use the paschal candle to light their own candles and then share their light with the remainder of the congregation. While this happens, a deacon processes the paschal candle around the people, singing, "the Light of Christ, the Light of Christ, the Light of Christ," as the people respond, "Thanks be to God."[2] What begins in darkness and silence ends in light and song, as the people sing the *Exsultet*, which includes lines referencing the light of Christ, such as "This is the night that with a pillar of fire banished the darkness of sin . . . this is the night of which it is written: the night shall be as bright as day, dazzling is the night for me, and full of gladness . . . Christ your Son, who coming back from death's domain, has shed his peaceful light on humanity . . ."[3]

For those who have experienced it, this opening section of the Easter Vigil is one of the most beautiful and powerful expressions of Christian worship, and at the very heart of the *Lucernarium* is the claim that Christ is the Light. But what does the claim that Christ is the Light mean? Is light a dead metaphor that no longer has any meaning? Is light an empty symbol that points to ancient modes of thought that no longer have any relevance today? Or is there something to the claim that Christ is the Light that is central to the Christian understanding of who Jesus Christ is and what he accomplished in his life, death, and resurrection? What might it mean to follow in the light of Christ? This book will investigate how one of the Church's most important theologians, Thomas Aquinas, used light language to answer those questions

1. U. S. C. C. B., *The Roman Missal, 3rd Altar Edition* (Catholic Book Publishing Corp., 2011), 200.

2. Ibid.

3. Ibid., 207–9.

by exploring and explaining the mission of the Son, the second person of the Trinity. In explicating Aquinas's thoughts on the theology of light we will see how light appears consistently in his writings across all of his theology; to explore Aquinas's theology of light is to explore the whole of his theology.

It should be no surprise if the theological language of light is mostly a dead metaphor in contemporary Christianity, unable to stir our minds to contemplate the connections between God and light. If Christians are unable to stand in awe of how Christ the Light illumines our minds by teaching us who God is, of how we are to love God, and of how we are to live with respect to God, it is because we have become unable to see the light that is all around us.

At a sheer physical level, Thomas Edison's invention of the electric light bulb means that humans have been able to make light a commodity, something that we can easily produce so as to conquer the darkness on our own. Modern humans, especially those in the developed world, have no fear of the dark, and we rarely consider light with any awe and instead focus on light as something to be explored for instrumental purposes. As with much of the rest of the natural world that humans have conquered, light no longer captures a special place in our imaginations, no longer points to a reality beyond our own, and no longer sets the boundaries on human interaction.

At a philosophical level, light and illumination began to disappear from the theological vocabulary in the late medieval period,[4] but its real descent into theological oblivion began with the Enlightenment, which co-opted light language for its own rhetorical purposes and limited the idea of illumination to what humans could know only by thinking for themselves. Those who relied on revelation or authority were deemed to be in the dark, while those who lived by reason alone were the ones who were enlightened. Immanuel Kant's famous essay, "What Is Enlightenment?,"[5] which made these arguments, signaled the end of light and illumination as meaningful and effective symbols in the Christian tradition.[6] Now, when the *Lucernarium* is completed, we turn

4. Robert Pasnau, "Henry of Ghent and the Twilight of Divine Illumination," *Review of Metaphysics* 49, no. 1 (1995): 49–76; Lydia Schumacher, *Divine Illumination: The History and Future of Augustine's Theory of Knowledge* (Malden, MA: Wiley-Blackwell, 2011), 181–216.

5. Immanuel Kant, "What Is Enlightenment?" in *What Is Enlightenment: Eighteenth-Century Answers and Twentieth-Century Questions*, ed. James Schmidt (Berkeley: University of California Press, 1996), 58–64.

6. I find it interesting that Pope Francis's first papal encyclical, *Lumen Fidei*, which does an outstanding job of reclaiming light imagery in the service of the church, places the blame for this at Nietzsche's feet, rather than Kant, who preceded Nietzsche. See *Lumen Fidei* sections 2–3.

the lights back on and ignore light with reference to God for another year, or at least until Epiphany, the other Christian feast of light.

In an attempt to recapture and explore the theological language of light in the Christian tradition, we will investigate how Thomas Aquinas uses light language throughout his theology. The goal is to use Aquinas's thought as a means of reopening and reengaging light language in the larger Christian tradition. Light language pervades all of Aquinas's work, yet it has been neglected as a means of entering into his thought.[7]

In looking at Aquinas's use of light I am attempting to meet two goals. First, light language can be found in every aspect of Aquinas's work, from his description of theology, to his understanding of God, to his discussion of angelic and human nature, to his treatment of morality, to his comprehensive Christology. By tracking the use of light language we can get a fairly comprehensive overview of Aquinas's systematic theology. By approaching Aquinas's theology through this key image, we get a broader view of his theology and so this book can serve as something of a partial introduction to his thought through the thematic exploration of light. The second goal of this book is to reinvigorate our understanding of light as a theologically rich image that speaks to the deep reality of the Christian experience of the revelation of God made through the life, death, and resurrection of Jesus Christ. While the first goal looks backward, it does so for the purpose of restoring to contemporary use the meaningful language that has in the past served the church so well; Aquinas can help make light theologically meaningful to us. The book will primarily focus on the first goal, but the constructive purpose found in the second goal is implicit in the whole work. Light language in the past is only interesting if we can reclaim it and use it with all of its theological richness in the future.

Why Aquinas?

For some it may seem strange to use Aquinas as a means to explore and reinvigorate light language in the Christian tradition. His contemporary, the great Franciscan theologian, Bonaventure, is well known for his descriptions of illumination. Likewise, Aquinas's predecessors in the Patristic period deployed light language effectively throughout their work. Why Aquinas instead of one of his contemporaries or predecessors?

7. As Lydia Schumacher points out, there has been very little done to give a systematic account of Aquinas's theology of light and illumination. Schumacher, *Divine Illumination: The History and Future of Augustine's Theory of Knowledge* (Oxford: Oxford University Press, 2011), 174.

Aquinas works well in this regard for several reasons. First, because Aquinas was deeply immersed in Patristic writings, he serves as an excellent example of someone who retrieved the light language from the past for the purposes that were required for his own time. His engagement with John Chrysostom, Origen, Jerome, Augustine, and, above all, Pseudo-Dionysius, makes Aquinas an excellent mediator of light language to theologians of his own day and to ours. Second, the modern renewal of Thomistic studies that has emerged since Leo XIII's *Aeterni Patris* in 1879 (in section seventeen he even praises Aquinas using light language: "like the sun he heated the world with the warmth of his virtues and filled it with the splendor of his teaching")[8] has made Aquinas's thought relevant to contemporary theologians as well. Aquinas remains an important theologian in our own time, and engaging with the fecundity of his thought continues to provide theologians with important theological and philosophical resources for their work. Aquinas, then, serves as a bridge that links Christian theology with the past and with the present, especially with regard to light. A third reason to approach an understanding of light through the thought of Aquinas is because he serves as an excellent model for the integration of scripture and theology. While he is best known for the *Summa Theologiae*, his main academic work was as a commentator on Christian scripture and his commentaries on scripture offer surprising insights into his understanding of light. Finally, Aquinas also serves as an excellent example of a theologian who used the best science available to him as a means of understanding God. While medieval understandings of light may seem antiquated to us, Aquinas's methodology is still relevant, so by attending to how his understanding of light shapes his theology we might see how we can follow his method without having to embrace his medieval physics.

Why Light?

A second question that might arise is why we should focus on light in Aquinas's thought. After all, Aquinas uses a variety of different images in his work that might be fruitfully explored instead of that of light. He often uses heat and health, to name just two frequent images, as explanatory models that help us understand his thought, so why choose light?

First, Aquinas considers corporeal light—the light made on the first day of creation—to be of a higher spiritual nature than any other created object.[9]

8. Pope Leo XIII, "Aeterni Patris," August 4, 1879, http://www.vatican.va/holy_father/leo_xiii/encyclicals/documents/hf_l-xiii_enc_04081879_aeterni-patris_en.html.

Second, Aquinas makes a direct link between physical and spiritual light, where the light we see with our eyes is a "certain image" of spiritual light.[10] Third, he goes even further and describes intelligible light as an attribute of God, and here he does not seem to be speaking metaphorically.[11] For Aquinas, light tells us something absolutely crucial about God.

Additionally, half a century ago M. D. Chenu spelled out the importance of investigating Aquinas's light language. He describes the variety of images that Aquinas uses, and Chenu argues that of all of those images, "the image most frequently recurring, because the most spontaneously arising, is the analogy of light used in describing intelligence."[12] Chenu goes on to describe the payoff and method for approaching the investigation of a particular image:

> It has been justly observed that an attentive examination of the images employed by Saint Thomas would open the way to a genuine deeper penetration into the understanding of his thought. This is an indication, therefore, that these images should be reinvestigated, imagined anew, in line *with the outlook customary to the medieval mind*; that they should be followed up in their refined, suppled, interknit forms; that they should be freed from elements alien to what they would convey; that they be dematerialized.[13]

While Chenu pointed to the importance of Aquinas's use of light imagery almost half a century ago, very little has been done since then to systematically investigate this image. There are two reasons for this neglect. First, Aquinas is typically understood to have rejected Augustine's theory of divine illumination (TDI). The standard account of Augustine's TDI understands Augustine to have argued that any act of human knowing requires a new divine illumination in order for the knowledge to be truthful; God acts extrinsically on the human in any act of truthful knowing.[14] In an enormously influential article, Etienne Gilson described why Aquinas felt a need to criticize and amend Augustine's

9. ST I 69.1.

10. *In Ioh.* 8.2 §1142.

11. DDN 4.3 §304.

12. Marie-Dominique Chenu, *Toward Understanding Saint Thomas*, trans. A.-M. Landry and D. Hughes (Chicago: H. Regnery Co., 1964), 171.

13. Ibid., 172. My emphasis.

14. I am simplifying this summary a bit, as there is significant scholarly discussion on just what Augustine understood illumination to be. As Rudolph Allers pointed out in "St. Augustine's Doctrine on Illumination," *Franciscan Studies* 12 (1952): 27, "This lack of agreement is largely the result of the scant explanation St. Augustine himself gives of his idea."

TDI.[15] Gilson's argument has generally held sway, with the consequence that scholars have neglected Aquinas's understanding of illumination or have only treated it from a philosophical perspective.[16] If Aquinas rejected Augustine's TDI, his theology of illumination, understood as operating intrinsically, is often taken as unimportant. The main exception to this neglect is the attention to Aquinas's description of the agent intellect, but this is rarely treated theologically, and usually understood as an adoption of Aristotle over Augustine and as a response to Avicennian ideas of an extrinsic agent intellect. Thirteenth-century Franciscan scholars, most especially Bonaventure, are usually understood as having more interesting things to say about illumination.

A second reason for this neglect is Aquinas's rejection of the light metaphysics of his time. Both Robert Grosseteste and Bonaventure had developed a light metaphysics that held light to be a substantial form. As we will see later, Aquinas rejects this position for several reasons in favor of a more restrained understanding of light. But, as with the case with Augustine's TDI, because Aquinas rejects this alternative, he is often seen as having nothing interesting to say about light. When we combine his rejection of Augustine's TDI with his rejection of the light metaphysics of the thirteenth century, we can begin to see why scholars have largely ignored his teachings on illumination, especially theologians; several of Aquinas's contemporaries would seem to provide more fruitful opportunities for engagement with a theology of light.

Yet, as Chenu argued, light is a pervasive theme across Aquinas's work. Aquinas may not have held Augustine's TDI and he may have rejected thirteenth-century light metaphysics, but this is not to say that Aquinas has nothing important to say about light and illumination. In fact, as I hope to show, Aquinas has many interesting things to say about light and illumination, especially when viewed theologically rather than philosophically. Light, then, provides important insights into Aquinas's theology because it appears across the whole of his theology and because it represents an important contact between the spiritual and material worlds. As Chenu points out, however, we

15. Étienne Gilson, "Pourquoi Saint Thomas a critiqué Saint Augustin," *Archives d'Histoire Doctrinale et Littéraire du Moyen Âge* 1 (1926–27): 5–127.

16. Thus Stephen Marrone, in his excellent two-volume study of illumination, *The Light of Thy Countenance: Science and Knowledge of God in the Thirteenth Century; Volume One, A Doctrine of Divine Illumination* (Leiden and Boston: Brill, 2001), which focuses on the Augustinian tradition of illumination in the thirteenth century, does not treat Aquinas's theory of divine illumination at all, though he does mention Aquinas. Even though he does not engage Aquinas directly, his study is enormously helpful for understanding the theological and philosophical issues that would have influenced Aquinas.

have to understand light on Aquinas's terms, not ours, in order to understand the full import of the image.

Central Arguments

The argument of this book revolves around three interlocking theses, which I will introduce here and develop over the course of the book. First, for Aquinas the proper understanding of illumination is that it "is the manifestation of truth with reference to God, who illumines every intellect."[17] All too often discussions of illumination with regard to Aquinas focus on our ability to know objects and realities that are evident to our senses and fit with our natural abilities. Part of this focus on our natural light is a holdover from Augustine's theory of illumination, which seems to suggest that we need illumination to know any truth, for instance that I would need illumination to know that there is a tree outside of my window and illumination to know about the way the bark, roots, and leaves work together or any other of the natural features of that tree.[18] For Aquinas, however, illumination properly understood provides us truths about those realities with reference to God. So while I can know those natural truths of the tree by the light of nature, illumination properly understood provides the knower with the idea that the tree was created by God, who serves as both its beginning and end, and that the tree was given by God for human flourishing. Illumination with respect to the tree might even extend further, teaching us that humans fell into sin by taking the fruit from a tree and that humans were restored to life by the death of the Incarnate Son on a tree. None of these theological truths can we know under our own power, without divine illumination.

This leads to the second thesis, which is that Aquinas posits three kinds of illumination, all of which find their origin in God's light: the light of nature, the light of faith or grace, and the light of glory.[19] Philosophers and theologians have for the last century focused on the light of nature, particularly with regard to the idea of illumination, while generally neglecting the light of faith/grace and the light of glory. Much of this important philosophical and theological work finds its origin in an effort to find in earlier Christian

17. ST I 106.3 and I 107.2.

18. Lydia Schumacher has recently called this understanding of Augustine's theory of divine illumination into question, arguing that Augustine's TDI is intrinsic, and so Aquinas is the best interpreter of Augustine in this regard. Schumacher, *Divine Illumination: The History and Future of Augustine's Theory of Knowledge*, 25–65.

19. ST I 106.1 ad 2.

sources philosophically and theologically acceptable ways to understand human knowing. These efforts to develop a robust Christian epistemology in the face of alternative modern and postmodern approaches have been helpful, but often neglect the larger role and understanding of illumination in Aquinas's theology; they only tell one-third of the story. One of the goals of this book is to show how the natural light of the intellect is only one aspect of human knowing and that for the human intellect to fulfill its purpose, which is to know and love God, it requires more than just the natural light, but also the light of grace and the light of glory. Aquinas does not so much have a theory of divine illumination as he has a theory of divine illuminations.

The third thesis builds on the previous two and is the most important of the three. The central idea in this book is that the illumination of our minds is primarily the mission of the Son,[20] who became incarnate for our sakes and who manifests the truth about God for our salvation. For Aquinas's theology of illumination to be properly Christian, it must be rooted in the life, death, and resurrection of Jesus Christ. Because of the overemphasis on the natural light of the intellect among Thomistic philosophers, this key aspect of Aquinas's theology of illumination has been eclipsed. Yet when we attend to what Aquinas says in both the *Summa Theologiae* and his scriptural commentaries, we will find that illumination properly understood is not the product of a vaguely theistic God, but rather is found in the mission of the Son. Christ is the light.

This third thesis came as a complete surprise to me in the course of my research. I had originally planned to do one chapter on the illumination provided by Christ, but as my research proceeded it became obvious that it was the light of Christ which makes possible our ability to do theology, to know God, to live a moral life, and so on. Everywhere Aquinas touched on the theology of light with respect to humans, Christ was there providing the illumination we need. Theologians are beginning to pay attention to the Christological elements of illumination, in particular Lydia Schumacher, who has recently made the case that Augustinian illumination must be understood in its proper Trinitarian and Christological context, but for the most part the illumination provided by Christ has been neglected by contemporary theologians. This book is one attempt to rectify that oversight.

20. ST I 43.5 ad 2 and 3.

The Approach

Let me briefly describe how we will engage these issues. For the most part we will follow the course of the *Summa Theologiae*, beginning with the illumination necessary for and provided by the practice of *sacra doctrina*, moving to the role of light in our theological language, in the life of God, in creation, in morality, and finally concluding with a discussion of some Christological elements of illumination. There will be two exceptions to following the plan of the *Summa*. First, after introducing the question of *sacra doctrina*, I will discuss the physics of light in Aquinas's thought, with the goal of understanding how Aquinas's medieval physics of light is different from modern physics, which will allow us to understand his use of light language more accurately. Second, while the book ends with a chapter on Christ the light, all of the other chapters, with the exception of the aforementioned chapter on physics, will also end with discussion of the Christological elements of light with regard to each particular chapter's concerns. The purpose in incorporating into each chapter the role of Christ in our illumination is to strengthen my overall case that Aquinas's theology of illumination is deeply Christological by showing the pervasive place of Christ in his theology of light. The Son gives us the light of nature in creation, we acquire the light of grace through his teaching and receive grace in the sacraments, and it is the Son who makes the light of glory possible for us and enables the beatific vision.

While the book will roughly follow the plan of the *Summa*, it does not rely only on the *Summa Theologiae* for its argument. For Aquinas, one of the ways that God's illumining self-knowledge is made available to humans is through the revelation of Christian scripture, and so, much of this book incorporates Aquinas's thought on the theology of light as described in his commentaries on scripture. For the larger part of the last century Aquinas's scriptural commentaries have been neglected as sources for understanding his theology; only recently have students of Aquinas begun to mine his commentaries for their rich theological descriptions of the Christian faith. That the genre of commentary seems less systematic than that of disputed questions does not mean that scriptural commentaries are any less relevant for those who are interested in exploring Aquinas's theology.[21] In several cases we will see how Aquinas's scriptural commentaries allow us to understand from a different perspective a topic he takes up in the *Summa*. Of all of these commentaries

21. Though if we pay attention to the way that Aquinas organizes his scriptural commentaries and divides the texts, we can see that in many ways his scriptural commentaries are quite systematic. One wonders if the idea that scriptural commentaries are somehow nonsystematic is a modern conceit.

on scripture, the one that will come to the fore is his commentary on the Gospel of John, which was written roughly at the same time as the *Summa*. In his commentary on John's Gospel, which begins with a rich exploration of the *Logos* as light, Aquinas fully develops his Christology of light and does so in conversation with other important voices in the Christian tradition, most especially Augustine.

What This Is Not

The primary goal of this book is to provide systematic account of Aquinas's theology of light by roughly following the plan of the *Summa Theologiae* in conversation with his scriptural commentaries. This task is sufficiently complicated in itself because of its scope, so it necessitated making some choices about what not to include. First, as is not uncommon in the study of Aquinas, this book will focus on his later and more mature systematic work, the *Summa Theologiae*. There will be cases where some of his earlier works, such as his commentary on Peter Lombard's *Sentences*, will be engaged because those earlier works provide a perspective that is lacking in a later work or because it clarifies a concept, but for the most part the emphasis will be on Aquinas's mature thought. Second, this book is meant to serve as a description of Aquinas's theology of light, so by choice I have limited my discussion about some of the more significant contemporary disputes about Aquinas in favor of describing Aquinas's understanding of light; the emphasis is primarily exegetical. In doing so I am under no illusion that my account is anything other than my own interpretation of Aquinas. My own questions and interests are always in the background and so shape this study. I wrote this because the topic is relevant and interesting both to specialists and nonspecialists in Aquinas, but I have intentionally focused on describing his theology of light.

Finally, one element that will seem to be missing from Aquinas's theology of light is the Holy Spirit. Aquinas has sometimes been accused of having a pneumatological deficit and of ignoring the important role of the Holy Spirit in the Christian life; the virtual absence of the Holy Spirit in this book (with a rare exception in chapter 4) might feed into this perception. The absence of the Spirit, however, is because of the way that Aquinas understands the missions of the Son and the Spirit. While the mission of the Son, as I have already indicated, is to illumine our intellects, the mission of the Spirit is to inflame our affections with love for God.[22] Whenever one sees Aquinas mention the role of inflaming

22. ST I 45.3 ad 2 and 3.

our affections for God, there the Spirit is. This book, then, only covers one of the two divine missions, and a book detailing the mission of the Spirit would be a nice companion to this one. For Aquinas, knowledge of God alone is not sufficient for our salvation, for we also need to love what we come to know about God. Nevertheless, the two missions are related and relevant to each other. As we come to know more about God we come to love God more, and as we come to love God more we want to know more about God.

So this book is written to help us know more about how Christ comes to give us knowledge about God, to make God more manifest to us. It will be up to the Holy Spirit to inflame our affections in response to this knowledge.

1

The Gift of Illumination

The *Principium* of Light

In the late spring of 1256, a young Dominican priest stepped in front of his colleagues at the University of Paris to give his inaugural lecture, *Rigans Montes*, as a Master in Theology. While his intellectual talents were already well known and some of his work had already been made available to his contemporaries, as the young Thomas Aquinas stepped to the lectern he was formally embarking upon a public career that would shape the theology of the church for the next eight centuries. In this first public lecture Aquinas would describe an understanding of theology and the task of the teacher—what we might think of as his "teaching philosophy"—that he followed for the rest of his career, so that "in this exposition we can see luminously the ideal he is setting himself for his life's work."[1] One of the key themes of his talk, and a theme he would develop for the rest of his career, was that of light and divine illumination. The purpose of this book is to follow that theme and attempt to understand the theology of Thomas Aquinas with regard to the light language he deploys throughout his work.

One of the key features of Aquinas's work that quickly becomes evident is how important beginnings are to him. Most of his works have substantial prologues in which he details either what he is doing, with regard to his original works, or what he thinks another author is doing with regard to his scriptural and philosophical commentaries. One ignores Aquinas's introductory comments and his division of the text of a work at the risk of misunderstanding what follows as he expounds on his introduction.[2] Further, with regard to how one comes to deep knowledge (*scientia*) of a subject, Aquinas thinks one must work toward an understanding of the key principles from which one begins.

1. Simon Tugwell, *Albert & Thomas: Selected Writings*, The Classics of Western Spirituality (New York: Paulist, 1988), 270.

2. John F. Boyle, "St. Thomas Aquinas and Sacred Scripture," *Pro Ecclesia* 4, no. 1 (1995): 100–101.

Principles are a kind of intellectual beginning or starting place in the "order of teaching"[3] for Aquinas, even if he acknowledges that we often have to work backward to get to them.

It is worth noting, then, that the technical name for Aquinas's inaugural lecture was *principium*, a word with a variety of implications for Aquinas. In his Trinitarian discussion of whether it is adequate to call the Father the *principium*, Aquinas pithily suggests that "anything from which something proceeds in any way is said to be a *principium*."[4] In a more extended discussion of the term, fittingly found at the beginning (*principium*) of his commentary on the Gospel of John, Aquinas notes five possible meanings for *principium*, but all of them imply "an order of one thing to another,"[5] and so can be found in ordered things such as quantity, time, teaching, and the production of things, and in the mind of those who generate things. The key *principium* here is the third one, of teaching. For Aquinas our very ability to learn is Christological, proceeding from both Christ's divinity and his humanity. With respect to Christ's divinity, "the beginning and principle of our wisdom with respect to our nature is Christ," since our natures are formed by the "Wisdom and Word of God"; with respect to Christ's humanity, Christ is our *principium* of teaching through his incarnation.[6] Any learning that we have finds its beginning in Christ's divinity, through our created natures, and through his humanity, that is, through his teaching of us in the flesh. With respect to teaching, the principles from which Aquinas starts are decidedly Christological. Indeed, as Aquinas tells us in *Rigans Montes*, Christ is "the teacher of teachers."[7]

One of my key theses is that Aquinas's understanding of illumination is not just broadly theistic, but primarily Christological. Philosophers and theologians have for too long focused on Aquinas's discussions of illumination in his

3. ST prologue.

4. ST I 33.1: "[T]he word 'principle' (*principium*) signifies only that from which another proceeds: since anything from which something proceeds in any way, we call a principle; and conversely."

5. *In Ioh.* I.1, §34: "Since the word *principium* implies a certain order of one thing to another, one can find a *principium* in all those things which have an order."

6. Ibid.: "Third, order is found in learning; and this in two ways: as to nature, and as to ourselves, and in both cases we can speak of a 'beginning': 'By this time you ought to be teachers' (Heb 5:12). As to nature, in Christian doctrine the beginning and principle of our wisdom is Christ, inasmuch as he is the Wisdom and Word of God, i.e., in his divinity. But as to ourselves, the beginning is Christ himself inasmuch as the Word has become flesh, i.e., by his incarnation." Cf. *In Ioh.* VIII.3, §1183.

7. *Rigans Montes*. Cf. ScG IV.13, "Necessarily, then, it is by the Word of God, which is the knowledge of the divine intellect, that every intellectual cognition is caused. Accordingly, we read in John (1:4): 'The life was the light of men,' that is, because the Word Himself who is life and in whom all things are life does, as a kind of light, make the truth manifest to the minds of men."

theological syntheses and disputed questions, without paying much, if any, attention to the Christological elements of illumination found in his commentaries on scripture, especially on the Gospel of John. Likewise, even in a work like the *Summa Theologiae*, writers seldom seem to get much further than the *Prima Pars* in their study of illumination, and they neglect key elements like the light of faith.[8] Yet to neglect Aquinas's commentary on scripture and his Christological focus is to ignore the fact that Aquinas consistently points to scripture as the starting point for theological reflection, as well as the priority of revelation over natural reason; by ignoring scripture we do violence to Aquinas's own understanding of what the theological enterprise entails. This is not to say that anything that has been said about Aquinas's understanding of illumination from the broadly theistic or philosophical view is incorrect, but only that it is incomplete. Nor is it to pit faith against reason, a position that Aquinas would reject. Aquinas's theory of illumination is, however, thoroughly Christological, as he suggests by saying that the effect of grace that derives from the invisible mission of the Son is the "illumination of the intellect."[9] This follows on a previous response, which connects the mission of the Son to the instruction of the intellect.[10] In both cases, the purpose of the illumination and instruction provided by the Son is to inflame our hearts with affection for God, which is the effect of grace given by the Holy Spirit. The temporal expression of divine light, and thus the primary human experience of illumination, reaches its perfection in the person of Jesus Christ.

Indeed, for Aquinas, one cannot love what one does not know, and the more one knows about a good worth loving, the more one can love that good. Aquinas's theological work can sometimes appear sterile or emotionally remote for those who are put off by the scholastic method or the questions that interested him, but for Aquinas the connection between knowledge and love is so intimate—rooted in the divine relations of the persons of the triune God and their temporal missions in the world—that his quest for deeper understanding of

8. See, for instance, Matthew Cuddeback, "Light and Form in St. Thomas Aquinas' Metaphysics of the Knower" (Ph.D. dissertation, Catholic University of America, 1998). This is an excellent and helpful dissertation on the metaphysical elements of Thomas's understanding of light, but intentionally focuses upon questions 44–119 of the *Prima Pars*. Cuddeback summarizes and extends his argument in "Thomas Aquinas on Divine Illumination and the Authority of the First Truth," *Nova et Vetera (English Edition)* 7 (2009): 579–602.

9. ST I 43.5 ad 3: "If we consider mission as regards the effect of grace, in this sense the two missions are united in the root which is grace, but are distinguished in the effects of grace, which consist in the illumination of the intellect and the kindling of the affection."

10. ST I 43.5 ad 2: "Thus the Son is sent not in accordance with every and any kind of intellectual perfection, but according to the intellectual illumination, which breaks forth into the affection of love."

God is best understood as a Christologically centered act of profound love and a love that continued to grow as he learned more. If "love follows knowledge,"[11] then Aquinas was a man deeply and profoundly in love with God, a love that was made possible through the illumination and teaching provided by Christ.

So while there is always a risk in reading too much into the different meanings of Latin terms, the multiple meanings of *principium* might lead us to reflect that this lecture was not just a beginning in the sense of an inauguration, but that it also spelled out many of the basic principles that would shape the rest of Aquinas's career as a teacher. In this beginning, we can see two key elements of Aquinas's thought that are relevant to his understanding of light. First, Aquinas shapes his *Rigans Montes* lecture in conversation with the three main theological sources that shape his theology of light—scripture, Augustine, and Pseudo-Dionysius. Second, Aquinas in several places suggests that theology itself is a function of God sharing his divine light with those who seek to do theology, so that sacred doctrine is a process of illumination from God to humans and humans to each other; as just suggested, this is accomplished through the teaching of Christ.

Theological Sources: Scripture and Tradition

Aquinas's use of light language in his theology is by no means unique; rather his work is the continuation of a long Christian tradition of speaking about God in terms of light. Scripturally, the account of creation at the beginning of Genesis had long been a topic of interest to theologians, with a particular concern being how to understand the creation of light on the first day and the creation of the sun, moon, and stars on the fourth day. The adoption of the psalmody as the basis of the daily office among monastic and other religious communities provided opportunities for theologians to reflect routinely on key verses such as Ps. 35:10,[12] "in your light we see light," and Ps. 4:7, "Let the light of your face shine on us, Lord."[13] The opening verses to the Gospel of John provided the basis for a Christological link between God and light, and the declaration in 1 John 1:5 that "God is light and in him there is no darkness at all" further warranted a close link between God and light in the tradition that Aquinas

11. *Lectura romana* 17.1.1: "Love follows knowledge, since nothing is loved except it is known." Aquinas picks up this idea from Augustine (*De Trinitate* X.1.2), who he quotes to this effect several times in the *Summa Theologiae*. Cf. ST I 60.1 sc, I 60.2 ob 2.

12. Psalm 35:10. I will follow the Vulgate numbering of the Psalms.

13. Psalm 4:7.

inherited. These are just a few key citations, but scripture is rife with light language that Christian theologians had long explored before Aquinas arrived on the scene.[14]

It was not, however, just the contents of scripture that served as the basis for the light language that Aquinas would employ in his work, but the very nature of scripture itself that served to support the light language. For Aquinas, following Pseudo-Dionysius, scripture serves as "the ray of divine revelation"[15] by which God makes God's own knowledge of himself available to humans, who are restricted in their ability to know God due to their dependence on their senses and because of the obstacles caused by sin. The title of his compilation of Patristic commentary on the Gospels, *Catena Aurea* (*The Golden Chain*), bears with it the imagery of a golden ray of light that pulls one up toward an understanding of an incomprehensible God. For Aquinas and those who came before him, scripture by its very nature and content brings light into human darkness.

Prior to Aquinas, the Christian tradition had produced a number of theologians whose work prominently featured light. The Cappadocians used light imagery extensively, with Basil's *Hexaemeron* being one of the key texts for future reflection on the question of the origin of light on the first and fourth days of creation. Gregory of Nazianzus' *Fifth Theological Oration* and *Homilies on Epiphany* powerfully exploited the relationship between God and light. Anselm, who was at the forefront of a twelfth-century renaissance that expressed itself both theologically and aesthetically, would contemplate in his *Proslogion* what it meant for God to "dwell in unapproachable light" (1 Tim. 6:16).[16] Aquinas's contemporaries, Robert Grosseteste[17] and Bonaventure, would both reflect on the theological nature of light and deploy light language in their theology, but no theologians would have greater influence on Aquinas's

14. For a more substantial exposition of scriptural uses of light imagery, see Gerald O'Collins's essay in Gerald O'Collins, S.J. and Mary Ann Meyers, eds., *Light from Light: Scientists and Theologians in Dialogue* (Grand Rapids: Eerdmans, 2012), 103–21.

15. ST I 1.9 ad 2.

16. *Proslogion* 1 in Anselm, *Opera Omnia*, ed. F. S. Schmitt, 6 vols., vol. I (Edinburgh: Thomas Nelson & Sons, 1946–61), 98. See Giles E. M. Gasper, "Towards a Theology of Light in the Twelfth-Century Renaissance," in *Outside Archeology: Material Culture and Poetic Imagination*, ed. Christine Finn and Martin Henig, *BAR International Series 999* (Oxford: Archeopress, 2001).

17. For a translation of Grosseteste's *De Luce* and a theological exploration of the theme of light, see Iain M. MacKenzie, *The Obscurism of Light: A Theological Study into the Nature of Light* (Norwich, UK: Canterbury, 1996).

theology of light than St. Augustine and Pseudo-Dionysius, both of whom influenced the shape of this inaugural lecture.

In discussing Aquinas's inaugural lecture, *Rigans Montes*, Torrell claims that "the discourse is clearly inspired by Pseudo-Dionysius,"[18] and the Dionysian aspects of *Rigans Montes* are obvious from the opening lines of the lecture when Aquinas quotes the *Ecclesiastical Hierarchy*: "It is a most sacred law of the divinity that through first things, middle things are to be led to his most divine light."[19] We can note two things here, the first being that the goal of human life, its final cause, is the divine light. Aquinas begins his public career with reference to light. Second, it is through the outworking of divine providence that God achieves this goal. The universe is ordered so that God's (created) light of divine wisdom works through creatures to lead them back to the (uncreated) divine light.

Torrell sees this Dionysian principle as being the foundation for the whole lecture, where Aquinas explores the nature of the teaching of theology based on its exalted status, the standing of those who teach it, the position of those who would learn it, and the manner by which it is communicated. This claim by Torrell, however, is an overstatement, since it ignores the importance that Augustine had on both the theme and content of the lecture. As Peter Brown identified, light and mountains were an important influence on Augustine's theology:

> Mountains appear more often in his works: the light of the rising sun slipping down into the valleys; the sudden view of a distant town from the wooded slopes of a pass. Above all, he was surrounded by light. The African sunlight was the "Queen of all Colours pouring down over everything." He was acutely alive to the effects of light. His only poem is in praise of the warm glow of the Easter Candle.[20]

Biographical accounts of Aquinas's life tell us that prior to his inaugural lecture Aquinas was visited in a dream by a "venerable looking Dominican friar" who suggested the passage "From your lofty abode you water the mountains;

18. Jean-Pierre Torrell, *Saint Thomas Aquinas. Volume 1, The Person and His Work*, trans. Robert Royal, revised ed. (Washington, DC: Catholic University of America Press, 2005), 51.

19. *Rigans Montes*, prooemium.

20. Peter Brown, *Augustine of Hippo: A Biography, a New Edition with an Epilogue* (Berkeley: University of California Press, 2000), 23. One place where Augustine exploits the language of light most effectively is in his Easter homilies.

the earth is satisfied with the fruit of your work" as the foundational scripture of his lecture.[21] Whatever may be the reason that Aquinas chose Ps. 103:13 as the text upon which to base his lecture, the overarching theme of the lecture—that the "light of divine wisdom"[22] flows down to teachers (mountains) who then share that wisdom with their students—is as equally inspired by Augustine as it is by Pseudo-Dionysius. The first connection can be made through Augustine's *Homilies on the Gospel of St. John*, which Aquinas knew well,[23] and which begin with a discussion of how the apostolic author was able to speak of things that are beyond our understanding only because he was first illumined from above. Augustine describes how John was a mountain:

> Mountains are lofty souls; hills are ordinary souls. But then the mountains receive peace so that the hills might receive justice. . . . Lesser souls, however, would not receive faith unless greater souls—called mountains—were illumined by Wisdom herself, so that they might pass on to ordinary souls what these ordinary souls can grasp, and thus live from faith as hills because the mountains receive peace.[24]

Augustine expands on this theme with regard to scripture in general:

> When we lift up our eyes to the scriptures, because the scriptures have been provided by human beings, we are lifting up our eyes to the mountains from where help will come to us. Even so, because those who wrote the scriptures were human beings, they were not shining on their own, but he *was the true light who illumines everyone coming into this world* (John 1:9).[25]

A second connection can be made through Aquinas's citation of Ps. 75:5 in the *principium*: "You shine wonderfully from the everlasting mountains." Tugwell suggests that Aquinas is following a gloss by the Lombard in this interpretation,[26] but that gloss itself points to Augustine, among others, as its

21. Torrell, *Saint Thomas Aquinas. Volume 1, The Person and His Work*, 51.

22. *Rigans Montes*, prooemium.

23. Most of his lectures on the Gospel of John are in conversation with Augustine's homilies on John.

24. Augustine, *Homilies on the Gospel of John 1–40*, ed. Boniface Ramsey, trans. O. P. Edmund Hill, vol. 12 of Part III, The Works of Saint Augustine: A Translation for the 21st Century (New York: New City Press, 2009), I.2, 40.

25. Ibid., I.6, 43.

source,[27] so a more complete explanation would be that Aquinas was following Augustine's lead in his exposition of Ps. 75:5 in Augustine's *Enarrations on the Psalms*:

> Who are these eternal mountains? They are the people whom God has made to last forever; they are the lofty mountains who are preachers of the truth. You send your light, your own light, but you send it from the everlasting mountains, because those mighty mountains are the first to receive your light, and afterwards the earth is clothed in that brilliance which the mountains were the first to receive. Those great mountains, the apostles, caught it; the apostles intercepted the first glimmers of your rising light. . . . Listen, everyone: the light comes to you through the mountains, certainly, but it is God who illumines you, not the mountains.[28]

These Augustinian ideas about God, light, and mountains, whether received directly or indirectly, seem to be just as influential, if unstated, as the Dionysian influence upon Aquinas's lecture. The fact that the Lombard's gloss on Ps. 75:5 claims the eternal mountains are the apostles and other writers of scripture points to how pervasive these particular ideas of Augustine had become by the time Aquinas gave this lecture. This is not, however, to diminish the influence of Pseudo-Dionysius on the work, but rather to show how Aquinas could combine the ideas of these two authors into a coherent framework connected by ideas of light. Servais Pinckaers summarizes Aquinas's integration of the light of both scripture and tradition this way:

> In writing the *Summa*, Thomas is aware that he is listening to the Lord teaching on the mountain, in the company of the Fathers and the holy Doctors of the Church, in the same fellowship with all those, philosophers and others, who, without having been able to hear this voice directly, had nonetheless known how to welcome, even if imperfectly, the light of truth shining at the summit of their souls. For him, it is not merely a beautiful picture or ideal, but a living communion in the light of the truth poured into their hearts by the

26. Tugwell, *Albert & Thomas: Selected Writings*, 357, fn. 6.

27. PL 191:706CD.

28. Augustine, *Exposition of the Psalms 73–98*, ed. John E. Rotelle, trans. Maria Bolding, vol. 18 of Part III, The Works of Saint Augustine: A Translation for the 21st Century (New York: New City Press, 2002), 76.7, 59–60 (note that this text does not use the Vulgate numbering of the Psalms).

Spirit, who had already hovered over the waters at the beginning of creation.[29]

Theology as Illumination

Having looked at how scripture and tradition mediated ideas of illumination in this inaugural lecture, we can now look at the second element of this lecture, which is how theology is itself an illuminating enterprise. Much recent discussion in Thomistic circles has revolved around the question of whether or not holy teaching (*sacra doctrina*)[30] qualifies as an Aristotelian science (*scientia*) and whether Aquinas has sufficiently made the case that it is such. Lost in the discussion is the idea, as Aquinas suggests in *Rigans Montes*, that the work of holy teaching both requires and provides illumination. Perhaps the neglect is the result of a peculiar modern theological aversion to talking about enlightenment and illumination in any kind of realistic manner, especially in the wake of Kant's argument against the darkness of church thinkers and his demand that we dare to think for ourselves. Also important is the priority that scientific knowledge, though understood in the modern rather than the Aristotelian sense, bears in contemporary thought.[31] To suggest that our knowledge of God requires anything other than our own intellectual resources or personal intuitions is a kind of heresy to the modern secular mind.

Yet illumination is at the heart of Aquinas's conception of holy teaching, and to understand both what he is up to in general, and the "scientific" nature of holy teaching, we must attend to the illuminating effect of this teaching. Theology as illumination and theology as *scientia* are not concepts opposed to each other, but rather concepts that understood together can increase our understanding of Aquinas's project.

29. Servais Pinckaers, O.P., *The Pinckaers Reader: Renewing Thomistic Moral Theology*, ed. John Berkman and Craig Steven Titus, trans. Mary Thomas Noble, O.P. et al. (Washington, DC: Catholic University of America Press, 2005), 23.

30. "Holy teaching" is a better rendering of *sacra doctrina* than the usual "sacred doctrine" because it gets to the heart of the pedagogical task that is the emphasis of the *Summa Theologiae*, as well as the rest of Aquinas's works. The holiness of *sacra doctrina* points both to its source in the knowledge of God and the saints and to its function of making us holy. "Doctrine" tends to have, from a modern perspective, more rigid connotations that leave less room for dispute than was the norm in medieval scholasticism.

31. See Kant's essay, "What Is Enlightenment?" in James Schmidt, *What Is Enlightenment?: Eighteenth-Century Answers and Twentieth-Century Questions*, Philosophical Traditions, 7 (Berkeley: University of California Press, 1996), 58–64.

As John Jenkins has pointed out, given Aquinas's understanding of the Aristotelian notion of *scientia* found in the *Posterior Analytics*, in any *scientia* there is a considerable amount of intellectual preparation that must take place prior to grasping the demonstrations that provide the deep knowledge that constitutes *scientia*.[32] In order to achieve this knowledge, one must serve an apprenticeship under an experienced teacher, one who knows the principles from which all knowledge of a field flows.[33] But the very act of teaching is, for Aquinas, an act of illuminating others, and the act of learning is an act of being illumined, where one "can truly be called a true teacher inasmuch as he teaches the truth and illumines the mind."[34] Our modern description of this intuition is found when we describe light bulbs going on over our students' heads when they finally understand something, or grasp an illuminating example.

The Three Lights of Nature, Grace, and Glory

Aquinas was aware of the need for illumination not on a purely theoretical level, but as a reality that he lived in his daily work. In his prayer, *Ante Studium*, which Aquinas was said to have regularly prayed before working, he explicitly asks for God "to infuse into my darkened intellect the rays of your brightness and remove from me the twofold darkness of sin and ignorance into which I was born."[35]

This prayer gives us insight into the two problems that any theologian faces in the task of doing theology, which are two kinds of darkness that obscure the light of God. The darkness of ignorance is the consequence of the fact that human beings by nature are unable to know God as God is.[36] Our cognitive capacities are limited by both our distance from God and by the requirement that we must do all of our learning through our senses, which is a rather severe

32. John I. Jenkins, *Knowledge and Faith in Thomas Aquinas* (Cambridge and New York: Cambridge University Press, 1997), 46.

33. Ibid., 68.

34. DV 11.1 ad 9. See also ST I 113.5 ad 2, where Aquinas describes the role of guardian angels "to illumine by teaching" (*ad illuminationem doctrinae*).

35. Thomas Aquinas, *Opuscula Theologica*, ed. Raymundi Spiazzi, vol. II (Rome: Marietti, 1954), 285–86. My translation of "infundere digneris super intellectus mei tenebras tuae radium claritatis duplices in quibus natus sum, a me removens tenebras, peccatum scilicet, et ignorantiam."

36. Though God created humans in a state of grace that allowed them to know God. Through sin they lost this grace and so by nature are no longer able to know God. See ST I 94.1. For a full description of the metaphysical assumptions here, see A. C. Pegis, "In Umbria Intelligentiae," *New Scholasticism* 14 (1940): 146–80.

limitation for anyone thinking about a being, God, who is not directly available to our senses. The darkness of sin puts an additional obstacle between us and the source of divine light in the same way that the moon blocks the light of the sun during a solar eclipse, so without the light of grace removing the obstacle of sin, our ability to think correctly about God is limited. There is a direct link between the holiness of the theologian and his ability to do theology well, as Aquinas mentions in his *principium*.[37] There is a third darkness that Aquinas mentions elsewhere, the darkness of condemnation, but because of its eschatological character it is less relevant to the actual task of theology except, of course, as something to be avoided. All of these darknesses, these obstacles and limitations that obscure our ability to know God, cause humans to be unable to apprehend God as their final end. Under our own power it does not matter if holy teaching is a *scientia* or not, as we are unable to get any kind of theological project very far off the ground at all. On our own, we are lost.[38]

The counter to the three darknesses of sin, natural ignorance, and condemnation with respect to God is found in what we might think of as Aquinas's three light theory of theology. Aquinas sees three lights, "the light of nature, grace, or glory,"[39] as being crucial to the theological enterprise. First, we use the natural light of our intellect for two things—to understand something of God through his effects in the world and to understand the principles of theology revealed to us in scripture. This light is not an autonomous light, but one implanted in us by God and thus a participation in God's light, yet it also operates under the power of our will; to capture this dependence and independence, we might think of this natural light and its activity as flowing from a "created autonomy."[40] Second, theology proceeds by the light of grace or the divine light, which both removes the cognitive effects of our sin and elevates our intellects beyond their natural abilities for the purpose of overcoming our ignorance. Third, theology is ultimately aimed at participating in the light of glory found in the beatific vision, in which the discursive nature of theology will be replaced by the perfect and unmediated vision of the incomprehensible

37. *Rigans Montes*: "So all the teachers of sacred scripture ought to be high because of the high quality of their lives, so that they will be capable of preaching effectively . . . hearts cannot be goaded on or fixed in the fear of God unless they are fixed in an elevated way of life."

38. This is why the very first article of the *Summa Theologiae* deals with the necessity of holy teaching, not its status as a *scientia*. ST I 1.1: "But the end must first be known by men who are to direct their thoughts and actions to the end. Hence it was necessary for the salvation of man that certain truths which exceed human reason should be made known to him by divine revelation."

39. ST I 106.1 ad 2.

40. We will explore this natural light in chapter 5.

God. At the same time, the basis for holy teaching is God's own knowledge and that of the blessed which is experienced in the beatific vision—when this light is shared with us we come to know things about God we could not know in any other way.[41]

These three lights all come together in Aquinas's description of the *imago Dei*, based upon the aforementioned Ps. 4:7:

> Wherefore we see that the image of God is in man in three ways. First, inasmuch as man possesses a natural aptitude for understanding and loving God; and this aptitude consists in the very nature of the mind, which is common to all men. Secondly, inasmuch as man actually and habitually knows and loves God, though imperfectly; and this image consists in the conformity of grace. Thirdly, inasmuch as man knows and loves God perfectly; and this image consists in the likeness of glory. Wherefore on the words, "The light of Thy countenance, O Lord, is signed upon us" the gloss distinguishes a threefold image of "creation," of "re-creation," and of "likeness." The first is found in all men, the second only in the just, the third only in the blessed.[42]

Holy teaching, inasmuch as it involves humans, must involve our light as created, as re-created, and ultimately as full participation in God's light.

It would, however, be a mistake to consider these as three separate lights and set them off against each other. For Aquinas only God has light by essence and thus any illumination we experience is a participation in God's light.[43] While there is but one source of light, however, that light has multiple effects that are partially determined by how receptive we are to them. Just as the sun may have the multiple effects of causing some things to grow, some to decompose, and some to change, so God's divine light, which he has by essence, has multiple effects in our world. Thus the three light theory I am suggesting is perhaps better thought of as the three effects of divine light theory or as Aquinas's theory of divine illuminations. We can look at each in turn as it applies to the task of holy teaching.

41. ST I 1.2: "So it is that sacred doctrine is a science because it proceeds from principles established by the light of a higher science, namely the science of God and the blessed."

42. ST I 93.4. The gloss is from Cassiodorus and can be found in the *Glossa Ordinaria*, PL 133:849D.

43. *De Trin.* I.1 ad 6: "God is always the cause of the soul's natural light."

Natural Light of the Intellect

The natural light of the human intellect can know some important truths about God, even if such knowledge is insufficient to save humans and restore them to the love of God. Aquinas puts it succinctly:

> It is better to suppose that this is said to distinguish between knowledge of God obtained by other sciences and that obtained by faith. For the knowledge of God obtained by other sciences illumines the intellect only by showing that God is the first cause, that he is one and wise and so on. But the knowledge of God obtained by faith both illumines the intellect and delights the affections, because it not only says that God is the first cause, but that he is our Savior, that he is our Redeemer, that he loves us and that he became incarnate for us: all of which inflame the affections.[44]

By means of our natural light we can come to know, for instance, that God exists, that there must be but one God and some other basic truths, such as that God must be simple, immutable, good, and so on, but even these properties only tell us what God is not, which hardly gives one reason to love God.[45] This *de minimis* knowledge of God is made even more tenuous by the combination of the limitations of sin and ignorance mentioned above, so we are unable to know the most important things about God, those that lead toward our salvation, such as God's triunity, the Incarnation, and God as our final end. Even what we do end up knowing is the result of a long, slow, and inexact process that is rife with error.[46] As this passage from *In II Corinthios* indicates, the natural light of our intellect is not accompanied by an infusion of love with respect to God; what we can know by the natural light of our intellect is a cold, distant knowledge, and possibly even a hateful knowledge in the case of demonic knowledge of God.[47]

44. *In II Cor.* 2.3 §73. The "this" to which Aquinas refers in the first sentence is a gloss on 2 Cor. 2:14, which can be found in the *Glossa Ordinaria*, PL 114:553D–554A.

45. ST I 3 prooemium: "When the existence of a thing has been ascertained there remains the further question of the manner of its existence, in order that we may know its essence. Now, because we cannot know what God is, but rather what he is not, we have no means for considering how God is, but rather how he is not."

46. ST I 1.1.

47. See ST I 64.1 ad 2 for Aquinas's description of the natural knowledge of God that remains in the fallen angels: "Not even an angel can of his own nature know God's substance. Yet on account of the perfection of his intellect he can of his nature have a higher knowledge of God than man can have. Such knowledge of God remains also in the demons. Although they do not possess the purity which comes

One way to understand the intellectual limits of our human nature can be seen in Aquinas's treatment of the knowledge of Adam before the Fall. Aquinas argues that even before Adam had fallen into the darkness of sin, he needed a divine gift of grace, which Aquinas calls "original justice," in order to have knowledge of God. Adam, while unable to see and know God directly as in the beatific vision, was still able to have more perfect knowledge of God than we can, since Adam's reason was not prevented from its proper operation by being preoccupied with anything lower than the First Truth. Yet this knowledge of God was a gift given through grace and so was accidental to human nature—we could lose it and still remain human. What remains after grace is gone is our human nature as we have it now, though even this is diminished by sin.[48]

The cognitive limitation imposed on humans by the requirement that knowledge comes through our corporeal senses not only restricts our ability to know things about God, but it also means that we are unable to know everything that we are naturally disposed to know.[49] With regard to God, even angels, who are not restricted to knowledge via the senses, need illumination to know God.[50] Thus if humans were left to their own powers they would have a severely impoverished knowledge of God. This is not to say that the light of our natural reason does not play an important role in the task of sacred doctrine, since the tools of philosophy that result from the use of our natural light can help clarify and explain what we believe by faith, but rather that there are clear limitations that call for real humility in approaching theological work, so that "one knows God most perfectly who holds that whatever one can think or say about Him is less than what God is."[51] Under our own power, we are lost.

with grace, nevertheless they have purity of nature; and this suffices for the knowledge of God which belongs to them from their nature." As the corpus of the article makes clear, demons have been deprived of the grace that would lead to love of God.

48. ST I 94.1: "And man was made right by God in this sense, that in him the lower powers were subjected to the higher, and the higher nature was made so as not to be impeded by the lower. Wherefore the first man was not impeded by exterior things from a clear and steady contemplation of the intelligible effects which he perceived by the radiation of the First Truth, whether by a natural or by a gratuitous knowledge." See also ST I 100.1: "Now original justice, in which the first man was created, was an accident pertaining to the nature of the species, not as caused by the principles of the species, but as a gift conferred by God on the entire human nature."

49. *De Trin* I.1 ad 4: "In us the intelligible light is obscure, being overshadowed as it were by reason of conjunction with the body and with corporeal powers, and on this account is impeded so that it cannot freely and naturally behold the truth which is itself knowable."

50. ST I 57.5 and ST I 58.1.

51. *De Causis* 6.

Light of Grace

In the face of this obstacle to doing theology, for Aquinas the task of holy teaching is only made possible by the divine light, which both elevates the intellect and reveals the deep truths about God.[52] Aquinas thinks of this primarily in terms of God as a teacher who reveals to his disciples the information needed to attain salvation.[53] As our teacher, God is able to act interiorly as well as externally to teach us, whereas all human teaching is only external, by writing and speaking. An important principle here is that only God has perfect knowledge of God, and Aquinas believes that "only perfect forms can be the principle of action in something else."[54] That is, if God only had partial knowledge of himself, he would only be able to impart partial knowledge to us. This coincides with one of Aquinas's pedagogical principles, that "the truth of knowledge is the same in learner and teacher since the knowledge of the learner is a likeness of the knowledge of the teacher."[55]

There is a hint here of how we might understand the question of holy teaching as a *scientia*. If we take the question of whether sacred doctrine is a *scientia* from a human perspective, then it is quite likely that it cannot meet the criteria laid out by Aristotle in the *Posterior Analytics*: holy teaching, from a human perspective, deals with articles of faith that are not self-evident (*per se nota*) and are in many cases contingent rather than necessary.[56] At best, holy teaching is a subalternate *scientia* that derives its principles from a higher knowledge, that of God and the blessed.[57] But perhaps what Aquinas is driving at in ST I 1.2 is the claim that holy teaching is a *scientia* for God. God knows his existence *per se* and God is perfectly knowable to himself.[58] Aquinas never puts the question as to whether holy teaching is a *scientia* from just a human perspective, but he is quite clear that God and the blessed have *scientia* with

52. *De Trin.* 3.1 ad 1: "Although matters of faith considered according to man's natural powers are above him, they are not above man when he is illuminated by divine light; hence it is not necessary for man that he seek out such truths by his own power, but it is necessary for him to know them by divine revelation."

53. ST II-II 2.3: "Hence it was said above that man's ultimate happiness consists in a supernatural vision of God: to which vision man cannot attain unless he be taught by God."

54. ST I-II 5.6 ad 2.

55. ST II-II 171.6. Note that this assumes that the teacher actually does know the truth. Among humans this might not always be a sound assumption, but Aquinas feels quite safe in making it with regard to God's own self-knowledge.

56. On the role of *per se nota* principles and *scientia*, see Guy Mansini, "Are the Principles of *sacra doctrina per se nota*?," *The Thomist* 74, no. 3 (2010): 407–35.

57. ST I 1.2.

58. ST I 2.1 and I 12.1. See also ST II-II 1.5.

regard to God. As long as, one might argue, holy teaching meets the criteria of *scientia* with regard to someone's knowledge, it meets the criteria adequately; it only takes one successful instance of some being having divine *scientia* in order to make the case that holy teaching is itself a *scientia* in its strongest sense; it is because of God's perfect *scientia* that the human enterprise of holy teaching is able to proceed in its subalternate form.

Put in the context of teaching, this makes even more sense. A teacher's job is to have superior and intimate knowledge of the subject matter so as to impart it to her students. Inasmuch as the teacher knows the principles perfectly, she is able to know the conclusions of a science. This suggests that there is more continuity between questions one and two of the *Prima Pars* than we might have recognized. The question of the self-evidence of God's existence concludes that humans in their present state cannot know God *per se*, but that God surely does.[59] Thus in the realm of divine pedagogy, God knows the object of the *scientia* perfectly and intuitively and so is able to teach it perfectly. The first question of the knowledge of any *scientia* is the existence of the subject, the *an sit* ("that it is"); thus establishing the existence of God, which is self-evident only to God and the blessed, is the first step in the *scientia*. Unlike humans, however, God does not know this discursively, but this does not mean that God does not have *scientia*, only that God's knowledge is perfect in ways ours currently cannot be.

God's *scientia* is mediated to humans in a variety of ways. In one way God's own knowledge is the universal cause of the illumination of souls, as the sun universally illumines the earth.[60] Inasmuch as all creation both points to and contains the divine light, it reflects God's knowledge; by engaging in the study of this world, that is, through God's natural effects, we can ourselves gain some knowledge of God. This teaching, however, is nonverbal and so less explicit. In another way, God imparts wisdom to believers through revelation, for "we impart a hidden and secret wisdom of God, that is, which is God and from God. For although all wisdom is from God, as it says in Sirach (1:1), this wisdom, which is about God, is from God in a special way, namely, by revelation."[61] This comes in the form of explicit teaching, which Aquinas often equates with illumination and which has three stages to it, aligned with the three theological

59. ST I 2.1.

60. ST I-II 79.3: "God is the universal cause of the illumination of souls, according to John 1:9: 'That was the true light that illumined every man that comes into the world,' even as the sun is the universal cause of the illumination of bodies, though not in the same way, for the sun illumines by necessity of nature, whereas God works freely, through the order of his wisdom."

61. *In I Cor* 2.1 §85.

virtues given through grace: 1) the illumination of the intellect through faith, 2) the elevation of the mind through hope, and 3) the changing of affection through love.[62] While God alone, because of his power and omnipresence, is able to teach us interiorly, God may also teach us through exterior means, through the ministry of angels or other humans.[63]

As mentioned above, God is the supreme teacher because God has perfect knowledge, not just of himself, but also of all creation. We should not discount the latter part of that statement, for Aquinas believes that holy teaching not only teaches us about God, but in the process we learn more deeply about the nature of creation from the one who created it.[64] This teaching, of God and creation, comes to us from God adapted to our abilities; part of the gift that God gives us in teaching us is giving it to us through sensible means so that we can understand it. This teaching by God about God comes in the light of faith, a light that cannot fail precisely because it comes from God. There is a risk here in misunderstanding how Aquinas views theological certainty. We might think that the theological certainty that Aquinas finds in scripture, for instance, derives from its nature as scripture. For Aquinas, however, what makes scripture infallible, when properly interpreted, is its source in God. (We will discuss the role of scripture below, but the point here is to direct our attention to the infallibility of God as teacher.)

What God does as teacher is share his own goodness with us and constantly make himself manifest to us. One of the words that appears consistently in the context of illumination with regard to God is "manifestation," based on Eph. 5:13, "all that is made manifest is light."[65] Light, for Aquinas, makes things manifest to us and without it we cannot see. For Aquinas, God is constantly reaching toward us through a variety of means, internal and external, to communicate who he is and that we should love him. For all of his discussion of analogy and apophatic theology, Aquinas considers God to be the most manifest God possible; God is supremely knowable to God and shares that supreme knowledge with us, both through creation and revelation, out of the love of his goodness.[66] God is not some remote deity that ignores us, but

62. The sermon *Beatus Vir* in Thomas Aquinas, *The Academic Sermons*, trans. Mark-Robin Hoogland, The Fathers of the Church: Mediaeval Continuation (Washington, DC: Catholic University of America Press, 2010). On teaching as illumination, see fn. 34 above.

63. See ST I 117.1 especially ad 1; DV 11.1; DA II.11 §372; *In Iob* 33:14, lines 141–50, pp. 175–76.

64. See ST I 32.1 ad 3, where Aquinas argues that knowledge of the Trinity, given by grace, clarifies the nature of creation as contingent and the product of God's love of his own goodness.

65. Vulgate: "omnia autem quae arguuntur a lumine manifestantur omne enim quod manifestatur lumen est." Aquinas makes the connection between light and manifestation explicit at ST I 67.1.

one constantly reaching out to us. The primary gift of the Father of lights is our knowledge of God that comes from God's own self-knowledge. Holy teaching, then, is based on God's infallible self-manifestation to us, based upon his goodness.[67]

God's teaching and manifestation of his goodness functions primarily soteriologically and is a part of his providential care of creation. In his commentary on Job, Aquinas calls God's providence a lamp and his instruction a light;[68] part of God's providence is directly related to the salvation of individuals through their predestination.[69] Aquinas makes the connection between salvation and illumination explicit in several places. In ST III 44.3 ad 1 he argues that healing and justification lead to the illumination of wisdom;[70] in his commentary on John he says that salvation consists in participating in the light, who is Christ;[71] in his commentary on 1 Corinthians he claims that illumination by the Holy Spirit allows us to have sound judgment about salvation.[72] What

66. ST I 12.1: "God, who is pure act without any admixture of potentiality, is in himself supremely knowable." *In Ioh.* I.4 §116, God creates, "not, indeed, to add anything to himself, since he has no need of our good, but so that his goodness might be made manifest in all of the things made by him, in that 'his eternal power and divinity are clearly seen, being understood through the things that are made' (Rom 1:20). Thus each creature is made as a witness to God in so far as each creature is a certain witness of the divine goodness. So, the vastness of creation is a witness to God's power and omnipotence; and its beauty is a witness to the divine wisdom."

67. DDN 1.1 §13: "For that which is known by something alone, is not able to be thought or spoken of except as it makes itself manifest. It is fitting for God alone to have perfect knowledge of himself as he is. Therefore, no one is able to truly speak or know about God except by revelation from God."

68. *In Iob* 29:3, lines 31–39, p. 156: "and to express this he says, 'when his lamp,' that is, his providence, 'shown over my head,' that is, my mind, for he directed my mind toward many good things which my mind did not attain. In certain respects, however, he was directed by God as though instructed by him about what he ought to do, so he then says, 'in his light,' that is, by his instruction, 'I was walking,' that is, I was proceeding 'in darkness,' that is, in doubts."

69. ST I 23.1.

70. ST III 44.3 ad 1: "Now the end for which miracles were worked was the health of the rational part, which consists in the illumination of wisdom and the justification of man. The former presupposes the latter, since as it is written in Wisdom 1:4, 'Wisdom will not enter into a malicious soul, nor dwell in a body subject to sins.'"

71. *In Ioh.* 1.4 §122: "Now although John, of whom so much has been said, even including that he was sent by God, is an eminent person, his coming is not sufficient to save men, because the salvation of man lies in participating in the light. If John had been the light, his coming would have sufficed to save men; but he was not the light. So he says, 'he was not the light.' Consequently, a light was needed that would suffice to save men."

72. *In I Cor* 2.3 §118: "It is in this vein that the Apostle says here that the spiritual man judges all things, namely, because a man with an intellect enlightened by the Holy Spirit and set in good order by Him has a sound judgment about the particulars which pertain to salvation. But a person who is not

Aquinas seems to be saying is that we are saved when our minds are illumined by God so that we can know who God is, so that we know God is our final end, and so that our affections are enkindled for God. Our minds, in the darkness of ignorance and error, are unable to be saved and put on the path toward God without illumination by God. We must have God teach us by illumining our minds so that we can know what we must do to reach our final end. Without God's intervention through illumination, we would be doomed to the darkness of condemnation, and one of the key tasks of theology is to participate in this illumination to make salvation known to the world.

A natural objection to all of this would be that it is too cognitive an idea of salvation, and even of sin. Surely, one might object, humans as embodied souls are more than just their cognitive selves, and this view of salvation leads to an impoverished view of humans. Are we not putting reason above the whole person here? For Aquinas, however, this objection would be based on faulty anthropological assumptions. It is precisely our cognitive abilities that are what make us human and distinct from other corporeal creatures. Our ability to reason, to think abstractly, to think about our thinking, to contemplate the truth, and so on, are what differentiate humans from cats, dogs, horses, and all other animals. The Aristotelian notion that humans are rational animals naturally leads to the idea that what is needed for human salvation, and not canine and feline salvation, is what differentiates us from cats and dogs—our rational aspect. There is another reason why Aquinas sees salvation in these cognitive terms, which is that part of what it means to be made in the image of God is to be able to think abstractly and rationally—above all about God.[73] There are, in Aquinas's view of the universe, only three types of beings with this capacity—God, angels, and humans—and this cognitive ability demarcates us from other animals. This is not to diminish the importance of our bodies and our passions, but rather to see that they reach their fullest expression when they are placed under the control of our reason. When our passions and desires overrun our reason, according to Aquinas, the person is diminished and becomes more like other animals and thus loses some of the image of God that was imparted to humans from the beginning.

Beyond the anthropology there is another important reason why Aquinas emphasizes the cognitive aspect of our salvation. For Aquinas there is a distinct relationship between what we know and what we love, as we mentioned with

spiritual has his intellect darkened and his will disarranged, as far as spiritual goods are concerned. Consequently, the spiritual man cannot be judged by a man who is not spiritual any more than a man who is awake by one who is asleep."

73. ST I-II, prooemium.

regard to his *Lectura romana*.[74] In the *Summa Theologiae* he argues that "love is the term of knowledge" and that "to love God is something greater than to know him, especially in this state of life, it follows that love of God presupposes knowledge of God."[75] Our intellects must be illumined by God precisely so that we may love God. Otherwise, stuck in ignorance and error, we would not know who God is, that God loves us, and that we are made for God as our final end. In contemplating God we come to know that God loves us and that we should love God. But this is only possible if God makes himself manifest to us, since by our own powers we are unable to achieve this.

Those who engage in holy teaching must work within the context of the two lights of nature and grace, which explains why Aquinas is so sanguine about the relation between faith and reason. As we have discussed, all holy teaching proceeds from the divine light of God's own knowledge, while at the same time the natural light of our intellect must be applied to the data of revelation. The two lights, however, derive from the same source, the divine light, and so cannot be in conflict with each other, since that would mean that "God would be the author of error."[76] What is made known by divine revelation is what we cannot know by nature, but we can apply our natural reason to once it has been revealed. Inasmuch as the arguments of natural philosophy are true, and thus not in conflict with revelation, Aquinas thinks they are a help to holy teaching, even as they are deficient in respect to holy teaching due to the uncertainty of the source. Conflicts between faith and philosophy, according to Aquinas, are the result of errors in reasoning in philosophy, which he calls "an abuse of philosophy." These are the result of either using philosophical ideas that are opposed to the faith (modern versions of materialism would fall into this category) or by subordinating faith to philosophy so that one only believes what can be proved by philosophic reasoning, rather than the reverse.[77]

Thus the divine light is crucial to the task of theology both from a soteriological point of view and from the perspective of our affections. We

74. See footnote 11 above.

75. ST II-II 27.4 ad 1 and 2.

76. *De Trin.* 2.3: "For although the natural light of the human mind is insufficient to reveal those truths revealed by faith, yet it is impossible that those things which God has manifested to us by faith should be contrary to those which are evident to us by natural knowledge. In this case one would necessarily be false: and since both kinds of truth are from God, God would be the author of error, a thing which is impossible."

77. Ibid.: "If, however, anything is found in the teachings of the philosophers contrary to faith, this error does not properly belong to philosophy, but is due to an abuse of philosophy owing to the insufficiency of reason."

think about God, contemplate his creation and goodness, so that we may love him—and this is our salvation.

Light of Glory

There is a third light, the light of glory, which plays a role in holy teaching, but is less important to it than the divine light of revelation.[78] The light of glory is primarily the light by which the blessed see God in the beatific vision and is given to the blessed as a permanent gift that allows them to see God through his essence.[79] The light of glory is also, on rare occasions, given to humans in this life as a fleeting possession or one-off experience that is known to Aquinas as rapture. The apostle Paul would be one person who was raptured into the light of glory and his experience would contribute to the task of theology, as a form of revelation, through his writings in scripture.[80]

We can summarize this three light theory with a simple diagram:

↕
Light of glory—beatific vision/rapture
Light of grace—justification and illumination; Adam's original justice
Light of nature—created status without grace
Darkness of ignorance—created status without grace
Darkness of sin—post-Fall
Darkness of condemnation—post-judgment

Humans, because of their nature as embodied souls, have by nature a mixture of knowledge and ignorance, though God overcame their natural ignorance by creating them in grace, or the state of original justice. After the Fall, humans exist in a mixture of knowledge and ignorance, with an additional impediment from sin that imposes additional darkness, especially with regard to proper moral actions; the darknesses of ignorance and sin, if left unaddressed, will result in the darkness of condemnation. God, who makes himself manifest to us out of his goodness, grants us the light of grace to overcome our darkness, which

78. We are, however, unable to attain the light of glory unless "we are taught by God." ST II-II 2.3.

79. An overview of some problems with the light of glory can be found in Michael M. Waddell, "Aquinas on the Light of Glory," *Tópicos. Revista de Filosofía* 41 (July 2011): 105–32.

80. *In II Cor.* 12.1 §455, "In another way the light of glory affects a human mind as a passing quality; this is the way Paul's mind in rapture was enlightened by the light of glory."

allows us to know God as our end and to engage in proper moral acts that merit our ultimate participation in the light of glory.

As mentioned above, these three lights are really the multiple effects of just one light, so they should not be taken as exclusive of each other. In fact, given their shared source we would be better to see them as each contributing to the task of holy teaching (and thus the upward continuity provided by the arrow). By applying the light of natural reason to the self-manifestation of God given through the divine light and the light of glory we can come to know God in a way that allows us to love God. We need, however, to have a better sense of how this self-manifestation through the revelation of God works.

Revelation as Illumination

Aquinas mentions the need for divine revelation from the very beginning of the *Summa Theologiae* and refers to revelation as an illuminating enterprise in four of the first five articles. In the first article of the *Summa Theologiae* he answers the objection that the discipline of philosophy is sufficient for the knowledge of God and so there is no need for an additional science of God found in holy teaching. In response, he notes that the same objects can be investigated by different fields of knowledge, so that we can investigate God by the light of our natural reason and by the light of divine revelation.[81] The comparison between the light of natural reason and the light of divine revelation continues in the next few articles. In article two he discusses how some sciences proceed from the light of the natural intellect and others (subalternate sciences) by the light of superior science, and what makes holy teaching a science is that it "proceeds from the principles known in the light of a superior science, namely that of God and the blessed," just as optics proceeds from the higher science of geometry.[82] What unifies holy teaching as a singular field of study is that it proceeds from this divine light and considers creation as it is knowable under that light.[83] Thus all of holy teaching is related to divine revelation and God's self-manifestation.

81. ST I 1.1 ad 2: "Hence there is no reason why those things which may be learned from philosophical science, so far as they can be known by the light of natural reason, may not also be taught us by another science known by the light of divine revelation." One of the curious features of the English Dominican translation of the *Summa Theologiae* is that the translator left the words for light untranslated in this passage and in ST I 1.4 (see below), so I have supplied them.

82. ST I 1.2: "There are some [sciences] which proceed from principles known by the light of a higher science: thus the science of perspective proceeds from principles established by geometry, and music from principles established by arithmetic. So it is that sacred doctrine is a science because it proceeds from principles established by the light of a higher science, namely the science of God and the blessed."

We can know something about a tree by the light of our natural reason, but we can know other things about it as it relates to God—that the tree is created by God contingently, that God gives it being, and even other things, for instance, that the wood of a tree was used to hang the Son of God in the flesh and that this wood was prefigured in the Old Testament.[84]

In the fifth article of this introductory question, Aquinas also uses the comparison between sciences that proceed from our natural light and those that proceed from divine light to understand the level of certainty available to those who practice each science. At one level, because God's knowledge is certain, so must holy teaching be certain for those who receive it, while teaching that proceeds from the light of human reason may be mistaken. On the other hand, Aquinas notes that while from a human perspective sacred doctrine has a level of uncertainty to it, this is not the result of an ineffectiveness of God or existential uncertainty that is natural to the subject. Instead, the perfect divine knowledge, like the perfect divine light, overwhelms our limited intellects, like an owl blinded by the sun.[85] Any confusion or uncertainty in sacred doctrine is the result of our weakness, not God's.

This comparison between a science that proceeds from the light of natural reason and one that proceeds from the divine light, which we find throughout the first question, may give us a sense of why we need revelation. What we do not get in the first question, however, is a full-fledged description of what revelation actually is. In article eight, the closest we get to a definition and description of revelation is when Aquinas says, "our faith rests on the revelation made to the apostles and prophets who wrote the canonical books, not on the revelation, if there were one, made to any other teachers."[86] The key here is that revelation is made to the apostles and prophets, who subsequently write it down. Scripture is authoritative for Aquinas, but the revelation is made to

83. ST I 1.4: "Sacred doctrine, being one, extends to things which belong to different philosophical sciences because it considers in each the same formal aspect, so far as they can be known through the light of divine knowledge." Cf. SCG 2.2.5: "Since, then, the Christian faith teaches man principally about God, and makes him know creatures by the light of divine revelation, there arises in man a certain likeness of God's wisdom."

84. Aquinas expertly explores the mystery of wood in his sermon *Germinet Terra* in *The Academic Sermons*, 259–80.

85. ST I 1.5 ad 1: "It may well happen that what is in itself the more certain may seem to us the less certain on account of the weakness of our intelligence, 'which is dazzled by the clearest objects of nature; as the owl is dazzled by the light of the sun' (*Metaphysics* II.1). Hence the fact that some happen to doubt about articles of faith is not due to the uncertain nature of the truths, but to the weakness of human intelligence."

86. ST I 1.8 ad 2.

the persons who then record what is revealed to them. God, Aquinas says, is the "author (*auctor*) of sacred scripture,"[87] but as I will argue later, this is not the same thing as engaging in divine dictation or divine writing, but is best understood as God being the principal cause and inspiration of sacred scripture, but a cause that allows for the causality of human beings in the process. To get a complete account of Aquinas's theory of revelation, we must look elsewhere, in his account of prophecy.

It may seem odd to look for a theory of revelation in an account of prophecy, but as we will see, Aquinas sees prophecy as encompassing broader areas of knowledge than we might, even as he also acknowledges different ways we talk about prophecy. Aquinas gives a full account of prophecy and revelation in five main places, *De Veritate* 12, *Summa Contra Gentiles* 3.154, *Ad Romanos* 12.2, *Summa Theologiae* II–II 171–74, and *In I Corinthios* 14.1. For our purposes we will concentrate on the latter two, as the discussions in *De Veritate* 12, *Ad Romanos* 12.2, and *Summa Contra Gentiles*, for the most part, are found in the other two works.

Summa Theologiae on Prophecy

Prophecy, according to Aquinas, "pertains to the cognition that exists above natural reason"[88] and is not just about future contingencies, but also about the past and present.[89] Aquinas argues that the subject of any kind of light is that which it makes manifest, so that the subject of the natural light of the sun is all colors and all things visible, while the subject of the light of the agent intellect is all things that are possible to know. The subject of prophetic knowledge, since it comes from divine light ("the form in prophetic cognition is the divine light"[90]), extends to all things, both natural and divine. Aquinas describes three degrees or levels of prophetic revelation, based on how remote they are from our natural ability to know. At one level is knowledge one person may have naturally that another person does not and requires the illumination of divine light to know, for example, by nature we may know that someone is in another

87. ST I 1.10.

88. ST II–II 171.2. The most useful commentary on Aquinas's theology of prophecy can still be found in Paul Synave, *Prophecy and Inspiration: A Commentary on the Summa Theologica II–II, Questions 171–178* (New York: Desclée, 1961).

89. ST II–II 171.3 sc: "Therefore, prophecy is not about future contingencies alone."

90. ST II–II 171.3 ad 3: "The formal element in prophetic knowledge is the Divine light, which being one, gives unity of species to prophecy, although the things prophetically manifested by the Divine light are diverse."

place, but because we are far away we may need God to reveal their location. At the next level are things that no human can know without the prophetic light, but that are intrinsically knowable, and Aquinas counts knowledge of the Trinity in this category, since the angels can know it (recall that God is intrinsically knowable to himself, but not to us). Finally, there is a category of things that humans cannot know and that are intrinsically unknowable, and these are future contingent events.[91] It is this last category that we typically think of as prophecy—the foretelling of future events—and Aquinas says that this is prophecy in its most proper form, but this does not preclude the other degrees of prophecy and revelation as being the subject of the divine light which makes unknown things knowable.

At its root, prophecy is a form of divine teaching, "a kind of knowledge impressed under the form of teaching on the prophet's intellect, by Divine revelation."[92] This form of teaching establishes an important relationship to the truth between the teacher and the student, as Aquinas operates under the principle that inasmuch as an instructor knows the truth, the instructor's students have the likeness of the same truth in them. If, to use my own example, a teacher knows the truth of the Pythagorean theorem and then teaches it to her students, the students will have a likeness of the truth of the Pythagorean theorem in them. The students, in turn, may be able to pass that truth along. With regard to the divine revelation found in prophecy, God obviously has complete knowledge of the truth of not only God himself, but of all created things as well, without any error. Therefore, those that God instructs via divine revelation will receive that teaching without any error.[93]

There is a caveat here, however, in that Aquinas accounts for two types of instruction by God, explicit instruction and a more mysterious instinctive form of revelation. This explicit instruction carries with it the impression of certainty, not only of the content but also of the very fact that it is a divine revelation; God gives the revelation and assurance that it is from God.[94] If this were not the case, then Aquinas thinks that our faith would rest on something very uncertain. In the second case, what a prophet knows by prophetic instinct, however, does not

91. ST II-II 171.3.

92. ST II-II 171.6

93. Ibid.: "Therefore, nothing false can come under prophecy."

94. ST II-II 171.5: "The prophet's mind is instructed by God in two ways: in one way by an express revelation; in the other way by a kind of instinct, to 'which the human mind is subjected without knowing it,' as Augustine says (*Gen. ad lit. II.17*). Therefore the prophet has the greatest certainty about those things which he knows by an express revelation, and he has it for certain that they are revealed to him by God."

come with such certainty and his knowledge is less than perfect, yet even here Aquinas sees one of the missions of the Holy Spirit as correcting these errors so that we come to know the truth.[95] God is to be trusted not to mislead us or to let us be misled with regard to divine revelation.

There is an additional component to prophecy that is crucial to Aquinas's account, which is the role that judgment and discernment play in prophecy and revelation. He points out that any form of knowledge has two components to it. First, we have things that we sense through their representations in our mind, such as seeing a person walking across the street from me. Second, we then make a judgment about these representations of sense data, such as judging whether the person we see is Mike or Scott. Our ability to make judgments by the light of natural reason depends on the strength of our intellectual light and training, so a trained entomologist can easily judge what kind of mosquito is biting her, while I only know that a mosquito is biting me. With regard to prophecy, we are given by God certain images or things represented in our minds, but we are also given an infusion of light that increases our ability to judge correctly on what has been revealed. The example that Aquinas uses is that of Pharaoh in Gen. 41:1-7, where the Pharaoh had the images impressed upon him in his dreams, but only Joseph had the divine light impressed upon him that elevated his understanding and allowed him to correctly judge the content of Pharaoh's dreams, so that only Joseph was operating prophetically.[96]

In I Corinthios on Prophecy

In his commentary on First Corinthians, Aquinas offers another perspective on prophecy and revelation that can help fill out our understanding of how he thinks it works. Here he bases his understanding of prophecy on an etymological description of its roots in the Greek word "pharos," which means "to see."[97] It follows, for Aquinas, that prophecy consists of seeing "things far off, whether they be future contingents or beyond human reason."[98] In order to see these things, he argues that there are four requirements: 1) bodily images formed in our imaginations, 2) an intellectual light that allows us to know

95. Ibid.

96. ST II-II 173.2.

97. This etymology is, unfortunately, incorrect. In ST II-II 92.1 ad 2, however, Aquinas is quite clear about the difference between etymology and meaning, so the initial move based on etymology should not detract from Aquinas's larger exposition on prophecy.

98. *In I Cor.* 14.1 §812.

things beyond our natural powers, 3) courage to announce what has been revealed, and 4) the working of miracles which provide the certainty, since things that surpass natural knowledge are more likely to be believed if they are accompanied by works that exceed nature.[99] These requirements lead Aquinas to note the various ways that we call someone a prophet, and by attending to the language of scripture he notes that some people can be called prophets just by being given the intellectual light that allows them to explain the visions of other persons, "to explain the sayings of the prophets or the Scriptures of the apostles . . . [or to] discern the writings of the teachers (*doctorum*)."[100] So for Aquinas, prophecy can include the gift of illumination that allows us to properly interpret scripture or the writings of the teachers of the church; there is a sense that we need revelation even to interpret scripture correctly, for without divine light we are likely to judge incorrectly.

Just as importantly, following Paul's lead, Aquinas points out that revelation is a gratuitous grace for the "the honor of God and the benefit of our neighbors."[101] Revelation's purpose with regard to others is threefold: 1) to build up beginners, 2) to encourage the proficient, and 3) to console the desolate; that is, revelation introduces people to the faith and makes it intelligible to

99. Ibid.: "Prophecy, therefore, is the sight or manifestation of future contingents or of things transcending human understanding. For such a sight four things are required. For since our knowledge is through bodily things and phantasms received from sensible things, it is first required that in the imagination be formed the bodily likeness of things which are shown, as Denis says that it is impossible otherwise for the divine ray to shine in us, unless surrounded by the variety of sacred veils. The second thing required is an intellectual light enlightening the intellect for knowing things shown beyond our natural knowledge. For unless an intellectual light be present for understanding the sensible likenesses formed in the imagination, the one to whom these likenesses are shown in not called a prophet but a dreamer. Thus, Pharaoh, who, although he saw ears of corn and cattle, which indicated future events, did not understand what he saw, is not called a prophet, but rather Joseph, who interpreted it. The same is true of Nebuchadnezzar, who saw a statue but did not understand it; hence, neither is he a prophet, but Daniel. For this reason it says in Dan (10:1): 'Understanding is needed in a vision.' The third thing required is the courage to announce the things revealed. For God reveals in order that it be announced to others: 'Behold, I have put my words in your mouth' (Jer 1:9). The fourth thing is the working of miracles, which lend certitude to the prophecy. For unless they did things which exceed the works of nature, they would not be believed in matters that transcend natural knowledge."

100. Ibid. §813: "But sometimes one who has solely imaginary visions is called a prophet, but in an improper sense and very remotely so. Again, one is called a prophet, if he has the intellectual light to explain even imaginary visions made to himself or someone else, or for explaining the sayings of the prophets or the Scriptures of the apostles. In this way a prophet is anyone who discerns the writings of the Doctors, because they have been interpreted in the same spirit as they were edited; and so Solomon and David can be called prophets, inasmuch as they had the intellectual light to understand clearly and subtly."

101. Ibid. §818.

them, it serves as a means to exhort faithful Christians to live a life of holiness through good actions, and it provides succor to those who are suffering. In short, revelation provides a pastoral ministry for the illumination of others and the full range of Christian experience.

The distinction between prophecy and revelation is really just a matter of temporality, where revelation is something that happens suddenly and prophecy is something that happens over time. We might think of Paul's Damascus Road experience as revelatory, in that it happened quickly, and Ezekiel's ministry as prophetic in that it occurred over a sustained period of time.[102] Otherwise there is no difference between the two.

The Illumination of Scripture

The source of revelation is always the divine light given by God, but its human expression is found in scripture. In *Summa Theologiae* I.1.10, Aquinas mentions that the "author (*auctor*) of sacred scripture is God." We might take this to mean that Aquinas is arguing for a kind of divine dictation that precludes any human input—if God is the author, then humans are purely passive receptacles of revelation, like tape recorders for the words of God. This, however, is to misunderstand *auctor*'s multivalent meanings and what Aquinas often means by *auctor*. To take just a few examples from the *Prima Pars*, Aquinas says that God is also the *auctor* of eternity (I 10.2 ad 1), of our intellectual power (I 12.2), of nature (I 22.2 ad 3 and I 91.1 ad 1), of the evil of penalty (I 48.6), and of both the light of grace and the light of nature (I 89.1). God as *auctor* extends even to the divine relations. Thus Aquinas claims that while "the Word has no beginning of duration, still he does not lack a *principium* or *auctor*, for he was with God as his *auctor*."[103]

The equivalence between a *principium* and an *auctor* provides an insight into how Aquinas understands the term in relation to the divine role in scripture. Elsewhere, Aquinas says that "the principal *auctor* of sacred Scripture

102. *In I Cor.* 14.2 §826: "They [revelation, knowledge, teaching, and prophecy] can be distinguished in another way according to the various ways that knowledge is from a supernatural source, namely, God, or from a natural, i.e., the natural light of the intellect. If it is from a supernatural principle, namely, by a divinely infused light, it can happen in two ways: because it is either infused by sudden knowledge, and then it is revelation; or it is infused successively, and then it is prophecy, which the prophets did not have suddenly but successively and by parts, as their prophecies show. But if the knowledge is acquired by a natural principle, this is either through one's own study and then it pertains to knowledge, or it is presented by someone else, and then it pertains to teaching."

103. *In Ioh.* 1.1 §48.

is the Holy Spirit," while humans were "the instrumental *auctor*[s] of sacred scripture."[104] What this suggests, along with equivalency of *auctor* and *principium*, is that Aquinas views God's role in the production of scripture as that of the principal cause and the human role as the instrumental cause, a position that he takes with regard to a number ways that God works in the world, but most especially in the sacraments. In Aquinas's view of efficient causality, there can be both principal and instrumental causes of the same act, without either one diminishing the causality of the other. The example that Aquinas often uses is that of a hand moving a stick in the dirt. It is the stick that causes the dirt to move, but it does so as an instrument of the hand, which is the principal cause of movement. This is an example of what is known in medieval discussions as "*per se* causality," where when the principal cause of something ceases to exist, all other causes cease to exist as well, so that if the hand drops the stick, the stick ceases to move the dirt. The other form of efficient causality is known as "accidental causality," in which the existence of posterior causes is not dependent on the continued existence of the prior cause, as is the case when a son continues to exist when the father dies.[105]

Aquinas clarifies the role of the Holy Spirit in prophetic revelation in ST II-II 173.4, where he takes up the principal and instrumental causality distinction in arguing that the human mind is moved by the Holy Spirit "as a deficient instrument with respect to the principal agent."[106] What makes the human defective is the simple fact that humans cannot know all that God intends in revelation—the layers of meaning may escape the one to whom God gives revelation. Aquinas suggests that in prophetic revelation there are three things that the Holy Spirit may move the human mind to do: 1) to apprehend something, 2) to say something, or 3) to do something, and these three can appear singly or in combination. In each action the Holy Spirit can either communicate that what is being given is revelation, and this is prophecy proper, or can just move the mind without communicating that it is the Spirit which is moving the mind, which Aquinas calls a kind of prophetic instinct.[107]

By differentiating between the Holy Spirit as the principal author and the human as the instrumental author, Aquinas is not making the writers of holy scripture to be mere mouthpieces or empty vessels through which God speaks; unlike inanimate sticks, humans have intellects and wills that must be used so

104. *Quodl.* VII.6 ad 5.

105. On these two forms of efficient causality, see Edward Feser, *Aquinas: A Beginner's Guide* (Oxford: Oneworld, 2009), 69–72.

106. ST II-II 173.4.

107. Ibid.

that the revelation can be communicated in a human way. Recipients of divine revelation must choose to speak and write and do so using their own language and imagery. Humans and angels are given by God "the dignity of causality," by which they are able to serve as causes that serve God's divine providence without in any way abrogating God's simultaneous principal causality.[108]

Unlike humans, however, God is able to work interiorly to speak to us, while all of our speaking is external. In fact, this "speaking" is not a kind of dictation, but rather a form of interior inspiration, as Aquinas notes in his commentary on Job, arguing that God speaks to men "by illuminating man and communicating wisdom through interior inspiration."[109] Some writers of scripture are seemingly not even writing under inspiration, but are what Aquinas calls "hagiographers" who write from their own perspective rather than God's.[110] This would include writers like Luke, who were writing secondhand, but we might conclude that there is still some illumination going on even here, as non-eyewitnesses still would need a light to discern the truth of the stories; illumination also provides an ability to judge properly what one comes to know by natural reason. This does not diminish the authority of Luke for Aquinas, but rather points to the fact that the revelation is found in what Christ revealed about God as relayed through the eyewitness accounts of others.[111]

108. *In Ioh.* 1.4 §119: "God wanted to have certain witnesses, not because he needed their testimony, but to ennoble those whom he appointed witnesses. Thus we see in the order of the universe that God produces certain effects by means of intermediate causes, not because he himself is unable to produce them without these intermediaries, but he deigns to confer on them the dignity of causality because he wishes to ennoble these intermediate causes. Similarly, even though God could have enlightened all men by himself and lead them to a knowledge of himself, yet to preserve due order in things and to ennoble certain men, he willed that divine knowledge reach men through certain other men." On the dignity of causality, cf. ST I 22.3.

109. *In Iob* 28:27, lines 343–46, page 155. Aquinas later goes on to describe the conversation between Job and God in the whirlwind as being either a literal discussion (and miraculous) or as a metaphorical expression of an internal inspiration.

110. ST II-II 174.2 ad 3: "It was this kind of prophecy [conveyed by an imaginary vision leading to a supernatural truth] that all those had who are included in the ranks of prophets, who moreover were called prophets for the special reason that they exercised the prophetic calling officially. Hence they spoke as God's representatives, saying to the people: 'Thus says the Lord.' But not so the authors of the sacred writings (*hagiographa conscripserunt*) several of whom treated more frequently of things that can be known by human reason, not in God's name, but in their own, yet with the help of the divine light."The content of the objection, which follows Jerome in dividing writers of scripture into prophets (Isaiah, Jeremiah, and others) and hagiographers (Job, David, and Solomon), would indicate that Aquinas's response includes the same division.

111. Even the "speaking" of the Holy Spirit is conceived of as an interior illumination of our minds. See *In Ioh.* 16:3 §2103 for a brief account of this.

All of this might still sound a bit too mechanical and a diminishment of human agency, but it may be helpful to remember that Aquinas treats the topic of prophetic revelation in his discussion of the gratuitous graces, which God gives to individuals for the salvation of others.[112] Thus the light of revelation is one of the effects of the light of grace that God gives to make our salvation possible. God's grace, as Aquinas points out, has both an operative and cooperative element to it. God operates in us interiorly, which only God can do, to move our will toward him. God also gives us the ability to participate with him cooperatively, which is an exterior movement of the soul.[113] Prophetic revelation, then, would have God's operative grace as the principal cause of revelation while the prophet would apprehend, say, or do what God has moved him to do cooperatively, with a free will and a range of possibilities. To understand the divine/human dynamic in revelation we must understand it within the context of how God works in the soul while maintaining the freedom that demarcates human acts.

Christ the Light of Holy Teaching

All of this—grace, revelation, illumination, teaching, and salvation—reaches its culmination in the visible and invisible missions of the person of the Son.[114] Christ, as Aquinas says in his *principium*, is the "teacher of teachers" and his divine mission, on which he is sent by the Father, is to illumine the human intellect.[115] As the "first and principal teacher of spiritual teaching and faith," Christ has all of the gratuitous graces, which make his teaching clear, in complete fullness.[116] Christ's teachings, which "both illumine and vivify," derive from the fullness of light which is in Christ.[117] Christ alone has light, not

112. ST I-II 111.1 and 111.4.

113. ST I-II 111.2.

114. Aquinas details two missions of the Son in ST I 43.2: "For the Son may proceed eternally as God; but temporally, by becoming man, according to His visible mission, or likewise by dwelling in man according to His invisible mission." Both of these missions have illuminative effects, so when I speak of the mission of the Son to illuminate, it will include reference to both of these missions—that of the Incarnation and of the Son's ongoing illuminative work.

115. *Rigans Montes* and ST I 43.5 ad 2.

116. ST III 7.7: "the gratuitous graces are ordained for the manifestation of faith and spiritual doctrine. For it behooves him who teaches to have the means of making his doctrine clear; otherwise his doctrine would be useless. Now Christ is the first and chief teacher of spiritual doctrine and faith . . . hence it is clear that all the gratuitous graces were most excellently in Christ, as in the first and chief teacher of the faith."

117. *In Ioh.* 8.1 §1118.

in a participated manner but essentially, since as God "he is light."[118] This illuminating privilege has the effect of driving away the darkness of sin and ignorance as well as the darkness of eternal damnation because his light is the light of life.[119]

The focal point of Christ's teaching and illumination is found on the cross. It is on the cross that Christ offers his deepest and most profound illumination by teaching us faith, hope, patience, devotion, and how to live.[120] Aquinas offers a striking image that links Christ's teaching on the cross with the kind of teaching that his students experience, explaining that "he carried his cross as a teacher his candelabrum, as a support for the light of his teaching, because for believers the message of the cross is the power of God, and believers do not hide their lights under bushels."[121] One imagines that the Paris masters must have had to supply their own light for reading and lecturing so that the candelabrum gave a physical manifestation of the intellectual illumination that was to take place in the medieval classroom. The cross of Christ plays that same role, with Christ carrying it as a physical manifestation of his illumination. This illumination that is the mission of Christ means that if we want to capture the secrets of divine wisdom it is Christ, as the source of light, to whom we must draw close.[122] The idea here is that the closer one gets to a light source, the more one is illuminated, and Aquinas's entire celestial hierarchy, derived primarily from Dionysus, is based upon this principle, with each layer of the hierarchy receiving illumination from God and the layer above it and then sharing the light with the next layers of the celestial (and ecclesiastical) hierarchies.[123]

This hierarchical principle leads us back to where this chapter began, with Aquinas's understanding of theology as an illuminating enterprise. The causal chain of illumination goes from God as the only being with complete and total knowledge of God in God's essence, to the ninefold hierarchy of angels, to humans, who are themselves arranged hierarchically by order of their own closeness to God. Each order in the hierarchy of closeness teaches the layers in the hierarchy below it, so that teaching is always a form of illumination

118. *In Ioh.* 8.2 §1141.

119. Ibid.

120. See the sermon *Germinet Terra* for Aquinas's discussion of how Christ teaches these things from the cross. Thomas Aquinas, *The Academic Sermons*, 278–79.

121. *In Ioh.* 19.3 §2414.

122. *In Ioh.* 13.4 §1807: "We can see from this that the more a person wants to grasp the secrets of divine wisdom, the more he should try to get closer to Christ, according to: 'Come to him and be enlightened' [Ps. 34:5]. For the secrets of divine wisdom are especially revealed to those who are joined to God by love."

123. *In Eph.* 1.7 §62; ST I 106.1; ST I 108.1.

for Aquinas. Returning to *Rigans Montes*, we can see how theologians must be represented by mountains because mountains are naturally closer to celestial bodies and thus receive more of the light. We should not, however, assume that what draws teachers closer to Christ is some sort of self-generated knowledge on the part of the instructor. Rather what makes one close to God, and thus able to receive the secrets of divine wisdom, is to be joined to God through love. There will always be, as we see in *Rigans Montes*, a requirement for theologians as illuminators to live a life of charity with regard to God and neighbors. Knowledge that is not ordered to and rooted in the love of Christ will, in Aquinas's understanding, have more of a demonic cast to it, since demons have greater knowledge of God than any human, but yet no love.

Holy teaching, then, has both an epistemological necessity and a moral necessity to it. Epistemologically it is necessary for our salvation that we be taught by God. Yet, because we are human, God as the supreme teacher instructs us by means that are geared to our creaturely status. The chain of teaching, from God to angels to humans, gives creatures both the dignity of causality in which they really participate in the means of revelation and an opportunity to participate in the light and reflect some of the divine splendor in themselves. The task of holy teaching is not to obscure, obfuscate, or mythologize what has been given by the divine light but rather to understand and communicate to others what has been given by divine grace.

The moral necessity of holy teaching is a result of the importance of sharing goodness. Aquinas argues that the more of God's goodness we have, the more of that goodness we try to share.[124] The light we are given is not to be kept to ourselves, but rather is meant to be shared with others. Part of this is driven as well by Aquinas's understanding of his mission as a Dominican. In reviewing the different forms of religious life, Aquinas contrasts the purely contemplative orientation typically found in Benedictine life, with which he was well familiar as a former child oblate, and the active life of the Dominicans. This active life begins with contemplation, but goes on to act upon that contemplation. Aquinas makes the comparison explicit using light language: "For even as it is better to illumine than to only shine, so it is better to hand on to others what has been contemplated than to only contemplate."[125] This argument, of course, presumes that the teacher has already been illumined.

124. ST I 106.4: "Every creature participates in the Divine goodness, so as to diffuse the good it possesses to others; for it is of the nature of good to communicate itself to others . . . so the more an agent is established in the share of the Divine goodness, so much the more does it strive to transmit its perfections to others as far as possible."

125. ST II-II 188.6.

There is also a pedagogical principle in play here. In a human *scientia*, the basic principles are self-illumining so that once we understand the terms of the principle we understand the principle itself. In metaphysics, for instance, the basic principle is that something cannot be and not be at the same time—the principle of noncontradiction. (I take this to be a metaphysical principle with logical repercussions, not a purely logical principle.) In holy teaching, the principles of the faith, which can be reduced to "God's existence and His providence over the salvation of man,"[126] are not self-illumining and known to humans *per se*, but are in fact the product of an ever greater illumination—God's; God knows his own existence *per se*. But once we understand the basic principles of holy teaching, which Aquinas lays out in QQ. 2–26 of the *Prima Pars*, we can begin to understand the rest of holy teaching, which culminates in Christ. Pedagogically this requires the teacher to understand and believe the basic principles of the faith better than the students.[127] The teacher, however, does not necessarily start by teaching the universal principles of the field of knowledge, but begins with more particular and contingent elements and works backward with the students so that ultimately they may understand the more universal principles of a science.[128] Teachers must work with the different lights given to each student and must share the illumination they have themselves received, whether from other teachers or from their own process of discovery.

Holy teaching, then, is a gift from the Father of lights, who is the principal teacher of all of us, primarily through the visible and invisible missions of his Son. The teaching of God, about God, is a process of illumination that we participate in by drawing close to God through his Son, and then sharing the goodness and illumination we receive from Christ with others. Aquinas starts his *principium* with these ideas, which continue to be a thematic focus of the rest of his career.

126. ST II-II 1.7.

127. ST II-II 2.6: "Men of higher degree, whose business it is to teach others, are under obligation to have fuller knowledge of matters of faith, and to believe them more explicitly." Perhaps a warning to all theology professors.

128. ST I 106.1: "Thus it is with us that the teacher, in order to adapt himself to others, divides into many points the knowledge which he possesses in the universal."

2

The Physics of Light

When Thomas Aquinas, or any of his medieval contemporaries, writes about light, we often import contemporary understandings of light into their discussions, but the fact is that Aquinas understood the nature of light very differently than we do. He completely rejected two of our understandings of light, since he believed that light could not travel as fast as it does and that it could not travel through a vacuum. When Aquinas writes about light, if we think that he understands it the same way we do we are at serious risk of misunderstanding him.

The purpose of this chapter, then, is to describe in detail Aquinas's understanding of light, so that when we turn to his theological application of light we will be able to understand him on his terms, without the anachronistic imposition of modern understandings of light. Additionally, by understanding how Aquinas thinks about light, we can observe how he uses his knowledge of the natural world to expand his understanding of God, since he believes that we can come to know some truths about God from God's created effects.

The study of physical light is important in understanding Aquinas's theology of light because he makes a direct connection between physical light and spiritual light. For Aquinas it is fruitful to understand physical light as a means of understanding spiritual and theological light:

> Sense perceptible light, however, is a certain image of spiritual light, for every sensible thing is something particular, whereas intellectual things are a kind of whole. Just as particular light has an effect on the thing seen, inasmuch as it makes colors actually visible, as well as on the one seeing, because through it the eye is conditioned for seeing, so intellectual light makes the intellect to know because whatever light is in the rational creature is all derived from that supreme light "which illumines every man coming into the world." Furthermore, it makes all things to be actually intelligible inasmuch as all forms

> are derived from it, forms which give things the capability of being known, just as all the forms of artifacts are derived from the art and reason of the artisan.[1]

To see how Aquinas thinks light works we will look primarily at three texts, *De Anima* II.14–15, *De Sensu* 2–6, and *Summa Theologiae* I 67. Additionally, we will look at the role that light plays in vision, because Aquinas's discussions of light invariably are intertwined with discussions of vision and because our final end is the vision of God, which requires the light of glory. As David Lindberg notes, "Before 1600 the science of optics tended to coalesce around two interrelated, yet distinguishable, problems—the nature and propagation of light, and the process of visual perception."[2] Light and vision go together, both from a scientific perspective, and in the case of Aquinas, from a theological perspective.

At the outset, let me point out that among medieval theologians there is nothing especially novel about Aquinas's understanding of light. Unlike his teacher, Albert the Great, Aquinas, while not ignorant of the natural world, generally kept his constructive, noncommentary work focused on theology. His commentary on Aristotle's *De Anima* is dependent upon Albert's work as well as that of Themistius and his commentary on *De Sensu* is reliant upon a commentary by Alexander of Aphrodisias.[3] This is not to say that there was one shared concept of light and vision among medieval theologians, or that others did not consider Aquinas's thoughts on light of interest. His treatment of light in *De Anima* II.14 was broken out and published as a separate tract, *De Natura Luminis*, which had its own manuscript history, so his contemporaries did think that he had something important to say about light.[4] Additionally, there were alternative understandings of light and vision that were live options in the thirteenth century, particularly the theory of extramission that came from the

1. *In Ioh.* 8.2 §1142.

2. David C. Lindberg, *Theories of Vision from al-Kindi to Kepler* (Chicago: University of Chicago Press, 1981), x.

3. On the reliance upon Albert and Themestius, see Robert Pasnau's introduction in: Thomas Aquinas, *A Commentary on Aristotle's De Anima*, trans. Robert Pasnau, Yale Library of Medieval Philosophy (New Haven: Yale University Press, 1999), xiv. On the reliance upon Alexander, see ———, *Commentaries on Aristotle's "On Sense and What Is Sensed" and "On Memory and Recollection,"* trans. Kevin White and E. M. Macierowski, Thomas Aquinas in Translation (Washington, DC: Catholic University of America Press, 2005), 161, fn. 6. For Alexander's commentary see: Alexander of Aphrodisias, *Alexander of Aphrodisias: On Aristotle's "On Sense Perception,"* trans. Alan Towey (Ithaca, NY: Cornell University Press, 2000).

4. On this see volume 45-1 of the Leonine edition of the *De Anima* commentary, pp. 271–75 of the appendices.

Platonic tradition through Augustine, an understanding that Aquinas rejected. The question of novelty, however, is not important here; rather, what is at stake is our ability to understand Aquinas when he speaks about light without being confused by our modern understandings of light.

Aristotelian Commentaries on Light

With regard to his commentaries on Aristotle, Aquinas looks at light in both *De Anima* and *De Sensu*. While there is some overlap in the topics taken up in the two commentaries, we might roughly divide them by viewing the text of *De Anima* as investigating the nature of light in general and the text of *De Sensu* as investigating the application of light to the senses, particularly that of vision. The main passages on the nature of light appear in Aquinas's commentary of *De Anima* in book two, lectures 14 and 15, in which he not only gives his typical line-by-line commentary on the text, but also extends the discussion to give his own views on light.

Light, according to Aquinas, "is the actuality of the diaphanous considered as diaphanous,"[5] an obscure definition to modern ears and one that will take some explication. Basically put, Aristotle observed that we are able to see objects, specifically colors, across distances because what is between us and the colors we see is transparent. If, for instance, there was an opaque obstacle, say a black box, immediately in front of us, we would be unable to see any colors that might exist on the other side of the box. On the other hand, if the same box were made out of transparent plastic, we would be able to see the colors on the other side of the box. In the Aristotelian tradition, the main transparent bodies, usually called "the diaphanous," were air and water, along with some precious stones and other bodies. Both air and water are basically transparent and allow us to see the objects on the other side of them. But what makes us able to see the colors on the other side of the diaphanous, whether it is the trees across the street or the fish at the bottom of a pond, is light. Without light the transparent medium is dark and we are unable to see the colors around us, so when Aquinas says that light is the actuality of the diaphanous, what he means is that we are unable to see anything without light. There is more to it than this, of course, but with this overview in place we can look more closely at some of the alternative understandings of light that Aquinas rejects; that is, one way we can understand what light is for Aquinas is by first understanding what light is not. Call it an apophasis of light, if you will.

5. DA II.14 418b9, lines 113–14.

Light Is Not a Body

One of the opinions rejected by Aquinas was that light was a body, a theory held by the ancient Greek philosopher, Democritus, and one that sometimes still held sway in the thirteenth century. Aquinas tells us that the main reason philosophers had argued that light was a body was because of how we used light language. When we speak of light rays traveling through the air, or of light reflecting off a surface, or rays intersecting, we speak as if light behaved like a body.[6] Aquinas argues that such language is misleading, and he gives four reasons why light cannot be a body. First, light cannot be a body because two bodies cannot occupy the same space, and a diaphanous medium, such as air or water, is already a body. So if light were a body as well, there would be two bodies in the same place, which is physically impossible.[7] Second, bodies move from place to place by local motion, but according to medieval observations the sky lights up from east to west instantaneously and yet no one can see the body of light moving from east to west. It was inconceivable to these philosophers that something could move faster than they could see, especially if it was a body.[8] Third, and similar to the second, if light were a body it would seem difficult for it to multiply itself across the entire hemisphere at once. An example (of my own) of a body that multiplies itself over a distance would be water flooding a vast area in a very short time, which we can observe happening, no matter how quickly. Light, however, seems to flood the entire earth at once when the sun breaks the horizon, so it cannot be a body if we cannot see it multiply. Fourth, if light were a body it would seem odd that light would be destroyed or corrupted simply by the imposition of an obstacle between the light source and the eye; bodies would not be so easily corrupted.[9] Light

6. Ibid. 418b20, lines 207–13: "As is said in the text, some have been of the view that light is a body. They were moved to say this by certain expressions that we use in speaking about light. For we have become accustomed to saying that a ray passes through air, or that it is deflected, or that rays intersect one another. All of these seem to be features of bodies."

7. Ibid. 418b17, lines 153–58. Those who advocated for light as a body argued that it was able to pass through glass because the glass had holes or pores in it that allowed the bodies to pass through. See PA I.42.88a11.

8. Ibid. 418b20, especially lines 176–79: "But no local motion of any sort of body can be immediate or instantaneous. Therefore the illumination would occur not immediately but successively." The main idea here is that if light were a body, it would constantly need to be created each day and destroyed each night via generation and corruption.

9. Ibid., 418b20, lines 215–20. See *Meta.* IV.2 §551: "Generation is a process toward being, and corruption a change from being to non-being."

language implying that light is a body is, for Aquinas, metaphorical language that obscures its true nature.

In this regard, Aquinas's understanding of the nature of light is not far off from modern conceptions. Light, we now know, is a form of energy—electromagnetic radiation to be precise—and not matter. Einstein's theory of relativity shows how mass and energy are related, but it is clear that light is not made up of matter (what Aquinas would think of as a body), but is energy instead. The language is slightly different and the arguments are certainly different, but the end result is similar.

Light Is Not a Spiritual Nature

A second understanding of light Aquinas rejects is that light has some spiritual nature, an understanding whose origin he again accounts for in our use of daily language. When we talk about light with regard to intellectual things (which are immaterial and spiritual) we can mistakenly think that light is likewise something spiritual, where "spiritual" is here understood not in its religious sense, but in the more abstract sense of not being a physical reality. Aquinas rejects this view, which Pasnau attributes to Augustine and Bonaventure,[10] for the simple reason that we can see light with our eyes, and our physical senses are only able to see physical realities. Aquinas is happy to agree with anyone who differentiates spiritual light from corporeal light, but wants to draw a clear difference between the two.[11]

Here Aquinas sees the importance of light and its (mis)attribution as a spiritual reality as the result of the relationship between light and vision, which is the highest and most spiritual of the senses for Aquinas.

Two More Incorrect Ideas about Light

Aquinas rules out two more incorrect ideas about light. The third is that light is just the "evidence of color,"[12] but Aquinas easily dismisses this by pointing out that if this were true we would be able to see the color of luminous things at

10. See Pasnau's note in: Thomas Aquinas, *A Commentary on Aristotle's De Anima*, 217, fn. 6. Pasnau points to Augustine's *De genesi ad litteram* IV.28 and Bonaventure's *Commentary on the Sentences* II.13.1.1.

11. DA II 14, 418b20, lines 226–40.

12. Ibid., 418b20, lines 287–88.

night, which we do not. We need light to see color, for color cannot make itself evident without it.

Finally, Aquinas addresses the idea that light (*lux*) is the substantial form of the sun, and the light (*lumen*) that emanates from it exists as a kind of intentional being, where intentional being is the existence that something has in our mind as a likeness to the naturally occurring thing.[13] Here Aquinas is addressing the medieval distinction between *lux* and *lumen*, the two Latin words for light, where *lux* is the form or source of light and *lumen* is the illumination that comes from that source.[14] As Aquinas points out, however, the problem with suggesting that *lux* is the substantial form of the sun is that we cannot see the substantial form of anything with our senses. We can see, for instance, the particular shape of a chair with our eyes, but to "see" the substantial form of a chair—what makes it a chair in itself—is something we must do by abstracting away the particulars, which we can only do intellectually. So, if *lux* were the substantial form of the sun, we would not be able to see the sun's light physically. An additional problem is that things that have intentional being cannot cause change in other things. If they did, then every time we thought about a fire our mind would begin to burn, but Aquinas knows that light actually changes things by heating them, decomposing them, illuminating them, and so on.[15] Crucially, in rejecting the idea that *lux* is the substantial form of the sun, or that *lux* is any kind of substantial form, Aquinas is rejecting the light metaphysics that were central to Grosseteste and Bonaventure.

So we have eliminated four wrong ideas about light—that it is a body, a spiritual thing, an appearance of color, or the substantial form of the sun. With those possibilities eliminated, Aquinas turns to what he claims is the true nature of light. At this point in his commentary on *De Anima* II.14 he has concluded his line-by-line commentary on Aristotle's text and is now offering his own constructive thought on the nature of light.

13. For a discussion on Aquinas's four different uses of the term *intentio*, see Robert William Schmidt, *The Domain of Logic According to Saint Thomas Aquinas* (The Hague: Martinus Nijhoff, 1966), 94–129.

14. We will discuss Aquinas's use of light language in depth in the following chapter. The key text for this distinction is II *Sent.* 13.1.3.

15. Ibid., 418b20, lines 301–4: "The second is also false, because something that has only intentional being does not bring about a natural transformation. But rays from the heavenly bodies transform all of lower nature."

The True Nature of Light

Aquinas, in his typically compact way, defines *lux* "as the active quality of a heavenly body on the basis of which it acts."[16] Because light is a quality of a heavenly body, it may be helpful to summarize Aquinas's cosmology with regard to heavenly bodies, which is significantly different than ours. The medieval position was that stars and the sun were not hot in and of themselves; instead, the heat we experience was the result of their bodies being in friction with the air; stars and such were actually considered to be cold.[17] At the same time, the heavenly bodies were considered to be the first, in the sense of hierarchy, in the place of all corporeal beings, and as such they are the "first things altering"[18] in the medieval cosmology to act on other bodies. As Aquinas puts it, "heavenly bodies are the agent causes of the things that are here . . . [and] all substantial forms of the lower bodies come to be from the power of the heavenly bodies."[19] The primary way that these bodies act upon the lower bodies is through light, which is "the universal active power of heavenly bodies" and one that all heavenly bodies share (including, for instance, the moon).[20] Light produces effects in us. The power to produce these effects comes from light as a quality of these heavenly bodies. Aquinas here understands *quality* on the basis of Aristotle's *Categories*, where a quality is something that allows us to qualify something in a particular way,[21] often in the sense of applying an adjective to a noun, so that we talk about a hot fire or the taste of sweet honey. There are, for Aristotle, four different kinds of qualities, and light and heat fall into the third category. This third type of quality, according to Aristotle, "consists of affective qualities or affections,"[22] which means that the quality is capable of producing an affection in our senses, so the hot fire causes our fingers to burn and sweet honey changes our tongue to sweetness. These kinds of qualities, while being accidental, are not substantial but are nevertheless permanent, abiding, and hard to change, and are the basis for the action of things. So, as belonging to the third kind of quality, light (*lux*) causes a change

16. Ibid., 418b20, lines 306–8: "So light (*lux*) is an active quality of a heavenly body on the basis of which it acts and is in the third species of quality along with heat."

17. *De Caelo* II.10 §387: "He says therefore first that heat and light are generated by the stars by a certain stroking of, or friction with, air and not because they are of a fiery nature."

18. Ibid., §393.

19. Ibid.

20. Ibid.

21. *Categories* 8b25–26. Aristotle, *The Complete Works of Aristotle: The Revised Oxford Translation*, ed. Jonathan Barnes, 2 vols. (Princeton: Princeton University Press, 1995), vol. 1, 15.

22. Ibid., 9a29–9b9.

in our senses and is a permanent and abiding characteristic by which heavenly bodies act.

Unlike heat, however, light does not have a contrary. This is important for our understanding of light and its theological application. Aquinas tells us that the contraries of some qualities are what are known as simple or pure privations, and he typically compares light to heat in this regard. Heat has a natural contrary, cold, which is a quality of its own, and for some object to take on the form of heat, to become actually hot, the form or actuality of coldness must be removed. The natural contrary to heat will in some sense resist the heat, even if a substance is disposed to receive the form of heat, so that the heat does not enter into the object immediately, but over time. Anyone who has tried to heat a bottle of milk for a screaming infant at 3:00 a.m. understands this principle implicitly. Some forms take a while to enter into objects. So some qualities have naturally opposed qualities that resist their entrance.[23]

Light, however, does not have a contrary that resists its form. We might think that darkness is its contrary, and it is, but darkness is not something that actually exists in its own right, but rather is an absence or privation of light; there is no object that has darkness as one of its qualities. What this means is that when something is disposed to possess light, but is dark, it is able to take on the form of light instantaneously because there is no opposing quality to resist its entrance. Again, at 3:00 a.m., the bleary-eyed parent is fortunate that when the lights turn on, the light immediately fills the room, rather than taking a while to seep into the atmosphere.[24]

There are important theological and moral implications of this view of light, which we will look at in depth later, but briefly stated we can see how God as light is able to enter into any place that is dark without resistance, a principle that is in play with the light of grace, allowing the instantaneous conversion of sinners, and with God's power over the devil. Likewise, as our evil acts are privations of good and thus have a certain darkness to them, God's grace in its illuminating power is able to point us instantly toward the correct

23. See Aquinas's commentary on the *Metaphysics* for a discussion of this type of privation. *Meta.* V.20 §1072.

24. DA II.14 418b20, lines 309–18: "Light differs from heat in that it is a quality of the first body that brings about change—a body that has no contrary. Thus neither does light (*lux*) have a contrary, whereas there is a contrary of heat. But since there is no contrary of light (*lux*), there cannot be a contrary disposition in something to take it on. For this reason, the thing light (*lux*) affects, a diaphanous medium, is always perfectly disposed for that form; hence it is illuminated at once. Something capable of being heated, in contrast, is not heated at once."

acts, which accord with reason. Similarly, as a quality that acts, so light allows us to act correctly toward our final end.

So because light does not have a contrary, when light (*lux*) illumines the diaphanous medium, it does so instantaneously, and "the participation or effect of light (*lux*) in the diaphanous medium is called light (*lumen*)."[25] Aquinas explains two other names we have for light, rays and splendor, where a ray is what we call light when we see it go in a straight line, and splendor or brilliance is what we call light when it is reflected off of another object.[26]

In summary, Aquinas describes light (*lumen*) as a quality of heavenly bodies that have light (*lux*) by nature. Light serves as a kind of first cause among material objects, has no contrary, and when it enters a diaphanous medium it instantly illuminates it and makes objects available to our vision. The light that we see is a participation in the light of the heavenly bodies, but is not an abiding quality in itself, so that without the source of light, the illumination goes away.

The Nature of the Diaphanous Medium

Aquinas discusses the diaphanous in *De Anima*, but pays more substantial attention to the nature of the diaphanous in *De Sensu*. The diaphanous is, according to Aquinas, not something that has a nature of its own, in the way that a horse is the only being that has horseness. Rather, the diaphanous is a common nature, a property that is shared by more than one thing, with the two most common being air and water.[27] The first thing to note about diaphanous realities is that they are bodies. As Aquinas has argued, this means that light could not be a body, since bodies cannot occupy the same space. Those who did think that light was a body posited that diaphanous things had small pores in them through which light penetrated, but Aquinas rejected this in favor of the view of light described above.

What makes something diaphanous is that it can take on color, but in order to do that it must have no color of its own. Instead, Aquinas claims that as its formal principle, "light is the color" of the diaphanous.[28] In this sense, light is not only a color itself, it is the origin and source of all other color—a

25. Ibid., lines 314–19.

26. Ibid. This helps explain what it means to say that the Son is the splendor of the Father's glory.

27. *De Sensu* 5, 439a21, lines 106–8: "He [Aristotle] says that *what* is called *the transparent is not a property of* either *air or water or any* such body—for instance glass and other transparent bodies—*but is a common 'nature'* found in many bodies." The italics represent quotations directly from Aristotle.

28. *De Sensu* 5, 439a18, line 84.

view that coincides with our modern notions of light and the existence of the entire spectrum of color that is found in light. But the diaphanous does not have light in and of itself, but rather light must come from something outside of it, which means that diaphanous objects have light in them as accidental qualities. Without light, the diaphanous is dark and in potential to receive light. Here Aquinas distinguishes three ways that something is in potential to receive light, arranged hierarchically. First, those objects that are "receptive of light and totally filled with it, being, as it were, perfectly brought to actuality, so that it cannot receive any further quality or form of this kind."[29] Among corporeal bodies, Aquinas argues that the sun is the highest example of a body that has light in full actuality and no potentiality. Second, are things that do not have light in themselves, but are able to be filled with light, and are thus transparent. This is, according to Aquinas, found in other heavenly bodies, fire, air, water, and some bodies that are partially made of earth but are predominantly composed of other diaphanous materials (an example might be a diamond). Third, are things that are made primarily of earth and can only receive light on their surface.[30] Thus those luminous objects at the first level are both receptive of light and have light as a natural quality. Second-level objects are equally receptive of light, but do not have light as a natural quality, but depend on a light source for their luminosity.

There are two interesting things of note here. First, Aquinas suggests that while we normally think of the diaphanous as materials found at the second level of receptivity to light, he says that we commonly call "anything that can be receptive of light in any way" transparent.[31] This extended use of the term "transparency" leads to the second interesting point, which is speculation on my part, since Aquinas is never explicit about it. It would seem that these three levels of light receptivity are roughly analogous to the three levels of theological light. Only God has light by nature, but each level of creature is receptive to light by different levels of participation, where the first level corresponds to the light of glory received by the angels and saints who have been purified so that they may receive the beatific vision—their souls are perfectly receptive to God's light. The second level corresponds to those who have received the light of grace, where persons do not have the light intrinsically, but are receptive of it,

29. *De Sensu* 5, 439a21, lines 130–34.

30. Ibid., 439a21, lines 134–61.

31. Ibid., lines 162–67: "Now although it is only in the case of bodies in the intermediate level that one properly speaks of the 'transparent' or 'diaphanous' according to the proper meaning of the term, nevertheless, generally speaking, that can be called 'transparent' which is receptive of light in any way whatsoever, and it is in this sense that the Philosopher seems to be speaking here of the 'transparent.'"

especially since the darkness in them is a privation that can be instantaneously changed. The third level is analogous to the light of nature, which we are imbued with at creation and which allows us to receive God's light in its universal capacity, in the same way that the sun shines on all of us—but it is strictly exterior, not an interior light. Perhaps these different levels of (divine) light receptivity also track the Dionysian process of purgation, illumination, and perfection.

Diaphanous things are transparent, as we have mentioned, so that they can take on color, and Aquinas explores the relationship between diaphanous mediums and colors. First, he recognizes that diaphanous things have boundaries, and those boundaries are found where the diaphanous meets the exterior of a colored object.[32] What he is pointing to here is the fact that visible color is only found on an exterior surface of an object and is a quality of that object in that it can affect our senses. This may seem like an odd way of putting it, but actually follows our normal sense experiences. When we see a tree, we do not see the interior of the tree, but only its exterior surfaces, which are all colored. We can see the difference between the trunk with its grayish-brown color from the leaves with their green colors, but we also see the shapes of the leaves by the difference between the green surface and the transparent air. We see shapes at the boundary of the color on the surface and the transparent air. If something is not colored, we cannot see it.

Second, color moves the diaphanous medium that has been actualized by light in order to make itself visible. What happens here is that first the diaphanous medium must be actualized by light, so that it is no longer dark; without light we can see no colors at all. Once the light actualizes the medium, color can then alter the medium and act against it. Aquinas rejects one possibility of how color acts in the medium when he argues against the idea that the colored body changes the medium by local motion. That is, he rejects the idea that somehow the color moves from one place to the other, with all the points in between, in the exact same shape and size that it exists, so that an apple would approach our eye in the same shape and size as it has at its point of origin. Aquinas argues that if color moved through the medium that way, we'd be able to see it move from one place to the other, in the way we see, for example, a train move from place to place.[33] Instead, the medium is changed by an instantaneous alteration where the color exists in the medium "incompletely according to a certain kind of intentional being."[34] There is no

32. *De Sensu* 5, 439a25, lines 212–15: "*For* colored bodies are seen only at their limits, from which it is evident that *color* either *is the limit* of a body *or is on the limit* of a body."

33. *De Sensu* 15, 446a26, lines 44–47. My example.

successive motion of the color, but it alters the medium all at once.[35] As the color alters the medium, it is prepared to be received by our sense of sight.

The medium is important because of the general role it plays in Aquinas's theory of sensation. According to him, all sensation of objects comes through some form of mediation. Sound and smell are mediated through an exterior mediate of air, while touch and taste have an interior mediation;[36] vision, as we will see, is mediated through the diaphanous medium. What drives the importance of the medium in this view is the idea that for one object to change another requires them to touch,[37] a theory that, in the face of medieval observational limitations and their lack of understanding of gravity, makes complete sense. Sound has to touch one's ear, sweetness has to touch the tongue, smell has touch the nose, and heat has to touch the skin. Of course, one does not have to put one's hand in the fire to feel the heat, so the medievals posited the idea that the fire moved the air and communicated the form of fire through the air toward the hand—which, given what we know about how heat excites atoms, was not entirely far off. If every form of sensation comes from some kind of touch, this means that one of the implications of Aquinas's theory is that light could not travel across a vacuum, as it needs a medium in order to move.[38]

The Superiority of Vision

Within this theory of sensation, Aquinas consistently claims that sight is the most superior of the senses.[39] According to him, what we can know by one sense we can almost always know better by sight. When we hear a loud

34. *De Sensu* 4, 438b2, lines 45–49.

35. *De Sensu* 15, 447a1, lines 304–10: "Hence all alterations of which the termini are being and non-being, or privation and form, are instantaneous and cannot be successive, for in successive alterations the succession is noted by means of determinate intermediaries with respect to the distance of one contrary from the other."

36. *De Sensu* 4, 439a1, lines 265–71: "This does not prevent an animal from perceiving by means of touch through the whole of its body, because as other senses perceive through an external medium, touch and taste perceive through an internal medium, namely flesh. And just as the principle of sight is not on the surface of the eye, but within, the principle of touch is also within, near the heart."

37. DA II.15, 419a7, lines 91–92: "For bodies change one another only if they touch one another."

38. DA II.15, 419a15, lines 103–9: "It remains, then, that the organ of sight must be affected by the visible object through some medium. Therefore it is necessary that there be some medium between what is visible and sight. But, if this is a vacuum, then there is no medium able to alter and be altered. It remains, then, that if the medium were a vacuum, nothing at all would be seen."

39. My argument in this section, while necessary for my larger argument, could at the same time be seen as an indirect argument against John Milbank's suggestion that touch is superior for Aquinas. See

rumbling sound we may not know whether it is thunder or a large truck until we turn our eyes to the sky or street. If we feel something wet on our skin we can tell if it is water or milk only by looking at it. Sight is "the more universal power"[40] and one of its key characteristics is its more abstract nature, which lends itself to more intellective manipulation—we can conjure up in our minds an image of fire more readily than what fire actually feels like.

Aquinas first accounts for vision's spiritual superiority based on its object, because what we see we see as the result of things held in common between heavenly and earthly bodies. That is, for Aquinas, the celestial bodies in heaven—the sun, stars, the moon—are the most perfect of corporeal bodies, and when we participate in their powers, we are elevated as well (the parallels with the divine, angelic, and human hierarchy should be obvious here). Because it is the heavenly bodies that cast the light we use for vision, vision has a special standing among the senses. As Aquinas points out, the other senses use the elements found on earth, and so lack participation in higher beings.[41] The second reason for the superiority of sight is that vision takes place by a spiritual alteration when something is illuminated, which is superior to the manner of change in other senses. In Aquinas's account, other senses are changed by local motion, as when, for instance, someone rings a bell and the sound travels across the air to our ears. Aquinas had no idea that light could travel as fast as it does, and so rejected the idea that it too traveled by local motion. Instead, it was observed that the whole sky lit up simultaneously when the sun rose above the horizon.

Aquinas differentiates between what he calls a "natural alteration" and a "spiritual alteration." The former represents the kind of change that imparts a quality into a subject, so that the subject takes on some of the natural being of the agent that is imposing the change. This happens, for example, when a tea kettle is changed from cool to hot by the application of a stove burner. A spiritual alteration occurs when the recipient of the change cannot actually take on the quality of what is causing the change—my eye does not change into a tea kettle when it sees it. Instead, our eye is spiritually altered by taking in the species (form) of the object, but is not changed into it.

John Milbank and Catherine Pickstock, *Truth in Aquinas*, Radical Orthodoxy Series (London and New York: Routledge, 2001), 60–87.

40. *De Sensu* 1, 437a5, lines 235–39: "Also, the *common* sensibles *are better* known *by this* sense [vision], because inasmuch as sight has a power of knowing that is more universal and extends to more things, it is more effective in knowing, because the more universal any power is, the more powerful it is."

41. DA II.14, 418b19–26, lines 246–61.

While sight undergoes spiritual alteration, taste and touch undergo natural alteration, so that when we touch something hot, our skin becomes hot, or when we taste something sweet, our tongue takes on sweetness. With smell and hearing our sense organs are changed by what is affecting the senses. So sight is, for Aquinas, the most spiritual of senses, and along with hearing is "singly instructive" for intellectual matters.[42] When we talk about intellectual matters, Aquinas points out, we almost always use language related to sight. But while sight is the most spiritual sense, light is not a spiritual substance.

Specifics of Vision

When he turns his attention to corporeal sight more specifically,[43] Aquinas first has to deal with a theory of vision that was popular in his own time. This theory, which Augustine picked up from the Platonists and propagated in his own works, is the theory of extramission.

The theory of extramission makes its first and most important appearance in Plato's *Timaeus*.[44] Plato claims the gods formed humans with a fire inside of them that flows through the eyes. When the fire leaves the eyes in the daylight, the fire from the eyes meets up with the surrounding daylight to "make a single homogeneous body aligned with the direction of the eyes."[45] Part of what makes this work is the idea that like things can combine to strengthen each other, in the way that two streams of water can make a larger river. The now-combined stream of light then "strikes and presses against an external object it has connected with."[46] By pressing up against the object of vision, the object then causes motion in the stream of light which is transmitted back to the eye and the soul, where it is seen. Plato claims that at night the fire from our eye is insufficient to move things by themselves since it now no longer has access to the strengthening of the exterior light, with the result that the light dies out so much that we even begin to get sleepy, shutting in our internal fire.[47]

42. Ibid., lines 283–86: "This is why these two senses are the most spiritual and uniquely instructive, and why in intellectual matters we use [terms] pertaining to them, especially sight."

43. In his Pauline commentary, *In II Cor* 12.1 §451, Aquinas actually distinguishes between three kinds of sight, "namely, bodily, by which we can see and know bodies; spiritual or imaginary, by which we see likenesses of bodies; and intellectual, by which we know the nature of things in themselves." We are dealing with the first one here, though it has implications for the other two.

44. *Timaeus* 45b4–46a3 in Plato, *Complete Works*, ed. John M. Cooper and D. S. Hutchinson (Indianapolis: Hackett, 1997).

45. Ibid., 45c4.

46. Ibid., 45c5–6.

There are two important things to notice here. First, in this extramission theory sight happens by a form of touching, so that our eyes, through the fire they emit, literally touch the objects that they see. Remnants of this idea can be found in language where someone touches someone with their eyes, while the modern aphorism that we are to "look but don't touch," would seem very odd to Plato. Vision, along with all the other senses, is one by which we have direct contact with what we perceive. Second, vision is an active process by which we seek out and touch objects with our eyes so that they may move the light back rather than a relatively passive enterprise of just turning our eyes to an object to have it change us.

This theory of extramission made its way into the Latin west primarily through two avenues. First, via a fourth-century translation of the *Timaeus* by Chalcidius, which was widely circulated in the Middle Ages—Lindberg reports that there are some seventy extant manuscripts that date before the twelfth century.[48] Second, and more important theologically, via Augustine, who mentions extramission more than once, but most prominently in *The Literal Meaning of Genesis* IV.54. Speaking of the vision of the sun he says, "And undoubtedly this is a ray of bodily light, darting out of our eyes and touching things set so far away with a speed beyond comparison or calculation."[49]

Until the medieval rediscovery of Aristotle, the theory of extramission was the primary means by which Christian theologians thought of vision. Understanding this theory is helpful in understanding what comes before Aquinas theologically, and his response. An example of this, which we will explore in more depth later, is the Augustinian idea that humans need divine illumination in order to know any truth. In an extramission theory of vision, this makes sense, because the light from the eye needs the exterior light in order to see anything at all, as its interior light is insufficient to touch anything on its own. Aquinas, however, will argue that the light in our mind is sufficient to see things on its own, but before we talk further about his theory of vision, we should first look at the reasons he rejected extramission.

In *De Sensu* 2 and 3, Aquinas outlines several reasons why Aristotle rejects the theory of extramission. First, if the eye is able to see visible things, then

47. Ibid., 45d. Because the light leaves the eye and then returns, technically this is what David Lindberg calls an "extramission-intromission" theory of vision. Lindberg provides a nice summary of the Platonic theory of vision in Lindberg, *Theories of Vision from al-Kindi to Kepler*, 3–6.

48. Ibid., 88.

49. Augustine, *On Genesis: A Refutation of the Manichees; Unfinished Literal Commentary on Genesis; The Literal Meaning of Genesis*, ed. John E. Rotelle, trans. Edmund Hill (Hyde Park, NY: New City Press, 2002). Cf. I.31; VII.20.

it ought to be able to see the very fire that it emits. In this vein, Aquinas also argues that our senses must receive sensations through a medium. Proof of this is that if one puts an object on one's eye, it cannot be seen. You are unable to see it because there is no medium between the eye and the object, and with no medium there one should be able to at least see the fire that is in the eye.[50] Second, part of what drove Plato and others to argue for a fire in the eye was their observation that eyes shine in the dark, though they acknowledged the fire was insufficient to activate a medium. Aquinas wonders why, if this is the case, the eye does not see its reflection off of the medium when the eye moves from place to place.[51] Third, and perhaps most importantly, if a light goes out from our eye, Aquinas argues that we should be able to see in the dark. While Plato says that our light is extinguished by the dark, Aquinas argues that fire is only extinguished by cold or something moist, and darkness is neither;[52] as we mentioned above, since darkness is a privation of light, there is no substance in the dark that could extinguish the fire.

Aquinas offers several additional arguments against extramission. First, if we emitted a fire from the eye, then in order to see stars and other heavenly bodies, our fire would have to reach all the way to the heavens; as we mentioned above, this was what Augustine speculated. But fire, in Aquinas's understanding, is a body and if everyone were to look at the sun at the same time, then there would be a multitude of bodies occupying the same space, which was impossible. Plus, projections of bodies weaken over distance, so the fire should not be able to reach that distance. The only way for that fire to reach such a distance would be if it started off as a very large body, but the eye is too small to produce such a large body.[53]

Aquinas also addresses another element of Plato's theory, which is the idea that the fire from our eye leaves the eye and coalesces with the exterior light by which we see. Plato's theory is that the fire unites to the light in the air somewhere around the midpoint between the eye and the object we are attempting to see, but Aquinas argues that if the light from the eye were to coalesce with exterior light, it would make more sense for Plato to have argued that it does so directly on the eye, since if it were dark, the light would (on Plato's theory) be extinguished. And even if it did occur at the eye, Aquinas argues that there are three additional problems. First, bodies can be united since they exist on their own, but qualities cannot, since they exist in other subjects;

50. *De Sensu* 2, 437a26, lines 70–78.

51. Ibid., 437b5, lines 153–71.

52. Ibid., 437b15, lines 215–26.

53. *De Sensu* 4, 438a25, lines 149–81.

that is, they do not exist independently. For example, two pieces of grass can be united by our intertwining them, but we cannot unite the two qualities of green that exist on each piece of grass. Second, the two bodies of fire and light (allowing Plato's assumption that light is a body) are different, and only similar bodies can be united. Third, there is a membrane, the eye, between the inner fire and the outer light that prevents them from being united.[54]

In the place of an extramission theory of vision, Aquinas offers up Aristotle's alternative account, which is a theory of intromission. Vision, according to this account,

> requires light, which makes a body be transparent in actuality . . . and so, whether the medium that is between the thing seen and the eye is air that is illuminated in actuality, or whether it is light—light existing not in itself, since it is not a body, but in something else that is a body, such as glass or water—the movement that occurs through this medium causes vision.[55]

Unpacking this a bit, there are several elements of this terse account that are important. First, as we have seen before, vision requires a medium that is illuminated by a light source; the light makes the medium go from potentially visible and capable of making color visible to actually visible and making colors visible. Light serves as the active agent that makes vision possible. Second, the light can exist in the air or in some other kind of body precisely because it is not a body. Third, vision is caused by a movement in the medium. All of this happens outside of the eye.

This third aspect of Aquinas's account, that vision is caused by a movement in the medium, is the trickiest part for him to explain. As we have seen, he has eliminated the possibility that the color moves across the medium into the eye by local motion. In this section of *De Sensu* he summarizes three reasons that local motion makes no sense: first, bodies that emanate are reduced over distance until they are worn away; second, the eye would be damaged if bodies actually hit it continuously; third, the pupil would only be able to see small portions of the bodies, since the aperture of the pupil is so small and there would be no way an entire body could fit through it.[56]

Instead, Aquinas argues that the "movement is according to alteration; the alteration is motion to a form that is a quality of the thing seen, to which the

54. *De Sensu* 3, 438a29, lines 205–28.

55. *De Sensu* 4, 438b2, lines 10–20.

56. Ibid., lines 21–31.

medium is in potency inasmuch as it is actually lucid, because the diaphanous is unbounded (since color is the quality of a bounded diaphanous)."[57] What Aquinas is saying here is that the colors we see move the medium by changing it not through local motion, but by imparting a form (and not matter) to it. By taking on that form, which is a quality that can affect the senses, the medium (assuming it is illuminated) goes from being colored in potentiality to colored in actuality. Since a diaphanous medium, as transparent and invisible, has no boundaries (*interminatum*), the colors that are in the medium as forms bound it and make it possible to see things. The colors delineate our vision.

The form of the color that alters the medium exists in the medium in a different way than it does in the colored body. Here Aquinas differentiates between natural being and intentional being, where something's natural being is its physical existence in nature—the rock as it actually exists; intentional being is the known object as it has existence in our minds when we know it—the rock as we think about it. Color exists on a body naturally, but exists in the medium as a "certain kind of intentional being."[58] Aquinas makes two important remarks about the implication of color as existing intentionally. First, color existing intentionally in the medium allows more than one color to be there simultaneously. So while the same object cannot be simultaneously black and white by nature, the medium can be black and white simultaneously, which will allow us to see both colors at the same time. If this were not the case, you would only be able to see a blank page or just the letters on this page, but not both. Second, objects that exist in the intentional mode of being exist imperfectly.[59] That same rock as it exists in our mind when we think about it can go away, and in the medium it loses its intentional existence when the light no longer illuminates the medium. Again, there is a theological implication that we will explore in more depth later, but this concept of the inferiority of the intentional existence of an object in the medium explains why the beatific vision must be one that is unmediated. If we see God through a medium, we will always see God imperfectly.

Finally, Aquinas describes why, given all of this, there must be some light in the human that allows for vision. Just as there must be a transparent medium to allow for light to exist in the air, so there must be a transparent medium in

57. Ibid., lines 32–37. My translation.

58. Ibid., lines 45–49: "Thus color is in a colored body as a quality complete in its natural being, but it is in the medium incompletely, according to some (*quoddam*) intentional being." The *quoddam* here seems to indicate that Aquinas does not think the intentional being of color in the medium is exactly the same as the kind of intentional being other objects have in our minds.

59. Ibid., lines 45–57.

our eye that would allow for light and color to exist there. Aquinas argues that our eyes are therefore made out of water, so that "the light must also be in the eye."[60] This light illuminates the watery medium that exists in the eye.

Ultimately vision takes place in the soul, since Aquinas claims that vision is a power of the soul. Here his hylomorphism is important. Because the soul is the form of the body and each of its parts, there must be a connection between the power of sight in the soul and a body part, at least with regard to the part of our soul that engages with sensations, so that "the principle of an operation of soul that is exercised by means of the body must be in a determinate part of the body." Thus Aquinas concludes that "the principle of sight is within, near the brain, where the two nerves coming from the eyes meet."[61]

The crucial role of light in vision helps explain the phrase Aquinas uses for God giving sight to the blind (one of the miracles he typically cites as an example of miracles taking place by only God's power, the other being resurrecting the dead). The phrase is "*illuminatio caeci*" and is commonly translated as "give sight to the blind." As the Latin makes clear, however, what God does in this miracle is give *light* to the blind, that is, he makes the darkness of blindness go away by putting light back into the eye all the way through the optic nerve.

Light in the *Summa Theologiae*

So far in our description of Aquinas's theory of light we have concentrated on his commentaries on Aristotle, with the general assumption that Aquinas accepts Aristotle's theories with little, if any, change. What has made his commentary on Aristotle useful here is his more in-depth explanations and extensions of Aristotle that reveal his broader thinking. At the same time, in the *Summa Theologiae* we do have Aquinas's thoughts on light given without the restraints of Aristotelian commentary. The main text of the *Summa* dealing with light is in Aquinas's discussion of creation, particularly with regard to the creation of light on the first day.[62]

In comparison to the Aristotelian commentaries, Aquinas's discussion of light is greatly condensed here. He primarily deals with two issues: whether light is a body and whether it is a quality.[63] These two articles are sandwiched

60. Ibid., 438b5, lines 65–70.

61. Ibid., 438b8, lines 89–94.

62. ST I 67.

63. ST I 67.2–3.

between a discussion of whether light is used metaphorically and an article dealing with whether it was fitting for light to be made on the first day, which is the article toward which the others are leading.

With regard to the question of whether light is a body, Aquinas offers three reasons why it cannot be. First, because more than one thing at a time cannot be in the same place. Second, because if it were a body it would have to move by some form of local motion, which would not be instantaneous as we experience light, nor could it move so fast that we could not see the motion, and (this is new) things that move tend to move in one kind of direction—in straight lines, in circles, and such—yet light moves in all directions at once, filling a space. Third, he argues against light as a body based on the nature of generation and corruption, that is, with the idea that bodies come into being and out of being as substances by taking on other forms. If light were a body, then each day some material would have to be brought into existence to fill the darkness and each day the light would have to transform into some other physical substance. The transformation of that much material each day made no sense to Aquinas.[64] In response to objection three of the question, Aquinas also mentions that we use terms indicating motion with regard to light metaphorically.

In the article on light as a quality (ST I 67.3) Aquinas addresses a new argument, that light has an intentional existence in the air. Recall from our discussion of color that color does have an intentional presence in air and a natural presence in the object that it colors, where an intentional presence is a nonmaterial way of existing as a form or abstracted concept. Aquinas argues that light, however, must have a natural presence in air for two reasons. First, you can predicate light of air, but you cannot predicate color of air. That is, you might say "the air is bright" or "the air is illuminated," but you would not be correct in saying that "the air is red" or "the air is brown."[65] Second, light has a natural presence in the air because it causes a physical effect by providing warmth through its rays, something that intentional presences cannot do.

Aquinas again addresses the argument of whether light is the substantial form of the sun, reiterating a previous argument and offering a new one. He repeats the argument that substantial forms cannot be seen through the senses and instead are understood only in our intellects, and since light is visible it must not be a substantial form. He adds a new argument by differentiating between a substantial form and an accidental form, pointing out that "a substantial form is what makes a thing to be of a certain type, and therefore it is always found in everything of that type."[66] So if light were the substantial form of air, when the

64. ST I 67.2.

65. Unless, perhaps, you have been in a dust storm in Lubbock, Texas.

light source goes away, the air would also cease to exist. By implication it must therefore be an accidental form, appearing in the air only when the light source is available. Light, then, must be "an active quality deriving from the substantial form of the sun or any other self-illuminating body."[67] Moreover, because the sun is the material object that first produces substantial form—"the body first producing change"—the light which is its quality has no natural contrary, only a privation.[68]

We can see, then, that Aquinas in his own account accepts Aristotle's understanding of light and makes it his own by the addition of arguments he has not offered before. To summarize: the process of vision, according to Aquinas's account, is as follows. A diaphanous medium, usually air or water, is in darkness and thus in potential to illumination. When a source of illumination becomes present to the medium, the diaphanous medium becomes actualized and thus in potential to receive colors. The illumination of the medium takes place instantaneously, not by local motion, since light is not a body, but by alteration. In the presence of an illumined diaphanous medium, the colors that appear naturally on the surface of sight objects then move across the diaphanous medium to the eye that sees them, but instead of the color having a natural presence in the air, it has an intentional or spiritual presence that moves across the medium where it enters the eye. The eye itself is made up of a diaphanous medium, water, and has light inside of it as well, which illumines the eye. The color, in its intentional being, enters the eye, moves across it, and then imprints itself on the optic nerve, which senses it. In the process, the eye is touched or imprinted by the color, which accords with the general Aristotelian principle that all sensing is done by touching an object. Thus vision is not a process of light leaving the eye and coming back, but of light actualizing the medium so that color may move across it and enter the eye, which is a more passive process.

66. ST I 67.3.

67. Ibid.

68. ST I 67.3 ad 2.

3

Light and Language

While we now have a better understanding of the physics of light according to Aquinas, his theological use of light language varies. Just as we may misunderstand Aquinas's theology by misunderstanding his physics, so too we run the same risk by misunderstanding the variety of purposes for which he applies light language. In this chapter we will discuss some of the basic light terms he uses, including the often important distinction between the two Latin terms for light, *lux* and *lumen*, and then explore the three main uses of light language in Aquinas, those of metaphor, analogy, and model. We will conclude with a discussion of how Christ fulfills our understanding of the language of light.

Some Basic Light Terms

One of the drawbacks to reading English translations of Aquinas is that English only has one word for light, while Latin has two, *lux* and *lumen*, which have technical meanings for Aquinas.[1] In his commentary on Lombard's *Sentences*, he describes *lux* as "that which is in a lucid body that is in act, by which others are illuminated, as in the sun," while *lumen* is that which the diaphanous body receives for illumination.[2] Robert Pasnau explains that *lux* "refers to being a source of light, whereas the latter [*lumen*] refers to the illumination emitted by that source."[3] When applied theologically, to say that God or Christ is *lux* is to

1. For a helpful history of the Neoplatonic roots of this distinction, see Yael Raizman-Kedar, "Plotinus's Conception of Unity and Multiplicity as the Root to the Medieval Distinction Between *Lux* and *Lumen*," *Studies in History & Philosophy of Science Part A* 37, no. 3 (2006): 379–97. Cf. James McEvoy, "The Metaphysics of Light in the Middle Ages," *Philosophical Studies* 26 (1979): 126–45.

2. II *Sent.* 13.1.3.

3. Thomas Aquinas, *A Commentary on Aristotle's De Anima*, 218, fn. 8.

say that they are the source of all light, and to say that the apostles have *lumen* is to say that they receive their illumination from another light source.

Light rays (*radii*) are beams of illumination that travel in a straight line from their source, and are thus a species of *lumen*, while splendor (*splendor*, often translated as "glory") is the reflection of light rays off of one body onto a third.[4] The latter of these two terms is the more important, as Aquinas will often speak of Christ as the glory or splendor of God, suggesting that the Incarnation makes it possible for us to see God's light reflected from his Son, though Aquinas also believes that Christ, as the Incarnate Son, is true *lux*.

Finally, and perhaps more controversially, I would argue that the term "illumination" (*illuminatio*) has a different meaning than is usually acknowledged among students of Thomas. Often illumination is treated as if it applies to any form of cognition for Aquinas, most especially natural cognition. For instance, illumination is defined by Kevin Corrigan as "the natural activity of the agent intellect which lights up the essence of the sensible thing so that it becomes intelligible by the possible intellect";[5] Robert Pasnau describes illumination as the process "according to which human beings are illuminated by the 'unchangeable light' so as to attain the 'eternal rules'";[6] and Matthew Cuddeback argues that illumination "brings to bear on our truth-knowing the authoritative rule (*regula*) of the First Truth."[7]

Some of this is naturally the consequence of Aquinas's use of the idea of the light of the agent intellect in our natural cognition. Since what lights do is illuminate, then our cognitive processes would seem to be a process of illumination, especially when Aquinas speaks of our natural light. Additionally, Aquinas is modulating the theory of illumination that he and his contemporaries inherited from the Augustinian tradition, which held that any kind of knowledge required divine illumination. So philosophers and theologians have quite naturally conflated illumination with cognition, most especially our natural cognition.[8]

Illumination, however, in its most proper sense is a light or manifestation of the truth that orders our knowledge to God. Aquinas discusses this with

4. II Sent. 13.1.3.

5. Kevin Corrigan, "Light and Metaphor in Plotinus and St. Thomas Aquinas," *Thomist* 57 (1993): 198.

6. Robert Pasnau, "Henry of Ghent and the Twilight of Divine Illumination," *Review of Metaphysics* 49, no. 1 (1995): 50.

7. Matthew Cuddeback, "Thomas Aquinas on Divine Illumination and the Authority of the First Truth," *Nova et Vetera (English Edition)* 7 (2009): 584.

8. Pasnau calls illumination of supernatural realities "special illumination," a category that Aquinas does not use.

regard to the impossibility of demons being able to illumine each other, since "illumination, properly, is the manifestation of truth, as it [the manifestation] is ordered to God, who illumines all intellects."[9] Demons can know a variety of facts, but their sharing of information will always be in an attempt to lead others away from God. The distinction here is between illumination in its proper sense and its extended sense.[10] For Aquinas, the proper sense of illumination is a light that leads us toward God, while we use illumination in an extended way when we speak of any kind of manifestation of the intellect.

In the demonic example here, Aquinas points out that demons can communicate ideas to one another without illumining each other; so that "not every kind of manifestation of the truth has the idea of illumination."[11] Not all cognition is illumination, for some of our cognition actually leads us into the dark. For example, if one robber were to tell another that a local bank had $1 million and no guards for the purpose of enticing him to join him in a robbery, he would be, in an extended sense, illuminating the mind of the other by telling him a truthful statement, but in its proper sense, he would not be illuminating him at all, as evil acts are not ordered to God. Rather, true and proper illumination leads us and orders our intellects to God. This means that illumination is one of the effects of grace, particularly the grace of faith.[12] Thus to discuss Aquinas's theory of illumination is by definition to engage in a theological discussion, since his understanding of illumination exceeds the limits of philosophy.

Light as a Metaphor

With this basic terminology in hand, we can now investigate Aquinas's overall theory of metaphor and then see how he deploys light language metaphorically by looking at a passage from his commentary on the *Divine Names*; we will repeat the process with regard to his theory of analogy. In this section on metaphor we will primarily look at his theory with regard to the use of metaphor in scripture, which is where he provides the most complete discussion of metaphor; additionally, it may help us understand some of the subtleties of his theological method.

9. ST I 109.3.

10. While Aquinas uses the language of a *proper* use of the term here, he does not explicitly discuss the extended sense of the term, but a proper use implies an extended sense, as we see, for instance, in ST I 67.1.

11. ST I 109.3 ad 1.

12. *In Ioh.* 12.8 §1714: "Therefore, illumination is an effect of faith."

While Aquinas is best known for his theory of analogical predication, he also speaks of metaphor as a means of speaking theologically, most notably in his defense of metaphor in the opening question of the *Summa*. In ST I 1.9, he deals with three objections to the use of metaphor in holy teaching: 1) that it diminishes the teaching, 2) that it obscures the truth, and 3) that created things we use to describe God should be objects that are by nature closer to God by means of having more perfections. Aquinas responds by first defining a metaphor as "something that is handed on under a likeness (*similitudo*),"[13] where the term *similitudo* is understood as a kind of image or likeness of something, that is, some corporeal image. Aquinas often uses the terms *metaphor* and *similitude* interchangeably when talking about theological language. Aquinas argues that God meets our intellectual needs by providing knowledge of himself in a manner fitting to the way we learn and in a way that is available to all people, and since we learn through our sense contact with corporeal things, God provides information about himself through images taken from these corporeal things.[14] While all persons are not able to understand the purely intellectual term "immutable," we are all capable of understanding what it means for God to be a rock, taken metaphorically, based on our common human experience of rocks of a certain size as being unmovable.[15] Metaphors serve a useful purpose in instructing us in a way that might cause us to seek to learn more about the truth of God.[16] Finally, the use of metaphor protects us from egregious errors in theological reasoning by reminding us that our knowledge of God is unclear and obscured since the images we use, like that of the rock, are so obviously far distant from the reality of God.[17]

In this passage Aquinas says that what is spoken of in scripture as a metaphor is explained more explicitly elsewhere.[18] Taking up the example of immutability and the rock, we might think of a clear scriptural proclamation of immutability at Mal. 3:6, "I am the Lord and I do not change," which helps

13. ST I 1.9 sc.

14. Ibid., corpus: "It is fitting that holy Scripture relate divine and spiritual realities under the likeness of bodily things. For God provides for all things according to the capacity of their natures. Now it is natural to humans to come to understanding through sensible objects, because all of our knowledge has its origin from the senses."

15. A metaphor explored in Psalm 18, for instance, but one that Aquinas was unable to explore in his commentary on the Psalms, as the version of the Psalms he was using did not include the rock language.

16. ST I 9 ad 2.

17. Ibid., ad 3.

18. Ibid., ad 2: "Hence those things which are related in one place in Scripture as metaphor are explained more explicitly in other places."

clarify the image of God as a rock, with the side benefit of refuting those who see immutability as a Greek metaphysical intrusion without basis in scripture.[19]

A natural objection to this would be to argue that in making this move, Aquinas sets up an opposition between metaphorical and literal senses of scripture, so that one could just ignore the metaphors and go to the more literal passages. There are two responses. First, in his response to objection 2 of ST I 9.9, Aquinas does not say that the metaphors are explained by the literal sense, only that they are explained more explicitly elsewhere, but this in no way diminishes the truth found in the metaphor. In this way scripture is seen as mutually reinforcing and able to communicate theological meaning through a variety of means. To say that "God is a rock" and that "God does not change" is to communicate the same basic concept of God in two different, but true, ways. If metaphor were unimportant to theology, we would expect Aquinas to ignore it in his work, but, as we will see with regard to light, Aquinas takes considerable time to explore the meanings created by metaphor. Second, and more importantly, Aquinas says elsewhere that metaphor is itself one of two ways of speaking literally, so that "the literal sense includes the parabolic and the metaphorical."[20] Aquinas mentions this again at ST I 1.10 ad 3, in his discussion of the parabolical sense of scripture, which we have just seen is equivalent to the metaphorical, when he puts the parabolical in the literal sense. The metaphorical and parabolical are not subordinate to or competitive with the literal sense, but rather should be seen as an important and complementary means of getting to literal truths about God, ones that fit our cognitive abilities. Aquinas's concluding statement, that "notST I 10hing false underlies the literal sense of scripture,"[21] indicates that the real target is the idea that metaphorical language is false and thus incapable of being used in holy teaching—Aquinas holds metaphor in high esteem and his endeavor in these articles is to find a rightful place for metaphor in holy teaching. Overall, this is a defense of the role of metaphor in scripture that seeks not to ignore or diminish it, but rather to make it available for theological work.

This is not to say that it is proper to use metaphors in propositions, for it would be odd to include a statement that "God is a rock," in any kind of argumentative process,[22] although what the metaphor signifies and the truth the metaphor reveals can be a part of that process. But that does not mean

19. Aquinas quotes this passage in his discussion of divine immutability at ST I 9.

20. *In Gal.* 4.7 §254.

21. ST I 1.10 ad 3.

22. See PA II.16 97b38 for a discussion of the prohibition against using metaphors in demonstrative arguments.

that metaphorical statements, for Aquinas, are meaningless or untrue. Rather, Aquinas uses what he sees to be metaphors to develop and understand important theological positions. Let's return to the question of immutability, where we have already seen that the verse from Mal. 3:6 provides sufficient scriptural support for the idea of God's immutability. Yet Aquinas also takes time to explore the text from James 4:8, "Draw nigh to God, and He will draw nigh to you," which objection three notes would indicate motion on God's part and suggests that God is mutable, since something that moves quite obviously changes.[23] In answering this objection, Aquinas uses the model of the sun's light, which assumes immutability on the part of the sun as the primary cause of corporeal things, to explain how something can be said to come or go without actually doing so. The metaphorical expression leads Aquinas to see that what happens is that we perceive God to draw closer to us when we receive grace—the "influx of his goodness"—and perceive God to be drawing away from us when we rebel (*deficimus*) against him.[24] The exploration of the metaphorical expression of James 4:8 helps us understand how God could be beyond change even though we seem to experience a change in God.

The risk in metaphors is not that we understand them as literally true, but that we understand them as signifying corporeal realities rather than spiritual ones. What makes them metaphorical is that the physical thing signifies a spiritual reality, rather than another physical reality. In several places Aquinas mentions that one of the fundamental theological mistakes that people make is thinking that a statement, such as "God is light," is true at a corporeal level, rather than a spiritual one. The group he tends to have in mind here is the "Manichees," which is his label for the Cathar heretics of his day.[25] He says of them, following Augustine:

> they said that God was a body; and a certain infinite light. Further, they thought that the sun that we see with our physical eyes was Christ the Lord. . . . But this cannot hold up, and the Catholic church rejects such a fiction. For this physical sun is a light which can be perceived by sense. Consequently, it is not the highest light, which intellect alone grasps, and which is the intelligible light characteristic of the rational creature.[26]

23. ST I 9.1 ob 3.

24. ST I 9.1 ad 3.

25. On Aquinas and the Cathars, see Fergus Kerr, *After Aquinas: Versions of Thomism* (Malden, MA: Blackwell, 2002), 4–5.

26. *In Ioh.* 8.2 §1142.

Aquinas explains the distinction in depth in his commentary on *De Anima* (II.14 415–16), where he remarks that people sometimes mistakenly think that the light we see has a spiritual nature because we use the term "light" with regard to intelligible things, although it is impossible for something that is spiritual to be sensed by corporeal powers. As long as we are clear that the intelligible light has a spiritual nature and is different than the light we see with our eyes, Aquinas is happy to assign the same name to both things.[27]

For all of the effort spent on understanding Aquinas's vision of analogy, one is hard pressed to find a sustained discussion of his theory of metaphor with respect to theology.[28] Some of this is probably a result of the idea that his theory is uncritically Aristotelian, but more likely it is the result of the influence of logical positivism and its diminution of metaphorical language, so that something becomes "mere metaphor." This dismissal of metaphorical language seems to find a parallel in Aquinas's description of the role of metaphor in ST I 1.9, compounded by some misinterpretations of his Latin terminology.

Commentators on Aquinas often put metaphorical language in opposition to literal language, but the distinction that Aquinas maintains is between the literal sense of scripture and its spiritual sense, which itself is broken into three subcategories of allegorical, moral, and anagogical senses. For instance, a recent commentator seems to equate the use of metaphor with the spiritual sense when he uses a text from ST I 1.10 ad 1, "for nothing necessary to the faith is said in a spiritual sense which is not explicitly stated in the literal sense elsewhere"[29] to justify his argument for Aquinas's use of the substitution theory of metaphor, "whereby the referents of the terms in a metaphorical expression and its truth value can be preserved after its substitution by a literal expression."[30] In Doherty's understanding, metaphorical expressions are subsumed in the category of the spiritual sense of scripture, rather than the literal. A very sophisticated interpreter of Aquinas, Brian Davies, makes a similar mistake, arguing that "metaphor, for Aquinas, is not a literal mode of

27. As we have discussed, strictly speaking, light is not a body either, but rather the active quality of a luminous body.

28. Two helpful exceptions can be found in Gregory P. Rocca, *Speaking the Incomprehensible God: Thomas Aquinas on the Interplay of Positive and Negative Theology* (Washington, DC: Catholic University of America Press, 2004), 318–24, and Ralph M. McInerny, "Metaphor and Analogy," in *Inquiries into Medieval Philosophy: A Collection in Honor of Francis P. Clarke.*, ed. James F. Ross (Westport, CT: Greenwood, 1971), 75–96.

29. Alexander J. Doherty, "Aquinas on Scriptural Metaphor and Allegory," *American Catholic Philosophical Association Proceedings* 76 (2002): 189. His translation.

30. Ibid.

discourse."[31] Here he points to an important text, ST I 13.3 ad 1, which is worth quoting in full:

> Some words that signify what has come forth from God to creatures do so in such a way that part of the meaning of the word is the imperfect way in which the creature shares in the divine perfection. Thus it is part of the meaning of "rock" that it has its being in a merely material way. Such words can be used of God only metaphorically. There are other words, however, that simply mean certain perfections without any indication of how these perfections are possessed—words, for example, like "being," "good," "living" and so on. These words can be used literally of God.[32]

This passage would seem to affirm the opposition between the metaphorical and the literal use of language—we can use one set of words, those based on corporeality, metaphorically, and another set of words, those based on certain perfections, literally. The problem, however, is that this all hinges on a mistranslation of what Aquinas actually says.

The last sentence of this passage reads in Latin, "*Et talia proprie dicuntur de Deo*," and both McCabe and the translators of the English Dominican translation render "*proprie*" as "literally," rather than as "properly." This is an odd translation, given that Aquinas seems to have a specific term, "*litteralis*," that he uses for "literal," which is sprinkled all throughout the first question of the *Summa*.[33] But the distinction that Aquinas makes in this question is between the metaphorical and the proper use of words, not a distinction between the metaphorical and the literal. Aquinas makes the same distinction in his discussion of light in ST I 67.1, where he says that the light we sense can be said to exist in spiritual things metaphorically, while light that makes things manifest (i.e., intellectual light) can be said properly (*proprie*) of spiritual things.

The question remains whether "properly" is equivalent to "literally" and just where metaphor might fall. For Aquinas, metaphorical expression falls under the category of the literal sense of scripture:

> Something can be signified in two ways through the literal sense of scripture, namely through the proper (*proprietatem*) way of speaking,

31. Brian Davies, *The Thought of Thomas Aquinas* (Oxford: Oxford University Press, 1992), 67.

32. Ibid., 67–68. Note that the translation Davies uses is from Herbert McCabe's version in the Blackfriars edition of the *Summa*.

33. Most especially ST I 1.10 ad 3.

> as when I say "the man smiles" or according to a likeness or metaphor, as when I say, "the meadow smiles" . . . both of these modes appear in sacred scripture . . . and so under the literal sense is included the parabolical and the metaphorical.[34]

Aquinas goes on to compare these two ways of speaking literally—the metaphorical and the proper—against the spiritual senses of scripture, which are the same three as enumerated in the *Summa*. So it appears that metaphor is a type of literal speech and that "proper" speech is also a type of literal speech, rather than its equivalent. The genus appears to be literal speech, with two species, metaphorical and proper. When Aquinas talks about the literal sense of scripture in ST I 1.10, he is including metaphor in that discussion, which is confirmed by his concluding response, ad 3, about the parabolic sense of scripture being contained in the literal sense. Aquinas explains that "the literal sense is not the figure itself, but that which is figured," and gives the example that "when Scripture names the arm of God, the literal sense is not that God has a physical limb, but that he has what the limb signifies, namely operative power."[35] Metaphor, when properly employed, points to a literal truth about God, and so metaphors are not false when understood as metaphors. But this does not strike me as strictly a substitution theory of metaphor, since the metaphor seems to point to a truth or signify some third thing that we might think of as a larger truth. In fact, given what we know about Aquinas's concerns regarding predication of God, to strictly substitute the metaphor, "God has an arm," with the proper expression, "God has operative power," runs the risk of causing us to think that the full meaning of God's work can be captured in this latter predication. And while Aquinas thinks we can make positive predications of God, the metaphorical statements reduce the risk of thinking that any of the literal things we say can comprehensively capture the nature of God.

In fact, metaphors can provide substantial insight into God and God's goodness, as we can see when Aquinas explores the idea of light as a metaphor for God.

Aquinas's account of the language of light in ST I 67.1 neatly summarizes how he understands the use of language with regard to sensible light. The question is whether the term "light" (*lux*) can be used properly with regard to spiritual things. Aquinas notes that we often start with one use of a word and then extend its use to other things, and he gives the example of how we use terms of vision to describe other acts of sensation. Likewise, he argues,

34. *In Gal.* 4.7 §254.

35. ST I 1.10 ad 3.

with regard to light, that because of our common experience of light, humans originally used light language to describe the light necessary for physical vision and then we expanded light language to intellectual understanding and vision. He concludes that when it comes to sensible light, we can only use language for it metaphorically with regard to spiritual things, since a term for a material being cannot be properly applied to something immaterial. Language for intelligible light, since it is immaterial, can be applied to spiritual things properly.

While we have established that the light we see can be used of God metaphorically, we have not discussed exactly how Aquinas understands the metaphor to work. Here we can turn to his commentary on Dionysius's *Divine Names* to see how Aquinas uses the metaphor of sensible light with regard to spiritual things to develop his understanding of God.

Light as a Metaphor: The Commentary on the Divine Names

Aquinas discusses the theology of light in his *Commentary on the Divine Names* in chapter four, lectures three and four, and begins by noting that Dionysius attributes the use of the term "sunlight" to God as a metaphor and that he also attributes the term "intelligible light" to God, so that the former is a metaphorical attribution and the latter a direct attribution.[36] The difference between the two is that sunlight is corporeal, seen by corporeal organs, while intelligible light is immaterial, seen by all beings that are capable of rational thought—God, angels, and humans. Aquinas begins with the sunlight metaphor, but does so in an unexpected way, from cause to effect. That is, in explaining how a metaphor might be attributed to God, one would expect him to start with the material object with which we are familiar—a rock, a lion, or in this case sunlight—and explain how its characteristics reveal something about God; in this way he would be moving from what we know to what we know less well, from effect to cause, as is typically his method. But in this passage he starts with knowledge of God and explains how sunlight has qualities similar to God, so that in this way it is our knowledge of God that expands our knowledge of corporeal light.

The relationship between the rays of the sun and God, and the basis for starting with knowledge of God to describe the nature of light, is that the sun's rays considered of themselves "exist out of that divine goodness and are sort of an image, that is, an expressed likeness of the divine goodness . . . for the divine

36. DDN 4.3 §304: "And first he [Dionysius] shows how the term 'sunlight' is metaphorically attributed to God; second, how intelligible light is attributed to him."

goodness is manifested in such light just as the archetype, that is, the principal figure and principal exemplar, is impressed on the image."[37] Aquinas, then, is basing his comparison on God's role as the exemplar cause of things, so that like the rest of creation, the natural form of corporeal light receives its form from the previously existing ideas in the divine mind.[38]

Corporeal light is good because it participates in the divine goodness which is its exemplar.[39] Aquinas explores this insight by describing three ways that Dionysius understands the divine goodness to be expressed: 1) through universal causality of all substances, 2) through the illumination of rational substances and the creation, preservation, and perfection of other substances (the effects of God's goodness), and 3) as the measure of all things.[40]

Dionysius, according to Aquinas, then shows how the sun manifests this goodness in similar ways. First, just as God is the universal cause of all substances from the greatest to the lowliest, the sun is transcendent over all other bodies, is able to illuminate all that are capable of receiving its rays, and is constantly shining. The sun reaches its rays across all of creation and in this sense its causality is universal.[41] Second, the sun's effects are similar to God's. God through creation gives existence and life, and preserves and perfects things in their existence; similarly, the sun gives existence to things through generation, causes things to move in a way that preserves their existence, and perfects the lower bodies through its power.[42] Third, just as God's goodness is the measure of all things with regard to this nobility of being, the light of the sun is the measure of things inasmuch as its motion is the basis for our measurement of time.[43]

Aquinas further explores the metaphor of the sun's light in Dionysius with regard to how things are ordered to the divine goodness as their final end, and again he starts with God and turns to the sun. God orders all things to him as their origin, as their conserving source, and as their ultimate desire.[44] Likewise, the sun, as the image of the Good, is desired by things as the origin of vision,

37. Ibid., §306.

38. See ST I 44.3 for Aquinas's discussion of exemplar causality, as well as Matthew Cuddeback's discussion of exemplar causality with respect to light in his dissertation "Light and Form in St. Thomas Aquinas's Metaphysics of the Knower" (Ph.D. dissertation, Catholic University of America, 1998), 120–31.

39. DDN 4.1 §270.

40. DDN 4.3 §308–10.

41. Ibid., §311.

42. Ibid., §312.

43. Ibid., §313.

44. Ibid., §316–18.

as the basis of their sustenance, and as the common desire of all living things.[45] In exploring this metaphor, Aquinas notes that the common mistake is to make the sun a god, but points out that while the sun is in a sense the creator of the sensible world, it is God who is the real creator.[46] Just as importantly, he explains that the basis of humans seeing the sun as a god comes from the natural theology found in Rom. 1:20, which makes God manifest through the things that are made. There is a sense in which Aquinas thinks it is a natural mistake to see the sun as a god, which would be one reason why we need holy teaching to correct the error.

This interesting passage indicates several things. First, light was in no way a dead metaphor for Aquinas, as one does not seek out meaning from dead metaphors. Instead, Aquinas takes this as an opportunity to explore the fecundity of the image of light as it relates to God, seeing God as the exemplar cause of sensible light and the means by which we can understand light's nature. Second, what makes this metaphorical is the corporeal nature of visible light; it is something both created and material and as such it cannot be predicated of God other than metaphorically.

Analogical Light

While Aquinas develops the metaphor with regard to sensible light here in the *Commentary on the Divine Names*, he goes on to do something that as far as I can tell he does not do at any other place in his corpus, which is talk about intelligible light with respect to God. Here it would seem he is not talking about intelligible light as a metaphor, but rather as a form of analogical predication, or as he terms it here, an "attribute" of God.[47] He initially makes this distinction in his original division of the text where he says that he will discuss how "the light of the sun is attributed to God metaphorically," and "how the intelligible light is attributed to him."[48] In leaving off the qualifier "metaphorically," Aquinas indicates that he must be speaking analogically, as intelligible light would not be something he would apply univocally and equivocation would not be

45. Ibid., §319.

46. Ibid., §320.

47. DDN 4.4 §321: "Now he [Dionysius] shows how intelligible light is attributed (*attribuatur*) to Him."

48. DDN 4.3 §304: "And first, Dionysius shows the way that the term 'sunlight' (*luminis solaris*) is attributed to God metaphorically; second the way that intelligible light is attributed to Him."

something worth exploring. Here, too, Aquinas will explore what the analogy tells us about God, but first it may help to recount briefly his theory of analogy.

In ST I 13.5 Aquinas explains that we cannot univocally predicate terms of God and creatures for the reason that effects that do not receive the full power of their cause fall short of their cause. Metaphysically, what seems to be happening here is that an efficient cause works by imparting a form to its effect, but only forms that are communicated perfectly can then be predicated univocally—we can predicate human nature of both my son and me because he received the perfect form of human nature from his parents.

Analogical predication results when two things have different natures, but yet are related to each other in some kind of proportion and have the same term applied to them. The examples that Aquinas uses are terms like "good," "wise," and others that we think of as representing perfections. As he describes it elsewhere:

> At other times, however, a term predicated of God and creature implies nothing in its principal meaning which would prevent our finding between a creature and God an agreement of the type described above. To this kind belong all attributes which include no defect nor depend on matter for their act of existence, for example, being, good, and similar things.[49]

The perfections that Aquinas seems to have in mind are immaterial or conceptual perfections that are not dependent upon material existence. Not just any perfection can be applied to God analogically, but only those transcendental perfections that apply to all categories of being. Analogy, then, would seem to be restricted to a limited set of perfection terms, those that exist as mental concepts that we apply to objects in the world.

It is in this sense that we can best understand Ralph McInerny's argument that analogy is a "logical doctrine"[50] that is the consequence of our thinking and naming of things, rather than due to the nature of the things themselves. We denominate perfection terms as the result of our thinking about them, and analogy arises out of our thinking about the logical, not metaphysical, relationship between two instantiations of a perfection. McInerny argues that

49. DV 2.11.

50. Ralph M. McInerny, *The Logic of Analogy: An Interpretation of St. Thomas* (The Hague: Martinus Nijhoff, 1961), 34.

> things which are named analogically are so named because of a community among them. This community is not simply one of the name, as is the case with pure equivocation, nor is exactly the same *ratio* signified by the name as it is predicated of each of them, as is the case with the univocal name. The analogous name names one thing primarily, and others insofar as they relate in some way to what it principally names.[51]

The problem, as Aquinas explains it, is that when we say "God is good" our intention is to say something meaningful about God—a substantial predication that nevertheless will always fall short of our full understanding; saying "God is good" is supposed to be a statement of true knowledge about God, not just a restatement of a negative, such as "God is not evil," nor a statement of God's causal primacy, such as "God is the cause of goodness."[52] If we say "God is good," we are saying something that gets to the essence of who God is, however imperfectly we understand it. At the same time, God's goodness is supereminent and so far beyond our conceptual abilities that "good" does not mean the same thing as when we apply it to creaturely terms, such as "that dog is good." Analogical predication is intended to represent the proportion of the lesser in the superior where "whatever is said of God and creatures, is said according to the relation of a creature to God as its principle and cause, wherein all perfections of things pre-exist excellently."[53] When we predicate "good" of God, this is to say that what we know as good is a participation in God's goodness as the effect participates in its cause, and that our idea of good preexists perfectly in God but only imperfectly and proportionately in the world.

Applying all of this to light, we can see how when Aquinas says, "the divine essence, which is pure act, is light (*lux*) itself,"[54] he is making an analogical predication. Aquinas, in passages like this, must be talking about what he calls "intelligible light," which is the kind of light that represents the attainment of intellectual truth or manifestation. It is not a corporeal or sensible light, but rather a spiritual, immaterial, or intellectual light that shines when we see the truth clearly. We know this light from our own experience, most often in the process of learning or discovery, when we "see" something clearly for the first time. This intelligible light that we see can also be predicated of God, who

51. Ibid., 78.

52. ST I 13.2.

53. ST I 13.5.

54. *In 1 Tim.* 6.3 §268.

has that same light supereminently and is, in fact, the exemplar cause of our own intelligible light. To say that "God is light" is to say that God is the First Truth, intrinsically the most manifest of all truths, and the cause of all truths in us. Yet we have a proportion of that light, even if imperfectly.

An analogy, like a metaphor, also provides an opportunity for reflection, though in this case what it allows is for us to see the relationship and similarities between God and his creatures while at the same time allowing for the dramatic distance between the two. It provides a chance to see how God causes good things in us while acknowledging our constant dependence upon God for their existence and operation.

Analogical Light

Aquinas begins his *Divine Names* commentary on intelligible light by discussing the causal nature of the intelligible light as found in God, which "designates in God the causality of intelligible light."[55] He notes that "God who is good through his own essence is named (*nominator*) 'intelligible light,'"[56] and points to John 8:12, "I am the light of the world," as a proof text. The "naming" indicates an analogical intent, as the questions of ST I 13 revolve around the naming of God. He points out that this light both causes the minds of the angels to fill up and provides knowledge of the truth. Aquinas goes on to explain that with relation to souls, meaning the souls of human beings, the intelligible light removes ignorance and error, two things that are impossible for angels to have, and that it gives a "holy light" to the soul *which orders us to know God*—this is the light of grace.[57] This reinforces our earlier definition of illumination as something that is properly understood to order or orient our mind to God; the light is from God and draws us to God. When we know who God is, because of God's self-revelation, we see things in a new light. In different ways, ignorance and error are part of both our human nature and of sin, and they put us in spiritual darkness that comes from not knowing the truth. The removal of ignorance and error comes from the intelligible light (i.e., the cognition of truth), which purifies our spiritual eyes, moves us toward acting well, and makes our eyes receptive to the light by desiring more of it; all of this takes place through grace.[58] The giving of a holy light, the light of grace that comes with the intellectual light, helps one attend to spiritual realities. Here Aquinas uses

55. DDN 4.4 §323.

56. Ibid., §325.

57. Ibid., §327: "Dionysius speaks of 'holy light' because it is emitted from God and because it directs (*ordinat*) us toward knowledge of God."

58. Ibid., §329.

the spiritual sense of taste to indicate that when, through the intellectual light, we get a taste of the truth, we desire it even more. As we desire it more, we get more of it, so that "a certain circular dynamic is noticed: for by the light the desire for light grows, and by the increased desire for it the light grows."[59] As we know more, we love more, and as we love more, we want to know more, until our capacity for both expands.

Aquinas goes on to explain the relationship between God and those things that are illuminated by the intelligible light. He argues that the Good, which is above both sensible and intelligible light, is nevertheless the fountain of all intellectual light in creatures. In this capacity the light diffuses itself into the minds of angels as assistants and ministers and into human souls, who are illuminated by nature and then through the lights of grace and glory. Note here the connection between light and the divine substance, since the divine light also exceeds all those who receive it, "because there is always a super-excess through its substance."[60] Finally, the divine light comprehends all things inasmuch as God knows all things by one simple power, instead of the variety of sensory powers by which we know things, and so God "does not acquire the power of cognition or teaching from anyone else, but all others get it from him."[61]

Aquinas concludes his analysis of the intelligible light by describing its final end, which is to unite all rational creatures in the truth. For Aquinas, there can be only one truth—here we can assume he is talking about God as First Truth—while there can be a multiplicity of mistakes that derive from being in the darkness of sin and ignorance. Another end of the intelligible light is to perfect humans and to convert them to the truth, "from opinion to certain knowledge."[62]

There are two things worth noting here. The first is the relation between causality and analogy. When Aquinas discusses analogy he often gives a brief description of how the same name can apply to different things and usually gives a brief example, most often around the term "healthy" or "good." Interestingly, in this passage we get a complete exploration of the analogical predication of intelligible light as it is applied to God, with an emphasis on God's causality. Because intelligible light is an essential property of God, it is God who, as exemplar, causes all intelligible light to exist, both as a creation in our nature and as created grace. He explains how God can have light

59. Ibid., §330.
60. Ibid., §331.
61. Ibid.
62. Ibid., §332.

supereminently and yet still diffuse it throughout the order of the universe, and how this same light ultimately brings us back to God. This emphasis on the causality of God brings to mind the importance of his participation metaphysic—none of our perfections operate autonomously or are self-created, but rather are created in us by God.

I wonder, and this is purely speculation, if there is something else revealing about this passage in the way he ends it. The notion that the final end of the intelligible light is to unite us to the truth perhaps indicates another reason why analogy is so important to Aquinas. Analogical predication is at one level a question of how we come to speak about God, but it is also a causal question, that is, Aquinas uses terms of equivocality and univocity with regard to causality just as he does with naming. Perhaps Aquinas is using the term "cause" analogically as well. If God were strictly an equivocal cause, causing things to come to exist that were so unlike him, then it would not be possible for them to be united to God; God could not be a univocal cause since that would lead to the creation of another God. Analogically predicated, causality would provide the means by which we could be united to God. Perhaps we can predicate these names and perfections of God precisely because we are also able to be united to God in the beatific vision. That is, for Aquinas the final cause is the basis of the other three causes, and if the final end of the intelligible light is to unite us to God, perhaps that is why analogical predication is so important, because it represents the possibility of our final end. In fact, Aquinas mentions that analogical terms are perfections found first in God, but he also sees the beatific vision as the human realization, through God, of those same perfections—perfections that we desire and seek our whole lives. All of those perfections are ultimately meant as our final end. This is, of course, speculation, since I am unaware of Aquinas specifically addressing this in any place, but given this long exposition of the analogy of the intelligible light as it flows from God and back to God, it is worth pondering the relation between the beatific vision and analogical predication, which Aquinas conveniently places next to each other in the *Summa*.

I am not arguing that analogical predication is only a matter of causality, a position that Aquinas rejects in ST I 13.5–6, where he argues that when we say "God is good," we mean more than that God is the cause of goodness, but that God really is good essentially, even as we cannot completely comprehend what that means. Rather, as Aquinas makes clear in these passages on the *Divine Names*, the basis for attributing light to God, which is done metaphorically with regard to corporeal light and analogically with regard to intelligible light, is that God is the exemplar cause of both corporeal and intelligible light. We can apply the name "light" to God because God first causes the light to exist around us and in us.

One question we might raise here is how much of this commentary expresses Aquinas's own understanding of light or whether this is a commentary alone, with which Aquinas neither agrees nor disagrees. The former seems to be the more likely case, for two reasons. First, Aquinas considered Dionysius to be the closest authority to the apostles and consistently cites him as an authority throughout his corpus. Second, there is nothing in these passages that disagrees with either Dionysius or with anything else that Aquinas has written about light or theological language. Instead, we can regard this as both an exposition of Aquinas's understanding of Dionysius and an extension of his own thought on theological language.

Light as a Model

There is a third way that Aquinas uses light language, which is as a model to explain other concepts. Aquinas has no theory of scientific modeling similar to modern accounts, so we cannot look to his writings for a theory of how we can use physical processes to model our understanding of other realities, yet it is something he does quite consistently. It is not anachronistic to use a contemporary explanation to understand one of the ways that Aquinas uses language, just as long as we are aware that he had no such theory himself that made him aware of what he was doing.

Instead, we can look at a recent account of modeling in theological language in the work of Janet Martin Soskice, who defines a model as "an object or state of affairs . . . [where] it is viewed in terms of its resemblance, real or hypothetical, to some other object or state of affairs; a miniature train is a model of the full-scale one, a jam jar full of cigarette ends is seen as a model for the lungs of a smoker, the behaviour of water is seen as a model for the action of electricity."[63] The source of a model is distinct from its subject and there are two kinds of basic models: 1) the homeomorphic model, "in which the subject of the model is also its source" such as a model train, and 2) the paramorphic model, "where source and subject differ (e.g. the use of billiard balls to provide a model for discussion of the property of gases)."[64] It is paramorphic models, according to Soskice, that primarily are used in science to construct and explain

63. Janet Martin Soskice, *Metaphor and Religious Language* (Oxford: Clarendon, 2002), 101.
64. Ibid., 102.

theories. Aquinas uses these kinds of paramorphic models quite frequently in his discussions, where light (and often heat) is one of the models of choice.

One place where Aquinas uses light as an explanatory model is in his doctrine of transubstantiation. In ST III 75.7, a metaphysical question is raised about how the bread can be changed into the body of Christ instantaneously. The first objection is that there are two instants in the process, one where the bread is bread and another where the bread has become the body of Christ. And yet, the objection goes, between every two moments of time there is another moment of time, which means that the bread is changed not instantaneously but over time. In essence, the objection is that there is no such thing as being instantaneous. The second objection presses the point, arguing that "in every change something is 'in becoming' (*fieri*) and something is 'in being' (*factum esse*)." The problem is that these also cannot be instantaneous, as something that is in the process of becoming is not already in being, which means that there is a "before and after" (*prius et posterius*, which happen to be two terms that are also used to explain analogy) and thus the change cannot be instantaneous. If the first objection is physical, that bodies must change over time, the second is metaphysical, as it deals with how "being" can be changed; both our knowledge based on the action of physical bodies and our intellectual understanding of being lead one to think that it is impossible for anything to happen instantaneously.

Aquinas responds with a discussion of substantial forms in themselves and substantial forms as they are received in their objects. Some forms are not substantial, that is, not forms that cause something to exist as a being with a particular nature. Health is not a substantial form, but a quality, while human nature is a substantial form that makes us human. Since health is not a substantial form, it is by nature something that happens over time, which anyone who has recovered from an illness knows from experience. Substantial forms are also received in their subjects differently than other forms. Some forms are received imperfectly, or as Aquinas puts it, "more or less," and the example he gives is of water being heated. Recall from the previous chapter that where there are already existing forms there is a tendency for the existing form to resist the entering form, meaning that the reception of the form requires time. So heat is resisted in a body that has the form of cold, requiring there to be a period of time for something to be heated.

Aquinas turns to light to explain that things that are disposed to receive a form perfectly are able to do so instantaneously. As we have discussed, there is no form opposed to light, since light has no contrary. Since there is no contrary, light can instantly fill a space. Finally, Aquinas notes that a being with infinite power can "instantly dispose the matter for the form." Aquinas turns again to light to reply to the second objection and explain how something can be "in becoming" and "in being" at the same time. Since he believes that light is not subject to local motion, illumination crosses space instantaneously, which means that the illumination is "in being" from the moment that the sun faces the hemisphere, but since it transverses space instantaneously, it also is "in becoming" at the same time, where "in being" with respect to illumination means that air already is illuminated, and "in becoming" means that it was not illuminated before. That is, for air (and by analogy, the bread and wine of the Eucharist) to be changed in one instant, it must be unilluminated at one moment and then completely illuminated the next, as we see when the first ray of light breaks across the horizon.

Here Aquinas is answering both the physical and metaphysical objections to transubstantiation at the same time. By giving a physical example he demonstrates that we do know of a physical example of something happening instantaneously, but it also explains the metaphysical possibility, since if it is physically possible it is clearly metaphysically possible. Thus for Aquinas, the questions of the timing of the change in substance are answerable.

What Aquinas would have argued if he knew that light actually had a measurable speed and was not instantaneous, we can only speculate. The larger point, of course, is just that light served for Aquinas as a model, not a metaphor or analogy, for the process of transubstantiation.

Another common use of light as a model is with regard to God's preservation in being of all creatures. Aquinas first mentions this in ST I 8.1 with regard to God's existence in all of creation. Here he mentions that light is only in the air when the sun is there; no matter how perfectly disposed the atmosphere is to receiving light, the light cannot exist in the air without the presence of the sun. Likewise, God is present to every thing inasmuch as it exists, and if God were no longer to be present, it would go out of existence. This is a remarkably intimate level of presence, since it suggests that God is universally present to all things at their deepest levels, those of their very existence. It suggests that no matter how hard we may try, we cannot escape the presence of God, any more than we can escape the presence of the sun.

Aquinas develops this idea in more depth in ST I 104.1, where he discusses God's governance, which is the outworking of God's providence. The question is whether created things must be kept in being by God. Much of the discussion revolves around the question of being and becoming that we just discussed with regard to transubstantiation. Here the argument is about God's essence and existence. The sun, Aquinas argues, has light by its very nature, whereas the air is illumined by participating in the light of the sun. Likewise, only God has existence essentially: "God alone is being in virtue of his own essence."[65] So just as only the sun has light by nature, only God has existence by nature; all creatures, therefore, must participate in God's existence in the same way that the air participates in the light of the sun. What Aquinas has done here is deepened the idea of God's presence in all things. The idea in ST I 8 primarily works in one direction, with God being present in all things, which receive God's presence in a purely passive way, as would metaphysically make sense given God's role as the perfect agent who acts on without being acted upon. The idea of participation, however, takes it a step further, implying that once we receive existence from God, we have an opportunity to participate in the life of God. Indeed, one of the key themes of the treatise on God's governance (ST I 103–19) is that God governs by giving his creatures "the perfection of causality."[66]

There is a further implication of this model, which, as far as I know, Aquinas does not work out explicitly. These previous two questions in the *Summa* revolve around God's presence and conservation of creation, but in *De Potentia* 5.3 ad 2, Aquinas takes up the question of whether God can annihilate creatures. The short answer is yes, but in his reply to the second objection he again resorts to the model of the sun's light, this time in a negative fashion. Whereas in the *Summa* questions he states that the air is illumined when in the presence of the sun, and likewise we exist due to the presence of the creator, in this question he argues that God does not have to actively destroy something to annihilate it, rather all he has to do is withdraw the action by which he gives something its existence; "thus the absence of the sun's action in illumining the air causes the absence of light in the air."[67]

Here Aquinas is talking about annihilation, which focuses in on the most fundamental level of existence, yet it would seem that the concept could be extended to other levels of being as well. One case where the model might apply is when God withdraws his support for processes that are part of our nature. In his commentary on Job, Aquinas discusses how God overcomes evil rulers "not because he leads them into false opinions but because he takes away his light from them so that they may not know the truth, and he clouds their reason so that they cannot find suitable ways to achieve the evils which they propose."[68] Just prior to this he makes the same basic argument with regard to philosophers,

65. ST I 104.1.

66. ST I 103.6 ad 2.

67. DP 5.3 ad 2.

68. *In Iob* 12:25 lines 380–99.

saying that God can confuse philosophers by withdrawing his grace from them so that they are unable to speak the truth.[69]

The point here is that there is a place where the model breaks down, as any model will break down in relation to God, for while the sun must of necessity illumine the world, since that is what it does by nature, there is no necessity in God that requires his conservation of our being or of those powers that are natural to us. While we might have the light of reason by nature, that nature is preserved in us by God, who is under no necessity to maintain it and can withdraw his grace in a way that diminishes our rational capacities. This is not annihilation strictly speaking, but any time our human capacities are diminished there is a correlative diminishment of being; the irony would seem to be that just when we think we can reason our way away from God, God can withdraw his support of our use of reason—thus Aquinas would read Rom. 1:21 as God withdrawing his light from the philosophers in a way that diminishes their being.[70]

Christ the Light of Our Language

One of the striking elements of Aquinas's discussion of analogy and its subsequent reception among philosophers and theologians is that the discussion centers upon how we can speak of God under the power of the natural light of our intellect. Aquinas argues that our ability to name anything is a consequence of our understanding of it, and since our understanding of God derives from our knowledge of creatures, our ability to name God starts with creaturely ideas, which we then improve upon by means of remotion and excellence.[71] All of this is based upon the idea that he established in the previous question, ST I 12, that we are unable to see God's essence in this life.

As long as we are talking about humans operating only by the natural light of their intellect this must be correct, but this is not the only state in this life in which our understanding of God operates, as Christians also operate under the light of grace. This light boosts our intellectual ability to know truths that are

69. *In Iob* 12:14–19 lines 313–19: "Philosophers excel in the consideration of the truth, and he says about them that he changes the truth from their lips, that is, from those who are keen to speak the truth; for sometimes God darkens their minds by removing his grace, so that they cannot find the truth and consequently cannot speak it."

70. *Ad Rom.* I.7, §126–30.

71. ST I 13.1: "Therefore it follows that we are able to name anything insofar as we can understand it. It was shown above that in this life we are not able to see the essence of God. But he is known by us from creatures as their principle, and through the modes of excellence and remotion."

normally above our natural ability to know, namely those that are unavailable to our senses.[72] We see something similar in Adam's knowledge of God prior to the Fall. Aquinas is clear that even here Adam was unable to see God's essence, since any being that sees God's essence is no longer able to sin. At the same time, Aquinas argues that Adam had a more perfect knowledge of God than we do under the power of our natural light.[73] If, then, we maintain the idea that we can name God only according to our knowledge of God, then the increased knowledge of God we receive through the light of grace and God's self-revelation would seem to improve our ability to apply names to God. This does not necessarily mean that we will move from analogical predication to univocal predication, but it would seem to suggest that at the very least our analogies would improve.[74]

All of this would suggest that the Incarnation, where God becomes man, would change our language of God and our understanding of light with respect to God. First, by becoming a human, God would now be available to our senses and so we would have additional knowledge of God that is fitting to our mode of knowledge. Second, the illuminating work of the Son is accomplished through his teaching, which is handed on through his disciples, again in a mode that fits our way of knowing.

This is worked out exquisitely in Aquinas's commentary on the Gospel of John. In three places Aquinas explores what it means when Christ is declared "the true light" (1:9) and "the light of the world" (8:12; 12:46) and in each of these places Christ is compared as the true light against other forms of light. In these cases it is light that is spoken of analogically with regard to Christ, because of his divinity, though other forms of linguistic comparison are mentioned as well. In his commentary on 1:9, Aquinas compares Christ as "true light" (*lux vera*) against three other ways of thinking about light—false light, figurative

72. ST I-II 109.1: "Higher intelligible things of the human intellect are unable to be known unless it is perfected by a stronger light, namely the light of faith or prophecy. We call this the light of grace, inasmuch as it is superadded to nature."

73. ST I 94.1: "So the first man was not impeded by exterior things from a clear and firm contemplation of the intelligible effects, which he perceived by the irradiation of the first truth, whether by natural cognition or grace. Whence Augustine says (*Gen ad. Litt.* XI), that 'perhaps God used to speak to the first man as he speaks to the angels, by sharing the unchanging truth by illuminating his mind, and yet without participating in the divine essence in the way the angels are capable of.' Therefore, through these intelligible effects of God, God was more clearly known than in our way of knowing."

74. Bruce Marshall has made the interesting argument that the Incarnation, which requires a naming of "God is man," requires univocal predication. See Bruce Marshall, "Christ the End of Analogy," in *The Analogy of Being: Invention of the Antichrist or the Wisdom of God?*, ed. Thomas Joseph White (Grand Rapids: Eerdmans, 2011), 280–313.

light, and participated light. The false light is represented by the light that the philosophers thought they had before Christ, but which actually darkened their hearts and made them fools. The figurative light is represented by the light of the teaching of the law, which the Jews gloried in, but actually pointed forward to the things [i.e., the true light] to come. The participated light is the light that angels and saints have through grace that enables superior knowledge of God. Aquinas concludes this comparison, arguing that "the Word of God is not a false light, nor a figurative light, nor a participated light, but true light, that is, through his essence. So he is called 'true light.'"[75] Aquinas then points out that a proper understanding of Christ as the true light prevents the mistake of Photinus, who believed Christ came into being through the Virgin, and the mistakes of Arius and Origen, who held that Christ participated in divinity. A true light, however, must be divine, so that "if the Word was the true light, it is manifest that he is true God."[76]

The next passage, the commentary at 8:12, again draws attention to Christ's divinity, which is made manifest by his driving away the darkness of sin by his light. Like the previous passage, Aquinas also draws attention to how knowing that Christ is the true and divine light prevents theological error. This time he draws attention to the Manichean error of thinking that God was corporeal "with a certain infinite light," and that the sun was actually Christ. Reiterating the argument of the commentary on the *Divine Names*, Aquinas mentions that the highest light is the intelligible light, not the sensible light, which is an image of the intelligible light. Christ, then, is not the sun, but the one who makes the sun. Aquinas sees another possible error avoided, that of Nestorius's indwelling, since if Nestorius was correct, the scripture would have read "the light of the world dwells in me."

In the final of these three passages, the commentary on John 12:46, Aquinas uses the fact that Christ has light by essence to give a reason for the Incarnation. Blending together several biblical texts, especially that of God dwelling in inapproachable light from 1 Tim. 6:16, Aquinas argues that if God does dwell in inapproachable light, then we are unable to reach him and it is for this reason that the Son had to come to us. Stuck in darkness, unable to approach the light, the true light had to come to us.

With respect to our language of God, then, Christ's light makes possible the further strengthening of our knowledge of God and thus our language about God. Metaphorical language about God, which originates in sense knowledge, is replaced by the presence of the Son in the flesh, who is available

75. *In Ioh.* 1.5 §125. Here and in the following quotation, Aquinas uses *lux* for light.

76. Ibid., §126.

to our senses. Models used to explain God or God's work are replaced by the Incarnate Son who is the model of all creation. Finally, Christ puts an end to analogy when we come to say, "God is man." The light of Christ illumines all of our language as it is ordered to God.

4

God is Light

Darkness and the Light of God

Having reviewed the physics and language of light and thus setting up a theoretical foundation for Aquinas's use of light, we can now turn to his actual application of light language in his theology, some of which we have hinted at already. In the remaining chapters we will roughly follow Aquinas's outline from the *Summa*, though we will do so in constant dialogue with his commentaries on scripture and other writings. We will begin, then, with God in both his essential attributes and in his Trinitarian relations, with the normal Thomistic apophatic disclaimers about the former and mysterious depths with regard to the latter.

We will also begin with God for the simple Thomistic reason that God is the final end of humans, and for Aquinas final causes are the causes of all other causes.[1] To understand what something is for or the end it tends toward is to understand the form it must take, the matter necessary for it to exist, and the things that cause it to move toward that end. Since all human existence is from God and all humans are made for God as their final end, we can best understand all that follows from God—creation, humans, morality, and salvation—by first understanding their divine source.

We will look at God as light under both the essential and Trinitarian aspects, then turn our attention to the beatific vision and the key role that the light of glory plays in the final human experience of God for the blessed and conclude with some brief Christological reflections. But before we do that, we should first look at a rather startling claim that has been made by several theologians to which this chapter is, in part, a response.

There is a recent trend among theologians to talk about "the darkness of God," and the darkness in which God dwells. I will argue that this is a

1. *Phys* II.5.186: "The final cause causes the other causes."

theological mistake, for "God is light and there is no darkness in him" (1 John 1:5), and to claim that Aquinas sees darkness in God is to misunderstand where the darkness resides and where the light is to be found. I will point to a variety of texts that show that for Aquinas, God's perfect light represents God's continued work to make himself manifest to the world.

To claim God's darkness is partially the result of contemporary efforts to recover apophatic theology and, with regard to Aquinas, partially the result of one of his early texts, which is worth quoting in full:

> The reply to the fourth is that all other names mean being under some other determinate aspect. For instance, "wise" means being something. But this name "he who is" means being that is absolute, i.e., not made determinate by anything added. Therefore Damascene says that it does not signify what God is—rather, it signifies an infinite (as though not determinate) ocean of substance. Hence when we proceed to God by "the way of removal," we first deny to him corporeal aspects; and secondly, also intellectual aspects such as goodness and wisdom, in the way they are found in creatures. Just "that (he) is" remains then in our understanding, and nothing more—hence it is, as it were, in a state of confusion. Lastly we remove from him even this very being itself, as present in creatures—and then it remains in a darkness of ignorance. In that ignorance, as far as the wayfaring state is concerned, we are best joined to God; and this is a dense darkness, in which God is said to dwell.[2]

Most of this is familiar Thomistic thought where Aquinas uses remotion to avoid anthropomorphic understandings of God based on material realities and then to avoid univocal concepts of goodness and wisdom. When only "being" is left, we have nothing left to anchor our ideas of God upon, and when we remove even that idea, we are in the darkness of ignorance. Aquinas says that in this life we are best joined to God in ignorance, and "this is a dense darkness, in which God is said to dwell."

Gregory Rocca picks up on this passage and adds one from the *Summa Contra Gentiles*, where Aquinas follows the thought of Dionysius to argue that we are completely unable to know God's essence in this life, so "to manifest

2. I *Sent.* 8.1.1 ad 4. Translation is from Joseph Owens, "Aquinas—'Darkness of Ignorance' in the Most Refined Notion of God," in *Bonaventure and Aquinas: Enduring Philosophers*, ed. Robert Shahan and Francis Kovach (Norman: University of Oklahoma Press, 1976), 70.

his ignorance of this sublime knowledge, it is said of Moses that 'he went to the dark cloud wherein God was.'"[3] Rocca uses these two passages to make the case that "God dwells in supereminent darkness, and the human darkness of unknowing is a direct consequence of God's excessive, dazzling light."[4] This is mostly right, but without further explanation it can leave us with the idea that there is darkness in God or that we are unable to know anything about God in this life. Taken without nuance or a deeper understanding of the light in God, we could approach the theological task only in despair of ever being able to know much about God at all. Theology would be the work of persons stuck in Plato's cave, not the work of those who have made it out into the light.

The darkness in this "darkness of ignorance," however, resides not in God, but in our own intellects. As Rocca points out, the darkness we experience when confronted with God is the result of a superabundance of light that actually blinds us in the same way that we would go blind if we were to stare directly into the sun for a prolonged period or were to experience the flash of an atomic bomb. As we will see later, Aquinas often compares the human intellect confronted by the essence of God to the eyes of a bat or owl in the daytime—God's essence overwhelms our mental faculties. So when Aquinas ends the passage from the *Sentences* by saying that "this is a dense darkness, in which God is said (*dicitur*) to dwell," the *dicitur* is the key, because it reflects a manner of speaking. We *say* that God dwells in darkness, but this manner of speaking really reflects the darkness of our intellects, for there can be no darkness in God or in those who dwell in God's presence and are filled with the light of glory. The darkness here is just a function of our limited intellectual abilities and is not anything real in God at all.[5]

Something that is dark is, to use Aquinas's metaphysical understanding, in potential for something else, but God cannot be in potential to receive something new or to change, so the darkness can only belong to intellectual creatures who have the potential to receive new forms, that is, either angels or

3. SCG 3.49.9: "And this is the ultimate and perfection of our knowledge in this life, as Dionysius says in the *The Mystical Theology*: 'We are united to God as the Unknown.' Indeed, this is the situation, for, while we know of God what he is not, what he is remains thoroughly unknown. Hence, to demonstrate his ignorance of this sublime knowledge, it is said of Moses that 'he went to the dark cloud in which God was.'"

4. Rocca, *Speaking the Incomprehensible God: Thomas Aquinas on the Interplay of Positive and Negative Theology* (Washington, DC: Catholic University of America Press, 2004), 29.

5. Aquinas is clearer about this in ST II-II 5.1 ad 2: "There was no darkness of sin or punishment in the original state of man and the angels, but there was a certain natural obscurity in the human and angelic intellect, in so far as every creature is darkness in comparison with the immensity of the Divine light: and this obscurity suffices for faith."

humans. Under our own power we are in the darkness of ignorance and God *seems* to dwell in darkness, because we are thoroughly ignorant of his essence.

Of course, the dwelling place could also be taken to be our heavenly experience of the beatific vision, but this too cannot be a dark place, precisely because it is filled with God's light and here the beatified humans and angels will have their intellectual powers boosted so that their minds are no longer overwhelmed by the light, but are enabled to see the light.

What follows in the remainder of this chapter, then, is a positive exposition of what it means for God to be light in the thought of Aquinas. While we may not be able to know the essence of God in this life, we can still know important attributes of God's essence both by reason and by revelation, especially because God reaches out to us in his self-manifestation through the mission of the Son, who illumines our understanding. Since it is not enough to merely argue against potential misunderstandings, the task of this chapter is to offer a full explanation of how God is best thought of as pure light.

We can begin by looking at three texts that directly link God and light.

God's Essence as Light

Aquinas directly links God and light when he tells us in his commentary on 1 Timothy that "the divine essence, which is pure act, is light itself."[6] This key insight regarding God's essence may seem odd given the apophatic moves that he makes with regard to God's essence early in the *Summa*. Surely, one might suppose, this is more a positive statement than one that says what God is not. There are at least two responses to this concern. First, one way to look at this is a denial of any darkness in God, which leaves only light remaining. By process of elimination, one can surmise that if there is no darkness in God, there must be only light. Second, as we mentioned with regard to Christ in the last chapter, apophatic statements resulting from our natural inability to know what God is would seem to be subject to supplementation by divine revelation. Our inability by nature to know what God is does not in any way preclude God from revealing to us something of his divine attributes. Even with divine revelation, we are "united to him as one unknown; still we know him more fully . . . according as we attribute to him some things known by divine revelation, which natural reason cannot reach."[7]

6. *In I Tim.* 6.3 §268: commenting upon 1 Tim. 6:16.

7. ST I 12.13 ad 1: "Although by the revelation of grace in this life we cannot know about God what God is, and thus are united to him in a kind of ignorance, nevertheless we know him more fully

Despite the additional information provided by divine revelation we lack complete knowledge of what God is; nevertheless, we still know more than we had before. Given this, Aquinas typically cites two scriptural texts to demonstrate God's essence as light: first, the text from 1 John 1:5, "God is light and there is no darkness in him," can be seen as divine revelation telling us something about God's essence, and second, 1 Tim. 6:16, "he dwells in inaccessible light, which no man may see." These two texts serve as the basis for Aquinas's claim that light is an attribute of God.

The statement that God is pure act and is light itself reveals several components of Aquinas's metaphysics that indicate important things about his understanding of God. Recall from our chapter on the nature of light that with regard to corporeal light, the heavenly bodies are the first agents of change. As such they have no contrary and are able to impart forms onto things. The light that is a quality of these celestial bodies acts on all things under heaven. These celestial bodies are similar to God in that way. God's light, like corporeal light, is able to act upon all things in the universe and as such there is no contrary to God—no power that exists that is capable of resisting or inhibiting God's action. Additionally, the description of God as "pure act" tells us as well that God is not in potential for anything. That is, nothing is able to act upon God in a way to change God or bring to God something that God does not already have; God cannot learn something new, have some power that God does not already have, attain some goodness that is not already in God. Just as corporeal light acts on everything and is the first agent of change among corporeal beings, God is the first agent of universal change and acts to bring things into being and sustain them. All of this is essential to God and an aspect of God's nature.

The second text is from his commentary on John, "for God is light itself and everything else is illumined by him."[8] Here we can note, besides the equivalency between God and light, that there is only one source of light, God. Others may seem to be sources of light, and may even think that they are their own source of light, but in fact they are illumined by the one source. This reflects back on our discussion of the proper understanding of illumination as a light that is ordered to God. Because ultimately there is only one source of illumination, all things that are properly illuminative must lead back to that

inasmuch as many and more excellent of his effects are demonstrated to us and inasmuch as we attribute to him some things from divine revelation, to which natural reason does not extend, such as God being three and one." Note that for Aquinas the influx of grace is one of the effects of God that we can come to know.

8. *In Ioh.* 8.6 §1250.

source, while things that are illuminative in an extended sense might be some manifestation of truth, but not the kind that leads us toward God.

This leads to our third text, also from the Johannine commentary, in which Aquinas says, "for to be light (*lucem*) is proper to God, and all others are illumined (*lucentia*), that is, they participate in light, but God is light (*lux*) through his essence."[9] Here Aquinas gives a more metaphysical account of how we are illumined by the one source of light, through participation, where participation is understood as receiving "something in a particular way which belongs to another in a universal way."[10]

Aquinas ascribes light to God and insists on the role of participation with the Manichean error in mind.[11] Aquinas in several passages mentions that with regard to light, the Manichees made the mistake of confusing God with corporeal light.[12] But for Aquinas, as we have described in the last chapter, God is an intelligible light rather than a corporeal light. Likewise, the Manichees believed that there were two principles of creation—one from light and one from dark.[13] This was not, for Aquinas, a historical heresy that only Augustine had to deal with, but a live option promoted by the Cathars of his time, many of whom still lived in Italy while he was there, which is why he occasionally refers to Manichees in the present tense and why he also argues in more than one place that there is only one principle of creation.[14] Aquinas's concern with light and dark, especially with regard to moral matters, might seem to the uninformed to be dualistic, but his understanding of light is consistently driven by a desire to *avoid* dualistic consequences of light. For example, as we mentioned in the second chapter, Aquinas views corporeal light as having no natural contrary, so that there is nothing to resist it at its point of origin; if he viewed light as having a contrary he might find himself pointed in a more dualistic direction. Or if, as we saw in his discussion of light language, he saw

9. *In Ioh.* 12.8 §1713.

10. *De Hebd.* II.70. For a detailed explanation of Aquinas's theory of participation, see Rudi A. te Velde, *Participation and Substantiality in Thomas Aquinas*, Studien und Texte zur Geistesgeschichte des Mittelalters, Bd. 46 (Leiden and New York: E. J. Brill, 1995).

11. For a brief discussion of Aquinas's awareness of the Cathar heresy, see Kerr, *After Aquinas: Versions of Thomism*, 4–5. For the larger context of the Dominicans with respect to the Cathars, see Roger French and Andrew Cunningham, *Before Science: The Invention of the Friars' Natural Philosophy* (Aldershot, UK: Scolar, 1996), 99–172.

12. See DM 16.1, *In Ioh.* 8.6, ST I 90.1.

13. See Antoine Dondaine, *Liber de duobus principiis: Un traité néo-manichéen du 13e siècle* (Rome: Istituto Storico Domenicano, 1939). English translation in Walter L. Wakefield and Austin P. Evans, *Heresies of the High Middle Ages: Selected Sources* (New York: Columbia University Press, 1991), 511–91.

14. See ST I 49.3.

corporeal light and spiritual light as being the same thing, he would again be headed in a Manichean direction. The adoption of an Aristotelian physics and metaphysics is crucial to combating the Cathar heresy, as it gave the Scholastics the necessary tools to affirm the goodness of the world and to understand its principles and causes.[15]

The key concept in this third passage is that of participation, which reinforces the idea that we are by no means self-illumining. Inasmuch as we are illumined at all, especially with regard to illumination in its proper sense, it is through participation in God's light, even if it is an unwitting participation. This is the result of the fact that only God has light as an essential property, which means that no other being can have it as such, since two things that share the same essence have the same nature. Other beings may have natures that can receive the light, as angels and humans do, but they cannot have light by their essence.

As the participation metaphysics might indicate, in addition to Aristotle, Aquinas was also deeply influenced by Neoplatonic thought. The Dionysian influence on Aquinas is well documented,[16] but with regard to light Aquinas connects light with the First Cause, who is God, quite explicitly in his commentary on the *Book of Causes*. Much of what he has to say here helps explain the texts we mentioned above. Aquinas says that the First Cause "is life and light itself"[17] and is an aspect of the simple goodnesses found in God. The human problem is that our intellect is unable to apprehend first causes, not because they are not intrinsically knowable, but because they are so luminous that we are blinded by them, like an owl's eyes in the sun.[18] The First Cause is pure act and so is pure light, "by which all other things are illumined and rendered knowable."[19] As such, it cannot be illumined by anything else, since

15. A detailed case is made for this in Roger French and Andrew Cunningham, *Before Science: The Invention of the Friars' Natural Philosophy* (Aldershot, UK: Scolar, 1996). See especially pp. 185–97 on Aquinas.

16. See Fran O'Rourke, *Pseudo-Dionysius and the Metaphysics of Aquinas*, Studien und Texte zur Geistesgeschichte des Mittelalters, Bd. 32 (Leiden and New York: E. J. Brill, 1992).

17. *De Causis* 16, 97: "Now, having established the order of things with regard to the infinite, he continues similarly with respect to other things, and says that all other simple goodnesses, namely life and light and the like, are the causes of things that have such goodnesses. For just as the first cause is the infinite itself, and all other things have infinity from it, so also is the first cause life itself and light itself, and from it the first created being, namely, an intelligence, has light and intellectual life."

18. *De Causis prooemium*, 2: "Our intellect relates to them [first causes] as an owl's eye does to sunlight, which it cannot perceive well because of the sun's excessive brightness."

19. *De Causis* 6, 45: "First, then, he shows that the first cause is not known in the first way, namely through a cause, when he says that the first cause does not cease to illumine its effect, while it is not

there is no other light above it. Aquinas argues that metaphorically we speak of that through which we know things as "light." We know things only inasmuch as they are in act, and so the actuality of something is in this sense its light. This implies that something is brought into act by some other cause—fire causes water to become actually hot, or a teacher causes the potential knowledge of Latin to become actual in a student. But while we know effects through their causes, the First Cause is not made known to us by any lower cause, but only through lower effects.[20] That is, causes lower than the First Cause do not have the power to bring the first cause into act any more than a candle has the ability to illumine the sun. Effects point back to their causes, and this is how we know about the causes, but with regard to God this is because God is constantly illumining the effects that he causes.

Causes work through participation, where "whatever abundantly participates in a characteristic proper to some thing becomes like it not only in form but also in action."[21] Aquinas understands form to be the principle of action, which means that particular forms have a tendency to act in predictable ways—something that has the instantiated form of a sphere is likely to act by rolling, and something that has had the form of heat applied to it is also capable of heating other things. Things participate in forms by having forms impressed upon them by some other agent that already possesses that form. The more we participate in that agent's form, the more we become like the agent. Aquinas offers two examples to explain this idea. The first is that of the illumination of the sun, in which we can participate in two ways, either by being seen (the illumination makes us visible) or by seeing other things illuminated by the sun, such as the moon, which by participating in the light of the sun also illumines other things. The second example is that of a knife, which has its natural form that lends to cutting, and a participated form, such as a heated knife, which it receives by an infusion of the form of heat. Aquinas argues that things that have a form naturally have them more powerfully than those that have a form by participation, so that the sun's light, which it has naturally, is more powerful

illumined by any other light because it is itself the pure light above which there is no light. To understand this we should realize that it is through corporeal light that we have sense knowledge of visible things. So we can speak metaphorically of that through which we know something, as if it were light. Now the Philosopher proves in Book 9 of the Metaphysics that every single thing is known through that which is in act. Therefore, the very actuality of a thing is, in a certain way, its light. Since an effect is such that it is in act through its cause, it follows that it is illumined and known through its cause. The first cause, however, is pure act, having no admixture of potentiality. Therefore, it is itself pure light, by which all other things are illumined and rendered knowable."

20. Ibid.

21. *De Causis* 23, 118.

than the moon's, which is participated. Theologically, this means that only God has light as a natural form and that all other lucid beings, inasmuch as they have light to varying degrees, have it as a participation in God's light. We may choose not to participate in the light and thus have our own vision obscured, but any time we have light, we have it from God acting in us.[22]

This understanding of causality also helps explain why Aquinas thinks that we can know some things about God just from an observation of nature. Effects that are infused with forms not only participate in their cause, but they also point back to it. Our participated light points back to God as the source of light.

Light and the Incomprehensibility of God

Beyond the unknowability of the First Cause, Aquinas quite often uses light to explain both God's incomprehensibility to us, with the operative principle of theological humility—that "one knows God most perfectly who holds that whatever one can think or say about Him is less than what God is."[23] This is not to say that we are unable to say anything about God, but rather that we must understand the limits of our statements. So while God "is pure act without any admixture of potentiality, and is supremely knowable in himself,"[24] this does not mean that other beings can know God in the same way that God knows himself; instead his excess of light renders us like bats in front of the sun due to the weakness of our intellect—a weakness, as we will see, that can be strengthened.[25] Aquinas says that our own light, when we come to the light of the divine essence, "is reflected back on itself by a more excellent light," and so is unable to penetrate into a vision of the divine essence.[26] This is not a pure apophaticism in which we are completely unable to know anything about God, but rather a qualified one that acknowledges human limits while at the same time asserting the intrinsic knowability of God to God and God's ability to strengthen our intellects to increase our knowledge of God.

22. Ibid.

23. *De Causis* 6, 43.

24. ST I 12.1.

25. Ibid. Note that in *De Causis* the animal was an owl, but here in the *Summa* the animal is a bat.

26. *De Trin.* 1.2: "The human mind receives its greatest help in this advance of knowledge when its natural light is strengthened by a new illumination, like the light of faith and the gifts of wisdom and understanding, through which the mind is said to be raised above itself in contemplation, inasmuch as it knows that God is above everything it naturally comprehends. But because it is not competent to penetrate to a vision of his essence, it is said in a way to be turned back upon itself by a superior light."

God's Light as Truth

This knowledge of God, limited though it may be in us, is a direct consequence of Thomas's idea that all knowledge and truth, which is manifested as intelligible light, derives from God's truth, which is an illumination of the intellect, for "God is light itself, and all things are illumined by him."[27] God is the "truth itself, and the highest and First Truth,"[28] which means something more than simply that all truth originates in God, which is not of itself trivial. Rather, the idea of God as First Truth carries within it a prioritization of truth, so that if one knows the First Truth first, one is more likely to know all the truths that follow. One may, for instance, know particular truths, including some that are eternal, as in certain mathematical formulas, yet not know a host of other truths that exist outside of mathematics. But because all truth is simply comprehended in the mind of God, knowing the First Truth means that ultimately it is possible to know all truths. Indeed, for Aquinas the perfection of the intellect is found in its knowledge of truth, as the perfection of any power is found when it reaches its end. The goal of the human intellect is truth,[29] which is ultimately found in the beatific vision in which all truths are known in the vision of God as First Truth. This idea that comprehending the First Truth leads to other truths is very similar to the idea that the conclusions of a *scientia* are found in its principles.

This light of the First Truth is given first in creation, and is a part of Aquinas's natural theology. In his discussion of the power of God, Aquinas says that "all knowledge derives from the uncreated light,"[30] and because of this we are all illumined (in the extended sense). For Aquinas, it is our pursuit of finite truth that leads us to the reality of an infinite and incomprehensible truth and thus gives us a means to arrive at knowledge of God, where "the first and supreme truth must be incomprehensible and infinite."[31] The idea here seems to be that when we consider the nature of truth and work backwards to see its source, the infinite number of truths lead us back to one truth that transcends those infinite truths, and so must be infinite itself. It would seem to be a version of the fourth way of proving God's existence from ST I 2.3, which

27. *In Ioh.* 8.6 §1250.

28. ST I 16.5.

29. ST I 16.1: "As the good denotes that toward which the appetite tends, so the true denotes that towards which the intellect tends."

30. DP 5.1 ad 18.

31. *In Ioh. prooemium* §6. In the prologue to his commentary on John, Aquinas lists four ways that philosophers attained knowledge of God by the use of natural reason. In important ways they parallel the famous five ways of ST I 2.3, yet also encompass different ideas, such as truth as a way back to God.

sees the gradation of things that require a perfect expression of its being, so that knowing that there is "something truest" would lead us to an understanding that God must exist.

There is a moral component to God's truth, in that not only is all truth measured by its conformity to God's knowledge, but God also does not lie to us—God knows the truth and speaks the truth. The comparison is always between God and the devil, who is the father of lies,[32] and between light and dark, so that Aquinas reads 1 John 1:5 as "'God is light,' that is, truth, 'and there is no darkness in him,' that is, lying."[33]

Our participation in the First Truth means that while the proper object of our intellect is the form of an object we have abstracted from its material instantiation, the perfection of our intellect is found when the existing form of objects, like stones, participate in a superior intellect, which Aquinas says is an intelligible light (implicitly referring to God).[34] So the measure of the perfection of a form is found in its divine origin in the mind of God, since God creates all forms. When we abstract a form from the particular matter in which it is found, the abstract form must have first existed in God before it existed in matter, and so the measure of its truth and perfection must first be found in God's intelligible light, where God is the exemplar cause of all forms.[35] Aquinas goes beyond a generic monotheism in this regard by arguing that all knowledge of truth is from the Holy Spirit inasmuch as he infuses the natural light in us and then moves us to use it.[36] Since our natural light is what allows us to abstract forms from objects and since the Holy Spirit also moves us to seek out truth, God is constantly at work in our mental actions, notwithstanding the fact that we also will our own thinking.

32. *In Ioh.* 8.6 §1250–51.

33. *In Ioh.* 5.6 §805.

34. ST I-II 3.6: "Consequently, the intellect is not perfected by the form of a stone, as such, but inasmuch as it participates in some likeness to that which is above the human intellect, namely the intelligible light or something of the kind."

35. See ST I 44.3 on God's exemplar causality.

36. ST I-II 109.1 ad 1: "All truth, spoken by anyone, is from the Holy Spirit as from an infusion of natural light, and moving us to understand and speak the truth, but not as dwelling in us by sanctifying grace, or as bestowing any habitual gift superadded to nature." For God's role in moving our intellect, see Matthew Cuddeback, "Thomas Aquinas on Divine Illumination and the Authority of the First Truth," *Nova et Vetera (English Edition)* 7 (2009): 579–602.

Light, Providence, and Evil

Aquinas's theology has a heavy emphasis on divine providence, and he often uses light as a model for how providence works. The Cathar argument that the material world is created by a dark principle, rather than one of light, means that Aquinas's theological response must account for a world that is continually illumined by God as a way of moving humans toward their salvation, while acknowledging the reality of evil. Aquinas sees the continued existence of everything as evidence of God's providential ordering of the universe, and consistently uses light as a model for how this happens. The existence of things, he says, is like the existence of light in the air in that it depends on a source outside of itself. Just as light in the air is dependent upon an illumining source, so our very existence is dependent upon the source of all existence—God.[37] God in this view is seen as constantly sustaining the world in existence.

This leads, in part, to Aquinas's understanding of how God knows good and evil. The question, simply put, is how a perfectly good being who knows all things perfectly is able to know anything about evil, which is not good and is by nature imperfect, especially if what we know is supposed to be in us as knowers. Aquinas argues that evil is accidental to a thing and not part of its substance; yet even so, God knows all accidents. His explanation again depends on light; God knows good and evil like we know light and dark. But since dark is no thing existing in itself, but rather an accidental quality of the diaphanous medium, it has no substance of its own. For God to know evil, then, is just for God to know the absence of the good in a thing. By participating in God's knowledge of good and evil, humans too are able to see evil as the absence of good in a thing.[38] There is no darkness in God, even in God's knowledge of evil.

God's providential ordering of the universe is not a matter of just starting the whole thing off and stepping back in the manner of a deistic God. Rather, Aquinas sees God operating in all of our actions by directing and moving our powers, including our intellectual powers. This means that our knowledge of truth is possible only because God is working in us through the light he has given us by nature—our natural light allows us to know the truth of sensible things, and we only need a *new* illumination to know things that exceed our

37. ST I 8.1: "Since God is very being by his own essence, created being must be his proper effect; as to ignite is the proper effect of fire. Now God causes this effect in things not only when they first begin to be, but as long as they are conserved in being, just as light is caused in the air by the sun as long as the air remains illumined."

38. ST I 14.10.

nature.[39] In this sense God's light shines on all of us by giving us the universal gift of cognition and the ability to know the truth of things.

At the same time, God also gives particular goods to those he chooses to give them, and while providence is about the universal ordering of existence, the particular goods of grace and glory fall under providence's subcategory of predestination. God offers new illuminations of grace and glory to his predestined elect who will be saved.[40] This saving illumination offers to humans the additional light above our nature that allows us to know the truth about God and how we should act in response to that knowledge.

There is an opposite to the gifts given by God's predestined grace, namely when God withdraws from us. Aquinas is clear that in order to achieve his purposes God can darken our minds by withdrawing even his universal benefits from us. In his commentary on Job, Aquinas notes that God is able to confound the abilities of those who oppose his plans "not because he leads them into false opinions [recall that God does not lie], but because he takes away his light from them so that they may not know the truth, and he clouds their reason so that they cannot find suitable ways to achieve the evils which they propose."[41] God even withdraws his light from philosophers so that they are unable to find and speak the truth.[42] In contrast to the philosophers whose minds have been darkened, God may intentionally give the light of wisdom to those who are ignorant as a means of demonstrating his power.[43] In this sense God draws us to him by bestowing these benefits on us.[44]

39. *De Trin.* I.1: "There are some intelligible truths to which the efficacy of the active intellect does extend, such as first principles which humans naturally know, and those truths which are deduced from them; and for such knowledge no new intelligible light is required, but the light with which the mind is naturally endowed suffices. But there are other truths to which these principles do not extend; namely the truths of faith and things that exceed the faculty of reason, such as knowledge of future contingent events, and the like; and these things the human mind cannot know unless it is divinely illuminated by a new light, superadded to the light of nature."

40. ST I 23.4. Note that the question of illumination arises in the first objection, where God's communication of goodness is compared to the universal illumination of the sun. The response, which mentions the particular gifts of grace and glory, does not mention illumination specifically, but both the objection and the role of the light of grace and the light of glory that we have previously described would indicate that God's election includes new illuminations beyond the universal light of his goodness. Cf. *Ad Rom* 8.6, especially §704.

41. *In Iob* 12:25 379–87.

42. Ibid., 313–20: "Philosophers excel in the consideration of the truth. He says regarding these, 'He changes the truth from their lips,' i.e., the lips of those who are eager to speak the truth. For God sometimes darkens the mind of those men by subtracting his grace so that they cannot find the truth, and, consequently cannot speak it, as Romans 1:22 says, 'Saying that they were wise, they have become foolish.'"

God's Illuminative Teaching and Its Soteriological Effect

Part of God's providential work is that of teaching, which Aquinas addresses in a number of places. The medieval discussion centered on whether or not anyone other than God could be considered a teacher. This question was the result of a dispute over how to deal with Matt. 23:8–10, which claims that Jesus' disciples are not to be called teachers (*magister* in Aquinas's Vulgate), since only God and the Messiah are the masters.[45] Were Aquinas and his teaching brethren claiming a title that was due only to God?

Aquinas, in his typically nuanced way, sees teaching as proceeding from two different directions, from within and from without. The interior principle of teaching is that which is in our nature, and Aquinas attributes this to the light of the agent intellect, which he says is responsible for understanding the basic principles of knowledge, such as the principle of noncontradiction. This light is given by God and he alone is responsible for teaching us interiorly by the creation of this light in us. God also gives us the interior impulse to seek out truth, which causes the intellect to act. The exterior form of teaching comes from our interaction with human teachers, who usually propose statements to us audibly, and in Aquinas's academic context almost exclusively so. One of the key differences between God who teaches interiorly and humans who teach exteriorly is that humans are unable to strengthen the light of their students; that is, they cannot make them smarter or more capable than they are. Aquinas recognizes that different people have different levels of intellectual ability and even the best teachers cannot make their students into something they are incapable of being. At the same time, human teachers are able to lead students from their limited particular knowledge to more universal understandings that

43. Ibid., 342–50: "As to those that are thought foolish and ignorant, he then says, 'he produces light in death's shadow,' for the shadow of death seems to be ignorance or foolishness, since the living are distinguished from the nonliving especially by knowledge. Thus, 'he produces light in death's shadow,' when he gives either wisdom to the ignorant or he shows those who were wise but whose wisdom was previously unknown to actually be wise."

44. *In Iob* 9:11 303–10: "Consider that in the Scriptures, God is said to come near to man when he lavishes his benefits on him, either by illuminating his intelligence, inflaming his affection, or bestowing any kind of good on him. So Isaiah 35:4 says, 'Our God Himself will come and save us.' On the other hand, God is said to withdraw from man when he subtracts his gifts or his protection from him." Note that the language of illumining intellects and inflaming our affections points to the invisible missions of the Son and Spirit.

45. This is the first objection in both DV 11.1 ob 1, and ST I 117.1 ob 1. In what follows, I refer to Aquinas's arguments in both articles, though primarily ST I 117.1.

for Aquinas demarcate superior understanding. God, on the other hand, as the author of our intellect is fully capable of boosting our natural ability to understand, so that we can begin to know God as well. This once again points to God as the providential source of all knowledge of God; God not only reveals himself to us, but strengthens our intellect by an infusion of light so that we are capable of understanding what is given to us through faith or direct encounter with God.[46]

One way of construing this idea of God as teacher would be to say that even though God works as an interior principle, his involvement in fact seems fairly remote. It seems that God gives us the natural ability to know and directs us to seek the truth—God winds us up like a mechanical toy and sets us off on our own. But this would neglect the soteriological aspects of God's teaching. As Aquinas mentions in one of his sermons, God's teaching is meant to help us not only by illumining the intellect, but also by moving our affections to love God. When we make ourselves students of God's inspiration, we become learners, and Aquinas says that this "pertains to justification."[47] In fact, he overlays the whole concept of teaching onto the three theological virtues of faith, hope, and love, when he argues that the divine teaching takes place in three stages: illumining the intellect through faith, elevating the mind through hope, and changing our affection through love.[48]

Given our post-Reformation worries about justification, it may seem odd to put God's teaching as the means by which we are justified, but in light of Aquinas's moral theory it perhaps makes more sense. Briefly put, for Aquinas, right actions are those that accord with reason, if only because all of God's acts are products of God's reason, which cannot err. As a result, God also cannot sin, since sin is a kind of spiritual darkness that is impossible in the God who is light.[49] When we sin we act against reason and against God, and so lack justice with regard to God. To be justified—to be made just—would naturally require that our future actions accord with reason. Sin is inherently unreasonable, and

46. In ST II-II 2.3, Aquinas argues that we cannot attain the beatific vision without first being taught by God, but as students, we must first believe the teacher, so our learning about God requires a prior act of faith. This reflects the kind of pedagogical insight that runs throughout the *Summa Theologiae*, for careful reflection on the teacher-student relationship should lead us to see the importance of trust in a classroom, for a student must trust that the teacher knows the truth and wants to communicate it in a nondeceitful manner. Without trust (or, in the case of holy teaching, faith), learning is less likely to take place.

47. *Beatus Vir* 2.2 in Thomas Aquinas, *The Academic Sermons*, 317.

48. Ibid., 317–18.

49. DP 1.6 sc: "On the contrary in 1 John 1:5 it says: 'God is light, and in him there is no darkness.' But sin is spiritual darkness. Therefore in God there can be no sin."

once we are in a state of sin we are no longer able to reason effectively about our actions. God's teaching allows us to know what we should do, and by learning this, along with receiving the grace to do it, we can become justified before God. Justification has not just a moral component, but also a noetic one, so that God's teaching heals our mind of our ignorance. In fact, the moral component of justification must necessarily follow the noetic one, since in all human acts we actually think about what we are going to do.

This illumination of God's teaching leads to a twofold judgment. On one hand, we both judge and know by the power of the natural light placed in us by God. This is the intellectual judgment we use when we ascertain the truth of sensible things, but the light that enables this judgment, while natural to us, is nevertheless a participation in God's light.[50] On the other hand, God's teaching results in an eternal judgment that ultimately illuminates and makes clear, as only God can, the things done in the darkness of our hearts.[51]

Summary

To summarize what we have said about the implications of God as light in his very essence, we have found that Aquinas uses light language both to describe how God makes himself manifest to us and how he also remains hidden from us. We have seen how the divine light has a universal causality that both creates and illumines the entire universe. God's light is connected to God as the First Truth and the teaching that goes with it, while also representing God's overarching providential care and predestined grace for the universe. God's light functions soteriologically to heal our minds while also casting judgment on our actions. Finally, humans, inasmuch as they have light, have it by their nature's participation in God's own light.

50. ST I 12.11 ad 3: "All things are said to be seen in God and in him all things are judged, because by the participation of His light, we know and judge all things; for the light of natural reason itself is a certain participation of the divine light; just as we are said to see and judge of sensible things in the sun, i.e., by the sun's light." Cf. DT 1.3 ad 1.

51. *In I Cor* 4.1 §196: "Secondly, he describes the perfection of the future divine judgment, saying: who, namely the Lord coming to judgment, will illumine the things now hidden in darkness, i.e., will make clear and manifest the things done secretly in darkness and will manifest the purposes of the heart, i.e., all the secrets of the heart."

Trinitarian Expressions of Light: The Divine Missions

The importance of light in the divine essence is also manifested in the relations of the three divine persons in Aquinas's Trinitarian theology. Generally speaking, Aquinas thinks that with regard to God "light by nature properly pertains to the realm of essence," yet that light can be used "to connote personal properties in virtue of the diffusive property of light."[52] To understand these statements we need to know what Aquinas is responding to. In this section of *Contra Errores Graecorum* he is interpreting the alleged statement by St. Epiphanius that "[t]he Holy Spirit is the spirit of truth, a light third in order from Father and Son."[53] Aquinas claims that any ordering of things is only possible where there is no unity of things, so since God is a unity, there can be no order of first and third. Aquinas argues that the "Father, Son, and Holy Spirit are one light, just as they are one God."[54] Calling the Holy Spirit a third light would be equivalent to making the Holy Spirit a third God. In spite of the name of the book, Aquinas stretches to find a charitable way to interpret this statement and so reminds us that light diffused from one source can also diffuse further light. Aquinas says that if we think about the diffusive properties of light we can then stretch it to "connote personal properties."[55] Using this extended language of light, we can say that while light pertains to the divine essence, it can be used to refer to properties unique to each of the divine persons. Aquinas, however, warns us not to press this too far and that the "Father, Son, and Holy Spirit should simply be confessed as one light."[56]

This creates a bit of a problem for Aquinas, as it immediately raises the question of how God can be essentially light, and yet light can also be a personal property of the Son. At the very least, the opening lines of John's Gospel would certainly imply that the Son must be called light. The solution to this problem can be found in the medieval idea of appropriation, which links the essential attributes of God to their manifestations in the Persons.[57] As Aquinas explains

52. CEG 1.3, 23–26. Translated in Thomas Aquinas, "Against the Errors of the Greeks," in *Ending the Byzantine Greek Schism*, ed. James Likoudis (New Rochelle, NY: Catholics United for the Faith, 1992).

53. Ibid., 5–7: Note that I use the term "alleged" because modern research has established that much of what Aquinas was responding to was not actually written by the authors to whom it is attributed in the *Libellus*. Aquinas, of course, could only respond to what was put in front of him and did so with his typical charity, always attempting to find some way to align the statements with orthodox positions.

54. Ibid, 8–9.

55. CEG 1.3, 23–26. See note 52 above.

56. CEG 1.3, 29–31.

57. A helpful summary of the history of appropriation and Aquinas's use of it can be found in Gilles Emery, *The Trinitarian Theology of Saint Thomas Aquinas*, trans. Francesca Aran Murphy (Oxford and New York: Oxford University Press, 2007), 312–37.

in his discussion of appropriation, we are able to know more about the essential attributes of God by the use of reason from our knowledge of creatures than we are about the personal properties, which require revelation for our knowledge.[58] Consequently, our knowledge of God's essential attributes, such as light, can help us better know who the persons are:

> As, therefore, we make use of the likeness of the trace or image found in creatures for the manifestation of the divine persons, so also in the same manner do we make use of the essential attributes. And such a manifestation of the divine persons by the use of the essential attributes is called "appropriation." The divine person can be manifested in a twofold manner by the essential attributes; in one way by similitude, and thus the things which belong to the intellect are appropriated to the Son, Who proceeds by way of intellect, as Word. In another way by dissimilitude; as power is appropriated to the Father, as Augustine says, because fathers by reason of old age are sometimes feeble; lest anything of the kind be imagined of God.[59]

Because light belongs to the essence of God, it can be appropriated to one of the persons, in this case the Son as Word. The intellectual illumination provided by the Son indicates both that the Son is divine and that illumination is an act proper to the Son. In this way we come to know more easily that God is light and is making himself manifest to us. Speaking specifically of appropriations that are fitting to the Son, Aquinas argues that the brightness or clarity of the Son "agrees with the property of the Son as the Word, which is the light (*lux*) and splendor of the intellect, as Damascene says."[60]

Even with the idea of appropriation helping us understand the way that essential attributes are expressed in the Persons, as we move from the divine essence to the Persons, it is helpful to remember the basic Trinitarian rule that all Persons in the Trinity are active in any of the divine actions in creation. To maintain the divine unity, all three Persons are active in the act of one of them, even if the act is made most manifest in one of them. For instance, in discussing sanctifying grace in ST I 43.5, Aquinas says that "the whole Trinity inhabits the mind,"[61] yet he carefully distinguishes the ways this comes to be

58. ST I 39.7: "Now the essential attributes of God are more manifest to us from the standpoint of reason than the personal properties, because we can derive certain knowledge of the essential attributes from creatures which are sources of knowledge to us, such as we cannot obtain regarding the personal properties, as was above explained."

59. Ibid.

60. ST I 39.8.

true, so that the Father is said to be in us without being sent, while the other two Persons are in us and are sent. In this particular article, Aquinas makes an important distinction about the mission of the Son with respect to the gift of sanctifying grace. Aquinas argues that all the gifts given through sanctifying grace are given by the Holy Spirit, who is the first gift of love. "Some gifts," however, ". . . by reason of their own particular nature, are appropriated in a certain way to the Son, those, namely which belong to the intellect, and in respect of which we speak of the mission of the Son."[62] This mission to conform the human intellect to God is not for every kind of intellectual perfection, so the Son does not perfect our intellect to know perfectly all the rules of mathematics (no matter how earnestly students might pray for it), but instead the Son is sent for a particular kind of "intellectual illumination that breaks forth in love."[63] This kind of illumination is one that properly orders our mind to God so that by our knowledge our will is led to see God as the good for which it is made and to love God for his intrinsic goodness. To be illuminated to know God is to want the friendship with God that is the apogee of human virtue found in charity. Both the gift of illumination and the gift of love are rooted in one divine grace, but the one cause has two effects in the two divine missions—the illumination of the intellect by the Son and the kindling of affection for God by the Spirit.[64]

Aquinas thus understands the primary mission of the Son to be the illumination of our intellects in ways that allow the Holy Spirit to kindle our affections. As a result, Aquinas has a theory of divine illumination quite different than anything that had come before it, because it is primarily Christological. Rather than a theory of divine illumination that requires God to intervene in every act of knowing, Aquinas thinks that we can know many things by nature because of the gift of the natural light of the agent intellect, which participates in the divine light (which is itself the light of Christ)[65] and is implanted in us at creation. Instead, his theory of divine illumination is focused on revealing to us knowledge of God, and this is primarily found in the person of the Incarnate

61. ST I 43.5.

62. Ibid., ad 1.

63. Ibid., ad 2.

64. Ibid., ad 3: "If we consider mission as regards the effect of grace, in this sense the two missions are united in the root which is grace, but are distinguished in the effects of grace, which are the illumination of the intellect and the inflaming of the affection."

65. *In Ioh.* 1.8 §188: "He was also full of truth, because the human nature in Christ attained to the divine truth itself, that is, that this man should be the divine Truth itself. In other men we find many participated truths, insofar as the First Truth gleams (*reluceo*) back into their minds through many likenesses; but Christ is Truth itself."

Son, who comes to illumine us. We can look at various ways that the Son illumines our intellects.

The Illumination of the Son

In at least two places Aquinas quotes Heb. 1:3, "Who is the splendor of his glory and figure of his substance," to establish that Christ "proceeds from the Father as splendor from light."[66] This piece of scripture, and the conclusion that Aquinas draws from it, is problematic because splendor is a kind of diffusion or reflection of light that is dependent upon a light source—it is more like *lumen* than *lux*—which means that it can diffuse itself in a variety of places and ways. If this is the case, then one possible consequence to this is that there could be more than one Son. Just as the sun can diffuse its light in many places, so could the Father diffuse his light into many Sons.[67] Aquinas's response is that corporeal light has its splendor diffuse from one place to another as a consequence of a division of matter (in the illumined subject, not in the source of light). In the case of God, however, there is no matter to be divided, and so the comparison does not apply.[68] The basic idea here is that material things are diverse in quantity by virtue of the same form appearing in the different individual pieces of matter, so that with respect to light different objects, like air and water, can receive the form of light and so the light exists in "diffuse" objects. But since God is immaterial, there is no matter that can receive the divine form and so no possibility of a diffusion of his form.[69] The relation between the Father and Son as one of light, for Aquinas, seems to have good scriptural support and does not necessarily subordinate the Son to the Father or make for multiple sons.

If the mission of the Son is to illumine us with regard to God, then he must possess light perfectly himself, and since light represents the perfection of knowledge, Christ must himself have perfect knowledge. Aquinas is concerned to address this issue in the Third Part of the *Summa*. Here the question is not whether the Son has light, but whether the Son united to human flesh, the human being Jesus Christ, has the light of perfect knowledge. How, one

66. DP 2.3 sc: cf. *In Ioh.* 12.5 §1662.

67. DP 9.9 ob 12: "The Son proceeds from the Father as splendor from the sun, as Hebrews 1:3 says, 'being the splendor of his glory.' Now one splendor can produce another splendor. Therefore the Son can generate another Son, and thus there would be several Sons in God and more than three persons."

68. Ibid., ad 12: "One splendor proceeds from another by the diffusion of light (*lux*) on to another subject. This is clearly due to a division of matter, which is impossible in God."

69. Aquinas explains this principle when he argues for the procession of the Spirit from the Son in DP 10.5.

wonders, could any being with human flesh not only be able to illumine another, but illumine others about a transcendent God? What happens when "the incorporeal light of the Divinity takes on the body of humanity"?[70] If Christ does not have perfect light, then he would seem to be unable to illumine us sufficiently about the perfect source of all light.

In another reference to the Son's mission, Aquinas gives a gloss on the Canticle of Zechariah at Luke 1:79, "to give light to those who sit in darkness and in the shadow of death," by suggesting that Christ came to take away our ignorance and to give light to those in darkness, and so "there was no ignorance in Christ."[71] A more substantial argument along these lines is found in ST III 10.4, where Aquinas discusses whether the soul of Christ, a created reality, sees the Word or divine essence more clearly than other creatures. Aquinas argues that

> the soul of Christ, since it is united to the Word in person, is more closely joined to the Word of God than any other creature. Hence it more fully receives the light in which God is seen by the Word Himself than any other creature. And therefore more perfectly than the rest of creatures it sees the First Truth itself, which is the Essence of God.[72]

He goes on to suggest that two people can know something via the same medium, but one can know more than the other by having a greater power to know. We might think of the way two people could know Einstein's theory of relativity, where a first-year physics student would know it to be true, but a professor of physics would know it to be true in a deeper way. Christ, argues Aquinas, will know the divine essence more perfectly than anyone else because his soul, united to God in the most perfect way a creature can be, is illumined more perfectly by God.[73]

In fact, in ST III 9 Aquinas uses the interaction of light with Christ's intellect to describe how Christ had beatific knowledge of God, infused knowledge of particulars, and acquired knowledge by the light of the agent intellect, that is, all three lights of glory, grace, and nature. Again, Aquinas is

70. ST III 32.1 ad 1.

71. ST III 15.3 sc: "Ignorance is not taken away by ignorance. But Christ came to take away our ignorance; for 'He came to illumine them that sit in darkness and in the shadow of death' (Lk. 1:79). Therefore there was no ignorance in Christ."

72. ST III 10.4.

73. Ibid., ad 1: "And in this way the soul of Christ, which is filled with a more abundant light, knows the Divine Essence more perfectly than do the other blessed, although all see the Divine Essence in itself."

operating from the presumption that Christ had a human soul that was united to the divine person, and this soul was fully functional so as not to unbalance the Incarnation. Without a human soul that was capable of knowing things, Christ would have been less than human.[74] The relation between the divine knowledge and the human knowledge, according to Aquinas, is not like two different illuminating bodies, such as the sun and a candle, where the light of the sun overwhelms the light of the candle, for to hold this would diminish Christ's humanity. Instead, the relationship is like that where one body illuminates and one is illuminated, such as the sun and the air, where the light of the air is strengthened by the light of the sun. In this way the divine knowledge strengthens the human knowledge of Christ.[75] Without saying it, Aquinas is relying on the fact that all human knowledge is made possible by God and that God can and does strengthen the intellect of other humans as well; in the case of Christ it was a perfect and abiding strengthening that was unobstructed by any sin or defect of nature, whereas in our case it will be an imperfect strengthening here through the light of grace caused by Christ's illumination, but one that still allows us to know more about God. Christ's divine nature perfected his soul through a participated light, which made possible the beatific vision of God while he was here. In fact, our beatific vision of God is caused by Christ's perfect beatific vision.[76] Likewise, Christ had infused knowledge, similar to that of the angels and to the infused light of grace, whereby God brought all of his passive intellect into act[77] and Christ acquired knowledge via the natural light of the agent intellect.[78] These three forms of knowledge track the three kinds of light

74. ST III 9.1c: "But it was fitting that the Son of God should assume, not an imperfect, but a perfect human nature, since the whole human race was to be brought back to perfection by its mediation. Hence it is proper for the soul of Christ to be perfected by a knowledge, which would be its proper perfection."

75. ST III 9.1 ad 2: "But if we suppose two lights, one of which is in the class of illuminants and the other in the class of illuminated, the lesser light is not dimmed by the greater, but rather is strengthened, as the light of the air by the light of the sun. And in this manner the light of knowledge is not dimmed, but rather is heightened in the soul of Christ by the light of the Divine knowledge, which is 'the true light which enlighteneth every man that cometh into this world,' as is written Jn. 1:9."

76. ST III 9.2c: "Now men are brought to this end of beatitude by the humanity of Christ, according to Heb. 2:10: 'For it became Him, for Whom are all things, and by Whom are all things, Who had brought many children unto glory, to perfect the author of their salvation by His passion.' And hence it was necessary that the beatific knowledge, which consists in the vision of God, should belong to Christ most excellently, since the cause ought always to be more powerful than the effect." And ad 1: "And therefore the soul of Christ, which is a part of human nature, through a light participated from the Divine Nature, is perfected with the beatific knowledge whereby it sees God in essence." I will discuss more on this in the last section of this chapter.

77. ST III 9.3c: "Besides the Divine and uncreated knowledge in Christ, there is in His soul a beatific knowledge, whereby He knows the Word, and things in the Word; and an infused or imprinted

we have discussed before—the light of glory, the light of grace, and the natural light of the intellect. By Christ perfectly having all of these lights in his human soul he was able to illumine us, since "he was given to be the Teacher of all."[79]

While Aquinas pays attention to Christ's knowledge and his mission of illumination in the *Summa*, it is in his commentary on the Gospel of John that his theology of Christological illumination reaches its apogee. Ignoring this commentary thus leaves one with an impoverished understanding of the role of light in Aquinas's theology. The immediate reflection on the opening Christological hymn of John provides for Aquinas a fertile place of reflection on Christ the light. We will begin by working our way through Aquinas's discussion of this passage. Aquinas mentions in his prologue to the commentary that the focus of this gospel is on Christ's divinity[80] and that John is the one "who sees the light of the Incarnate Word more excellently and expresses it to us, saying 'He was the true light.'"[81]

Aquinas picks up this theme in his reflection on John 1:4b–5, "and that life was the light of men. And the light shines in the darkness, and the darkness did not overcome it." He begins with a discussion on whether light is used properly or metaphorically with regard to spiritual things, a discussion we do not need to repeat. Aquinas understands the quote from verse 4b, "light of men," as a reference to the particular light of our intellect that makes us different from other animals[82] or to our salvation or to all rational natures.[83] This light of men is understood in two ways, as an object that only humans understand, namely the concept of truth, or as the light we participate in which makes the very vision of the Word or light possible. That is, as with corporeal light, an inner light is required for us to see light, which is why we say that God illumines the blind. In a gloss on Ps. 4:7, "the light of your countenance is shined upon us," Aquinas says that this refers to the Son, who is the face of God and makes God manifest.[84] Aquinas offers another way to understand how this light was the

knowledge, by which He knows things in their proper nature by intelligible species proportioned to the human mind."

78. ST III 9.4c: "It must be said that in Christ there was acquired knowledge, which is properly knowledge in a human fashion, both as regards the subject receiving and as regards the active cause. For such knowledge springs from the light of Christ's active intellect, which is natural to the human soul."

79. Ibid., ad 1.

80. *In Ioh. pro.* §10: "For while the other Evangelists treat principally of the mysteries of the humanity of Christ, John, especially and above all, makes known the divinity of Christ in his Gospel, as we saw above."

81. *In Ioh.* pro. §11.

82. *In Ioh.* 1.3 §97. Cf. *In Ioh.* 1.8 §188.

83. Ibid., §98.

life of men, in that we are illumined by Christ through grace. Christ comes to restore all rational creatures, Gentiles and Jews, by illumining them with grace and truth, so that life comes through this participation in grace, and light comes by knowledge of truth and wisdom.[85]

Aquinas goes on to compare Christ, "the existing light itself," with John the Baptist. For Aquinas, John participated in the light, whereas Christ, as the divine light itself, is able to give perfect testimony and perfect manifestation of the truth, while John and others are only able to do so inasmuch as they participate in the divine truth, who is Christ himself.[86] Aquinas claims that the Word is not only light himself, but he makes manifest everything that is able to be made manifest. Here he throws in a piece of metaphysics, by arguing that we know all things through their forms (which we know through the process of abstraction) and "all forms exist through the Word."[87] In this brief statement we can see how important the light of the Word is for created things. Without the light of the Second Person, we would be unable to know anything, since the Word gives them the forms by which we recognize them. Here we can see how the Word not only comes to illuminate us and save us, but how even in creation the Word was working to give illumination to us.

The comparison between Christ and John is telling, because it points to the difference between the divine possession of light and the human participation in light. John comes as a witness to the light, a witness that gives humans the dignity of causality, allows for testimony to be passed along across time,

84. Ibid., §101: "The light of men can also be taken as a light in which we participate. For we would never be able to look upon the Word and light itself except through a participation in it; and this participation is in man and is the superior part of our soul, i.e., the intellectual light, about which the Psalm (4:7) says, 'The light of your countenance, O Lord, is marked upon us,' i.e., of your Son, who is your face, by whom you are manifested."

85. Ibid., §104: "It was fitting to join light and life by saying, 'And that life was the light of men,' in order to show that these two have come to us through Christ: life, through a participation in grace, 'Grace and truth have come through Jesus Christ' (John 1:17); and light, by a knowledge of truth and wisdom."

86. *In Ioh.* 1.4 §117: "But Christ testifies in one way and John in another. Christ bears witness as the light who comprehends all things, indeed, as the existing light itself. John bears witness only as participating in that light. And so Christ gives testimony in a perfect manner and perfectly manifests the truth, while John and other holy men give testimony in so far as they have a share of divine truth. John's office, therefore, is great both because of his participation in the divine light and because of a likeness to Christ, who carried out this office."

87. Ibid., §118: "For as light is not only visible in itself and of itself, but through it all else can be seen, so the Word of God is not only light in himself, but he makes known all things that are known. For since a thing is made known and understood through its form, and all forms exist through the Word, who is the art full of living forms, the Word is light not only in himself, but as making known all things."

allows for different people to be reached in different ways, and allows for the especially weak-minded to understand Christ.[88] Aquinas argues that Christ came to humans not for the purpose of the light itself, but for the sake of humans, and reached us by first illumining some people who then were able to reach other persons "in a human way." Because of this we need the testimony of the prophets (those who are first illumined) for the cognition of truth.[89] If, however, we do not receive the message of the prophets, this is not because of a defect in their testimony, but rather is a function of our unwillingness to see the light.[90] Closing our eyes so as not to see the light is our own fault, not a fault of the light. Salvation, however, does not come from the light that prophets like John have, since theirs is a participated light, but only from the one who has light by essence, the Son. We are saved not by participating in the light of another participant, but by participating in the one light that has light by essence.[91]

Aquinas deals with a natural objection to this way of subordinating John's light to that of Christ, an objection found in Eph. 5:8 and Matt. 5:14, both of which say that we are lights, which Aquinas thinks refers to John, the apostles, and all good men. Aquinas replies that only God is *the* light, and all creatures are at best *a* light. Inasmuch as John participated in it, Aquinas thinks that it was fitting for John to testify to it, just as we would think that only someone who has actually witnessed an event could give accurate testimony to it.[92]

88. Ibid., §119. Here Aquinas is largely following Origen.

89. Ibid., §119: "And so the Lord chose to come down to them and to illumine certain men before others about divine matters, so that these others might obtain from them in a human way the knowledge of divine things they could not reach by themselves. And so he says, that 'through him all men might believe.' As if to say: he came as a witness, not for the sake of the light, but for the sake of men, so that through him all men might believe. And so it is plain that the testimonies of the prophets are fitting and proper, and should be received as something needed by us for the knowledge of the truth."

90. Ibid., §121: "One may object that not all have believed. So if John came so that all might believe through him, he failed. I answer that both on the part of God, who sent John, and of John, who came, the method used is adequate to bring all to the truth. But on the part of those 'who have fixed their eyes on the ground' (Ps 16:11), and refused to see the light, there was a failure, because all did not believe."

91. Ibid., §122: "Now although John, of whom so much has been said, even including that he was sent by God, is an eminent person, his coming is not sufficient to save men, because the salvation of man lies in participating in the light. If John had been the light, his coming would have sufficed to save men; but he was not the light. So he says, 'he was not the light.' Consequently, a light was needed that would suffice to save men."

92. Ibid., §123: "I answer that some say that John was not the light, because this belongs to God alone. But if 'light' is taken without the article, then John and all holy men were made lights. The meaning is this: the Son of God is light by his very essence; but John and all the saints are light by participation. So, because John participated in the true light, it was fitting that he bear witness to the light."

In *In Ioh.* 1.5, Aquinas provides a more comprehensive discussion of the sufficiency of the light. Here he is responding to a natural objection: if God's light is perfect and effective, then why are so many not illumined by it and live a life outside of the light? Aquinas argues that the Word's light is not false, as was the philosophers', or figurative, as was the Jews', or participated, as in the angels' or saints'. Instead, the Word is "true light, that is, light through his essence."[93] Saying that only the Word of God has light essentially might seem a bit of an odd way to assert the efficacy of the divine light, but it is important to remember that Aquinas's metaphysics understood that agents that have a quality essentially are able to act perfectly and so are able to act as perfect efficient causes. A true light is one that can perfectly illumine other objects because light is of its essence.

This means that "everything that shines must do so through him, insofar as it participates in him [Christ]"[94] and the Word's illumination "of every man coming into the world" (John 1:9) can be understood in two ways, as the light of knowledge and the light of grace. The light of natural knowledge that we all have is nevertheless a shared light that comes from participating in the true light, so our "intellect is derived from a source external to the world."[95] Taken as the light of grace, the illumination of every man in the world can be understood as the world of the church (Origen), the creation that Christ wants to save (Chrysostom), or those particular individuals who are illumined, rather than the universal illumination of our intellects (Augustine), but what matters most is that "no one is illumined except by the Word."[96] Aquinas adopts this starkly categorical statement from Augustine, and so calls into question all non-Christological theories of illumination (including Thomistic and Augustinian ones).

Aquinas sees this statement by John that Christ was "the true light, which illumines every man coming into the world," as providing a rebuttal to Manichean theories of two principles of creation, especially that creation was produced by the devil. If it were the devil that created humans, then we would have no light in us because we would not "be illumined by God or the Word."[97] This creation and illumination of the world by the Word does not mean that the Word is somehow contained in the universe or a part of it; rather he exists in the world as an "efficient and preserving cause,"[98] but one that works interiorly

93. *In Ioh.* 1.5 §125.

94. Ibid., §127.

95. Ibid., §129.

96. Ibid., §130. This is a quote from Augustine's *Enchiridion* 103.

97. Ibid., §131.

and mysteriously as a result of God giving existence itself to each creature—the most fundamental and internal gift that can be given and one that thus allows God to work interiorly.[99]

Christ's role in creation is, according to Aquinas's understanding of John, to make his own light manifest, "so the whole world is nothing else than a representation of the divine wisdom conceived within the mind of the Father."[100] And yet, "the world did not know him" (John 1:10). As a result of three things, then, the Son became incarnate. First, human nature had been so darkened by vice and ignorance that Christ came to illumine the dark.[101] Second, the illumination of the prophets and John, as participated light, was insufficient to illumine all and so "it was necessary that the light (*lux*) itself come and give the world a knowledge of itself."[102] Third, creatures by nature are unable to achieve knowledge of God, and so "it was necessary that the Creator himself come into the world in the flesh, and be known through himself."[103] This light came into the world and made itself present and evident, which is the natural effect of light—to make things manifest.[104]

Of course, the ultimate goal, the final end, of Christ's coming is not only to make us sons of God, but ultimately to confer on us the ability to see God's glory. Before the Incarnation humans were unable to see directly the glory of God, just as our eyes are unable to directly see the sun. Aquinas provides two explanations for this. Following Chrysostom, Aquinas says that we are able to see the sun when it is reflected off of a cloud or some other body and so prior to the Incarnation we were only able to see God in this same reflected way. Aquinas tells us that Augustine provides a different reason for our inability to see God directly before the Incarnation, namely due to the problem of sin, and draws the parallel between Christ healing our spiritual eyes in the same way

98. Ibid., §133.

99. Ibid.: "However, there is a difference between the way the Word acts and causes all things and the way in which other agents act. For other agents act as existing externally: since they do not act except by moving and altering a thing qualitatively in some way with respect to its exterior, they work from without. But God acts in all things from within, because he acts by creating. Now to create is to give existence to the thing created."

100. Ibid., §136.

101. Ibid., §141: "One is because of the perversity of human nature which, because of its own malice, had been darkened by vices and the obscurity of its own ignorance."

102. Ibid.

103. Ibid.

104. *In Ioh.* 1.6 §143: "He shows that the light (*lux*) which was present in the world and evident, i.e., manifested by its effect, was nevertheless not known by the world. Hence, he came unto his own, in order to be known."

that he illumined the blind.[105] In these two explanations we see a repetition of the two problematics of ignorance and sin that continue to be obstacles to our knowledge of God.

Aquinas takes up this twofold problem and its Christological solution again in his Johannine commentary, where he argues that since God dwells in unapproachable light (1 Tim. 6:16), it was necessary for God to come to us and "free us from error and dispel our intellectual darkness."[106] This illumination, however, while universally available still requires the light of faith that allows us to follow in Christ's footsteps.[107] Christ in this way operates as the one light source that lights our path and leads us from the twofold darkness to the eternal light. Aquinas explains just how we come to follow Christ in his commentary on Romans, where he says that we put on Christ by first receiving the sacrament of baptism and second by imitating Christ, since by imitating him we manifest his works.[108]

We have seen so far that the primary mission of the Son is to come to illumine humans through the Incarnation. Any possibility of the beatific vision for humans only comes through participating in the light and life of Christ, which takes place first through baptism and then through good works. But even our natural light, as we have shown, is Christological since it is based upon a participated light that is given to us in creation through the Word.

Illumination by the Spirit

While the primary mission of the Son is to illumine human minds to prepare them for the beatific vision, the primary mission of the Spirit is to kindle our affections for God, specifically for Christ.[109] For the most part, Aquinas sticks to these two basic missions when describing the actions of the Son and the Spirit. At the same time, basic Trinitarian logic requires that illumination be an act of all three persons. The Father, however, is not sent, but is the one sending, and so his role in illumination is to send the Son on the illuminating mission.

105. *In Ioh.* 1.8 §181–82.

106. *In Ioh.* 12.8 §1713.

107. *In Ioh.* 1.4 §120: "He says believe, because there are two ways of participating in the divine light. One is the perfect participation which is present in glory, 'In your light, we shall see the light' (Ps 35:10). The other in imperfect and is acquired through faith, since he came as a witness."

108. *Ad Rom* 13.3 §1079: "We put on Christ, first, by receiving the sacraments . . . second, by imitation . . . for a person who imitates Christ is said to put on Christ, because, just as a man is covered by a garment and is seen under its color, so in one who imitates Christ the works of Christ appear."

109. ST I 43.5 ad 2.

Aquinas, however, recognizes that the Spirit has a role in illumination as well, so we will look at the places where Aquinas speaks of the illuminating effect of the Spirit.

Aquinas's understanding of the illuminating role of the Spirit can be placed into three rough categories of: 1) general knowledge, 2) knowledge of Christ, and 3) the revelation, inspiration, and understanding that are among the sanctifying and gratuitous graces. The first, that of general knowledge, is a result of the light of natural reason with which all are endowed. Aquinas, in his treatise on grace in the *Summa*, tells us that "all truth is from the Holy Spirit inasmuch as he infuses the natural light and moves us to use it,"[110] but this is not, according to Aquinas, the same thing as the Holy Spirit indwelling us by sanctifying grace. The objection to which Aquinas is responding argues from a gloss on 1 Cor. 12:13 that suggests we can only know the truth through grace, but Aquinas argues that the natural light with which we are all endowed is itself a gift of the Holy Spirit, and our desire to understand the truth, which is the proper end of the intellect, is also a natural gift. But a natural endowment, that is, one that belongs to all humans, is different than an indwelling of grace.

If one ignores the objection to which Aquinas is responding, one might take Aquinas's claim that the Holy Spirit works in us whenever we know the truth about something as an argument that all of our knowing is graced, and that the nature/grace distinction is less defined in Aquinas than it might appear, since it implies that all of our intellectual gifts and our nature are kinds of gifts of God. In addition to ignoring the rest of his response, however, this objection would also be the result of mistaking contingency and grace. All of creation, in Aquinas's understanding, is contingent upon God's continued act of creation and sustenance of that creation. Our natures as humans, because they are dependent upon God for their most fundamental attribute of being, are wholly dependent upon God. All of human nature inasmuch as it exists at all is a kind of ongoing gift. Grace, however, is not just a gift, but a specific gift that goes beyond our nature, and while the one who bestows the gifts of nature and grace is the same, all humans receive nature, but not all humans receive grace. Or, to put it another way, all grace is contingent, but not all things contingent are graces.

The second way that the Spirit illuminates us is by giving us knowledge of Christ. This happens in a temporal progression. The first step in the progression occurred when the Spirit "illumined and inflamed the hearts of the apostles with

110. ST I-II 109.1 ad 1: "Every truth by whomsoever spoken is from the Holy Ghost from an infusion of natural light, and moving us to understand and speak the truth, but not as dwelling in us by sanctifying grace, or as bestowing any habitual gift superadded to nature."

the love of God."[111] The basis of this understanding is Aquinas's observation that before his crucifixion and resurrection, the disciples of Christ were ignorant of Christ's true nature. Instead, they were "attached to Christ corporeally."[112] They were, in a sense, materialists who were attached only to the material reality of Christ and the material works that he did. Only upon receiving the gift of the Holy Spirit were they able to grasp the divinity of Christ, and only by being illuminated by the Spirit about the divinity of Christ were the apostles able to understand in retrospect who Christ really was and the spiritual reality that was in union with his material reality.[113] The Spirit then gave the disciples the courage to preach and to accomplish mighty works, both of which testify to the divinity of Christ. It is from this preaching that we receive the teaching of Christ and about Christ, and teaching that is ordered to God is illumination.

The illuminating effects of grace given by the Spirit include inspiration and revelation, which are gratuitous graces for the building up of the church, and the gift of understanding, which is given to all Christians along with sanctifying grace. The first two, inspiration and revelation, we have discussed in the first chapter on sacred doctrine as an illuminating enterprise. We can just add here a few additional notes. First, Aquinas sees a difference in the way that the Old Testament and New Testament were given when he says that they follow the two modes of teaching—external and internal. The Old Testament was given "exteriorly by proposing words for our cognition," and here Aquinas seems to have in mind in particular the Mosaic Law and the messages of the prophets, all of which were given in some kind of exterior way. The New Testament, on the other hand, was given by the Holy Spirit in an interior manner by an interior infusion of the Spirit himself.[114] Aquinas goes on to say that knowing is not enough, but one must also act, and so the Spirit first illumines the intellect to know and then inclines our affections to act well. [115]

111. *In I Cor.* 2.2 §106.

112. *In Ioh.* 16.4 §2106: "'He will glorify me,' that is, give a clear knowledge of me. First, by illumining the disciples: for they were still carnal and attached to Christ in a carnal way, that is, in the weakness of his flesh, not realizing the majesty of his divinity. Later, they were able to grasp this through the Holy Spirit."

113. Ibid.

114. *In Heb.* 8.2 §404: "The manner in which it was given is twofold: in one way by externals, by proposing words suited to their understanding. This man can do; and that is the way the Old Testament was given. In another way by acting inwardly, and this is proper to God: 'the inspiration of the Almighty gives understanding' (Jb. 32:8). This is the way the New Testament was given, because it consists in the outpouring of the Holy Spirit, who instructs inwardly." Cf. ST I-II 106.1.

115. Ibid.: "But it is not sufficient to know, for one is required to act. Therefore, He first illumines the intellect to understand; hence, he says, I will put my laws into their minds. . . . Furthermore, He inclines

In this third way of illumining us, the Spirit provides both sanctifying and gratuitous graces. The key illuminating grace here is the gift of understanding, one of the gifts associated with the theological virtue of faith, and which is meant to move us to our final end by allowing us to know what our final end is, namely God—a knowledge that Aquinas claims from the very first article of the *Summa* as the most important and salvific knowledge we can have. The Holy Spirit can illumine our minds about the preambles of faith, but must also illumine our minds about what our final end is, and knowing the former does not necessarily result in knowing the latter. But even knowing the end is not enough; we must adhere to it as well.[116] As is often the case, demons may know that God is the last end, but through their own fall they no longer adhere to that end. Adhering to the end requires sanctifying grace, given by the Spirit, so the gift of understanding both illumines our mind about the end and helps us hold on to that end. In short, the Spirit, like the Father and Son, gives us all three lights—the light that applies to our natural knowledge, the light of grace that prepares us for the next life, and ultimately the light of glory that is found in the beatific vision, which is our last end. Because the beatific vision drives much of Aquinas's anthropology, soteriology, and ethics, which all concern our relation to the final end, God, the beatific vision needs to be addressed here.

The Light of Glory in the Beatific Vision

Aquinas forged his understanding of the beatific vision in his effort to reconcile two conflicting pieces of scripture. The primary objection to the beatific vision is found in John 1:18: "No one has ever seen God," a verse Aquinas lists as the first objection in a *Summa* question on the beatific vision.[117] This verse would seem to militate against any possibility of a beatific vision, in which we see God. In his Johannine commentary, Aquinas offers a detailed reading of this verse,

the emotions (*affectum*) to act well; hence, it is impressed on their heart. In regard to this he says, 'and write them on their hearts,' i.e., I will write charity on their knowledge."

116. ST II-II 8.5: "Accordingly then, the intellectual light of grace is called the gift of understanding, in so far as a human's understanding is easily moved by the Holy Ghost, the consideration of which movement depends on a true apprehension of the end. Wherefore unless the human intellect be moved by the Holy Ghost so far as to have a right estimate of the end, it has not yet obtained the gift of understanding, however much the Holy Ghost may have illumined it in regard to other truths that are preambles to the faith. Now to have a right estimate about the last end one must not be in error about the end, and must adhere to it firmly as to the greatest good: and no one can do this without sanctifying grace."

117. ST I 12.1 ob 1.

and includes a series of scriptural citations both for and against the possibility of the beatific vision.[118] In addition to John 1:18, another key scriptural objection is also found in 1 Tim. 6:16: "He dwells in unapproachable light, whom no man has seen or can see." Yet, as Aquinas points out, there are significant pieces of scripture that in fact point to just the opposite case, that the beatific vision is a possibility. For instance, the beatitude of Matt. 5:8, "blessed are the pure in heart, for they shall see God," and the throne account of Isa. 6:1, "I saw the Lord seated on a high and lofty throne," both contain a promise of the beatific vision and an actual example of such an experience (though Aquinas would likely categorize the latter as a product of rapture, in which the beatification is temporary and passing, but nevertheless a beatific vision of a kind, whereas the beatific vision proper has a permanence of eternity that is unable to be lost). Ultimately, Aquinas's logic follows Matt. 22:30: "The sons of the resurrection will be like the angels of God in heaven."[119] Aquinas surmises from this that if the angels can see God in heaven (from Matt. 18:10), then surely so can the sons of the resurrection, that is, humans.[120] But if humans can see God in the beatific vision, this leaves Aquinas with the puzzle of how to understand the statement that "no one has ever seen God." In his *Summa* response, Aquinas argues that this verse applies only to a comprehensive vision of God.[121] The basic idea is that we can apprehend something without comprehending it. For instance, one might be able to apprehend or perceive the grains of sand on the beach or all the stars in the universe in one sense, but in reality, a comprehensive understanding of them is beyond the human capacity to grasp—it is one thing to see a star or the sand, it is another to have comprehensive knowledge or really understand something that essentially escapes the bounds of our finite minds. While these normal sense objects exceed the scope of our minds, they do have a kind of created species that can exist in our intellects, making it possible for us to cognize particular expressions of them in our minds; we do this by abstracting their essence from their existence. God, however, cannot be represented by a created species for two very important metaphysical reasons. First, something infinite cannot be represented by something finite, and second, God's essence and existence are the same. "God is his own *esse*; therefore his wisdom and

118. *In Ioh.* 1.11 §210–14. Verses offered in opposition to the beatific vision are John 1:18 and 1 Tim. 6:16, while those offered in support are Isa. 6:1, 2 Sam. 6:2, Matt. 5:8, and Matt. 18:10 in conjunction with Matt. 22:30, 1 John 3:2, and John 17:3.

119. Ibid., §210.

120. Ibid.

121. ST I 12.1 ad 1: "Both of these authorities speak of the vision of comprehension." The authorities he references are Pseudo-Dionysius and John Chrysostom.

greatness and anything else are the same."[122] Aquinas thus comes to same the basic conclusion in his Johannine commentary as in the *Summa Theologiae*. "No one has ever seen God," is true of any kind of vision of God's essence in this life and of a comprehensive vision, though still of God's essence, in the next.[123]

The importance of the beatific vision for Aquinas is found partially in his understanding of the role of final causes in his overall explanatory framework of causes. For Aquinas, a final cause bears within it the formal, material, and efficient causes that are required to make the final cause come to be. If, for instance, one has the final cause of a house as a permanent abode that would effectively shelter one from the elements, it will require a certain kind of form (walls, room, foundation, etc.), certain materials, such as wood or stone, and an efficient cause: someone to bring the house into being by combining the material into the form. A final cause is "the cause of causes."[124] As a final cause, the beatific vision is the cause of all humans' need to attain it. It is Aquinas's understanding that at the deepest level we are made for friendship with God.[125] This friendship with God is only possible if we are able to know God, which requires a perfection of our intellect. Indeed, Aquinas argues that "the final perfection of the intellect is through union with God, who is the first principle of both the creation of our soul and its illumination."[126] The idea here is that created beings seek out the perfection of their nature. Dogs seek to be perfectly doglike, rocks seek to be perfectly rocklike, and humans seek to be perfectly human. The perfection of a creature is determined by its nature, so the perfection of a dog might be loyalty to its master, the perfection of a rock might be to fall, and the perfection of a human being is to have her intellect united with God. Again it is helpful to remember that for Aquinas it is our intellect and its ability to think abstractly that makes us human and differentiates us from other corporeal creatures. Without our intellectual capacities we would be more like that dog. This capacity for abstract thinking that makes us human finds its ultimate fulfillment in union with God. The drive for this fulfillment is, according to Aquinas, a built-in desire that comes from effects wanting to know their causes. So when, in this passage, Aquinas mentions that God is the

122. *In Ioh.* 1.11 §211.

123. *In Ioh.* 1.11 §214: "Using the above explanations, we can understand, 'No one has ever seen God.' First, No one, i.e, no man, has seen God, that is, the divine essence, with the eye of the body of or the imagination. Secondly, No one, living in this mortal life, has seen the divine essence in itself. Thirdly, No one, man or angel, has seen God by a vision of comprehension."

124. *Phys* II.5.186.

125. ST II-II 23.1: "It is evident that charity is the friendship of man for God."

126. ST I-II 3.7 ad 2.

first principle of our soul and our illumination, he implicitly understands this to mean that God is the final and efficient cause of our soul and its illumination,[127] which means that we will, by nature, want to understand what caused us to be. Since we have this innate desire to come to union with God, the full perfection of our intellect, and thus our human nature, can only be accomplished in coming face-to-face and in knowing the cause that brings us to be.[128] Only by resting in the contemplation of the divine essence, in which can be found knowledge of all of creation, can we find true happiness, and this is made possible by the light of glory.[129]

We should step back a bit and discuss just what the nature of the beatific vision is and why it is so important. Recall from the chapter on the nature of light and vision that vision is the most sublime of all the senses and the one that is most capable of dealing with intellectual and spiritual realities due to the spiritual image of the object that crosses the diaphanous medium into the eye. In the beatific vision the human or the angel directly sees God. This is not, however, a corporeal vision, for two reasons. First, God is not corporeal, so the vision must be an intellectual and not corporeal vision.[130] Second, the vision consists of the essence of God, yet even when we use our corporeal vision we are unable to see the essence of anything.[131] If I see a chair across the room, I do not see its essence; instead I must abstract an essence from the particular object I see. If we cannot see essences in our daily corporeal vision, then the beatific vision, where we will see essences, must not be corporeal. Instead, the vision is one that takes place in our incorporeal intellect. (This is one of the reasons that

127. Properly speaking, God cannot be the formal cause of a creature if one takes form to be in composition with material in a way that creates a unique creature, since God cannot enter into composition with matter. However, the Word does serve as an exemplar form for humans. See ST I 3.8 and ad 2 and *In Ioh.* 1.4 §118.

128. ST I 12.1: "For there resides in every man a natural desire to know the cause of any effect which he sees; and thence arises wonder in men. But if the intellect of the rational creature could not reach so far as to the first cause of things, the natural desire would remain void."

129. DT 6.4 ad 3: "The other [happiness] is the perfect happiness of heaven, where we will see God himself through his essence and the other separate substances. But this happiness will not come through a speculative science; it will come through the light of glory."

130. ST I 12.3: "For God is incorporeal . . . so he cannot be seen by the sense or the imagination, but only by the intellect."

131. In ST I 67.3, Aquinas says that no substantial forms are objects of the senses (*quia nulla forma substantialis est per se sensibilis, quia quod quid est est obiectum intellectus*), and in DA I.2 §236, that substantial forms belong to the essence or quiddity of something (*sed forma substantialis est de essentia, sive de quidditate subiecti*).

the soul and its powers must not be corporeal, for if they were, they would be unable to see God in any way.)

This vision of the essence of God by the intellect is the process by which we become deified. Aquinas says that "when any created intellect sees the essence of God, the essence of God itself becomes the intelligible form of the intellect" and that the light of glory is how "the blessed are made deiform, that is, like to God."[132] An intelligible form is closely related to the essence of a thing now seen in our mind. Humans gain intelligible forms through abstracting them from particular things that they sense. The process of abstraction, however, means that our intelligible forms are less universal than intelligible forms that are not tied to material objects. As beings move up the intellectual hierarchy they know more and more things by fewer and fewer intelligible forms, so that God ultimately knows everything through one simple intelligible form.[133] So when Aquinas says that the "essence of God itself becomes the intelligible form of the intellect," he is claiming that we will begin to know things through the same universal principle that God knows things. We become deiform because God unites his one universal form with our intellect. We become like God because through the beatific vision we begin to know as God knows.

There is, however, an additional problem here, which is that the vision itself must be unmediated and direct. As we mentioned in the description of Aquinas's understanding of the nature of light and vision in *De Sensu*, knowing in an unmediated way is superior to knowing in a mediated way.[134] The reason for this is that things are unable to exist in their natural being in a medium and so must take on a spiritual likeness or intentional being in order to make it through the medium and into the eye.[135] All human sensation, and to that extent all human knowing, is mediated. This would make the beatific vision problematic, for if we were to see God in any mediated way, we would not see God in his natural being and thus not really see God at all. In dealing with this problem in the *Summa*, Aquinas lists several reasons why the beatific vision cannot consist of a similitude or likeness of God as the object seen. First, superior things cannot be known by images of inferior things, so that an image of God is always going to be unable to communicate the entirety of God's

132. ST I 12.5.

133. See ST I 84.2 on how different beings see essences.

134. *De Sensu* III 438a27: "What can happen without a medium is better than what can happen by a medium, since it is better for something to happen by means of fewer things than more."

135. *De Sensu* IV 438b2: "Color is in a colored body as a quality complete in its natural being, but it is in the medium incompletely, according to an intentional being."

essence. Second, as we have mentioned above, God's essence is his existence, which is unlike a created form where the essence of a thing is separable from its existence (we can, for instance, know the essence of a unicorn or a chair without either one actually existing). Because any created form can have its essence separated from its existence, it is by nature incapable of representing the divine essence, which cannot be separated from its existence. Third, the divine essence cannot be circumscribed, yet any created likeness of the divine essence in our minds could only be signified by something that is itself somehow bounded, whether physically or intellectually.[136] Note that in each of these cases what limits the ability of the human intellect to see God is the natural limitations of the human intellect, not the intelligibility of God. Humans, by nature, have weak intellects that cannot know superior beings by images, can only know objects by abstracting universal essences from particulars, and must think about all objects in circumscribed ways.

If the overarching problem of the beatific vision is human intellectual limitations, not the intelligibility of God, Aquinas solves this problem by positing a divine gift of a created light of glory.[137] The purpose of this gift is to strengthen the intellect so that it may overcome these obstacles to the beatific vision. A key aspect of the light of glory is that it takes place directly in the human intellect, that is, without mediation, so that we are not dependent upon our senses to see God. This strengthening of the intellect allows us to know in the same way that God knows, in an unmediated and simple way. With the light of glory we can now know the superior being, namely God, without images, we can know created objects in their universal essences rather than through particulars existing as form and matter, and we can know the uncircumscribed God.

All of this takes place in the human intellect, and not through any kind of corporeal organ, though it is corporeal light and vision that Aquinas uses for his understanding of how the process works in the intellect. In fact, Aquinas makes it clear that no bodily eye can see God in his essence.[138] Even in the cases of rapture that we discussed previously, Aquinas assumes that the recipients of the

136. ST I 12.2.

137. Ibid.: "Therefore it must be said that to see the essence of God, there is required some likeness in the visual faculty, namely, the light of glory strengthening the intellect to see God, which is spoken of in Ps. 35:10, 'In Thy light we shall see light.'" An overview of the light of glory and some of the philosophical questions that arise from this idea can be found in Michael M. Waddell, "Aquinas on the Light of Glory," *Tópicos. Revista de Filosofía* 41 (July 2011): 105–32.

138. ST I 12.3: "It is impossible for God to be seen by the sense of sight, or by any other sense, or faculty of the sensitive power."

transient vision of God have been removed from their senses and experienced the beatific vision intellectually.

With respect to the role of light in the beatific vision, the key article in the *Summa* is I 12.5, where Aquinas takes up the question of whether we need a created light to see God. The crucial scriptural text is Ps. 35:10, "In your light we shall see light," which is the typical scriptural reference Aquinas uses for both the beatific vision and our natural light's participation in God. Here Aquinas explains that God's essence becomes the medium by which God himself is seen, so that the light of glory "is not the medium in which God is seen, but as one by which (*sub quo*) he is seen."[139] Again, Aquinas is navigating away from any possibility that we see the divine essence through some kind of mediation, which is not to see it at all. Instead, by the gift of the light of glory, which takes place in the intellect, God is both the medium and the object seen—the vision of God is intellectual and the light of glory is in our intellect as well.

To receive the light of glory we must be properly disposed for its reception, but this requires God to work in us, for we cannot dispose ourselves to something that exceeds our nature. God both prepares us to receive the form of the light of glory, which Aquinas calls the "intelligible form of the intellect,"[140] and imparts the form to us; the form imparted strengthens the power of our intellect to see God. The consequence of this is that God can impart the form, that is, give the light of glory, in different degrees. Just as our natural light of the intellect varies from person to person, so the light of glory will vary based on the amount of charity in each person.[141] Since Aquinas understands charity to be friendship with God,[142] as one has more and more friendship with God, one will receive more and more of the light of glory. Just as the punishment for sin is more and more darkness, the reward for charity is more and more light. One would think that this can become a self-reinforcing process, so that if, as Aquinas holds, the more you know about God the more you will love God, then as one receives more light one will come to love God more. There is no boundary on this love, as the infinity of the divine essence allows for the love of God to know no bounds.

139. ST I 12.5 ad 2.

140. ST I 12.5.

141. ST I 12.6: "Hence the intellect which has more participation in the light of glory will see God more perfectly; and he will have a fuller participation of the light of glory who has more charity; because where there is the greater charity, there is the more desire; and desire in a certain degree makes the one desiring apt and prepared to receive the object desired. Hence he who has more charity, will see God more perfectly, and will be more beatified."

142. ST II-II 23.1, see note 125 above.

Charity must exist in us prior to our actual reception of the beatific vision in the next life, and Aquinas notes three requirements for the beatific vision. First, we "must draw near to God," then we must actually lift up our eyes to see him, and finally, we "must take time to look, for spiritual things cannot be seen if one is absorbed by earthly things."[143] All three of these things are made possible by charity, which causes us to "join our soul to God . . . makes us look at God . . . and frees us from worldly matters."[144] It is not, however, enough merely to say that one loves God, since for Aquinas the love of God naturally results in obedience to God. One who loves something and intensely desires it will do everything necessary to attain that end, and it is the obedience that flows from charity that allows us to be put in a state ready for the beatific vision. True charity necessarily results in obedience to God's commandments.[145]

The important scriptural text here is the beatitude, "blessed are the pure in heart, for they shall see God" (Matt. 5:8). This is a key text for all Patristic and medieval understandings of the beatific vision, since it both contains the possibility of the divine vision and the requirement for it. The purity resulting from obedient love is a key concern for Aquinas, and the length and depth of the Second Part of the *Summa* sometimes obscures this important assumption behind his moral theology. Because we are made for the beatific vision and because it is only available to those who obey out of love, which is given by grace, Aquinas explores all the possible ways that we can obey and disobey. At the same time, we should remember that the Cathar heresy included leadership by the most pure members of the sect, and the Dominican order was founded to counter Cathar purity with a purity of its own. There were both theological and practical reasons for Aquinas to pay attention to purity.

We see this in a discussion of light. Light is better able to illuminate when the air is pure. Air filled with smoke, clouds, or fog is less able to receive light, while air clear of any particulate matter is able to receive all the light of the sun. As Aquinas points out, purity in humans and angels can be taken in two ways. In one way according to our natures, and in this way both angels and demons have a more pure intellect, since theirs is not limited by the obstructions of a body and the dependency on the senses. Theirs is a pure intellect and so by nature they are more illuminated than us. In another way, by the light of grace, demons and sinful humans are less illuminated than good angels and humans

143. *In Ioh.* 14.6 §1941.

144. Ibid.

145. Ibid., §1942: "And so, when a person's will is intent on God, who is its end, it moves all powers to do those things which obtain him. Now it is charity which makes one intent on God, and thus it is charity which causes us to keep the commandments."

who are full of grace, since the sin of demons and sinful humans puts an obstacle between them and God.[146] Our sin obstructs the light of grace just as fog or clouds obscure the light of the sun.

Christ the Light of the Beatific Vision

Given what we have said about the illuminating mission of the Son, it should not be a surprise that Christ plays a key role in our entry into the beatific vision and in the nature of the vision itself, even if his role has been neglected by theologians and philosophers. If the beatific vision is the goal of human life, the problem, as Aquinas spells out in the very first article of the *Summa*, is that we do not know that goal naturally. The beatific vision of the essence of God is a goal that exceeds our nature and requires God to not only make it possible, but also to make it knowable to us. Without God we are stumbling around in darkness, made worse by the further depredations of sin, which only deepen our darkness. The solution to our darkness is Christ, whose light we follow, for "one who does not walk in the light, not perfectly believing in Christ, but walks in the darkness, does not know where he goes, that is, to what goal he is being led."[147] To know our end we must perfectly believe in Christ. As Aquinas points out, the problem comes when we think we merit the light of grace and are instead deprived of it because of heresy.[148]

This is possible because Christ is the light and has light in his essence, while we can only participate in the light. The distance between these two points is covered through divine adoption, in which we become conformed to the Son so that we share in his splendor, since "by illumining the saints by the light of wisdom and grace he makes them conformed to himself."[149] By being conformed to Christ we are then able to receive the light of glory from him. Christ is not just a means to attain the vision, but is essential to what the vision *is*.

In the next life the saints will be illumined by the light of glory received from Christ, "on whom their glory depends."[150] In this light of glory the saints

146. DM 16.5 ad 9: "The uncreated light illumines spiritual substances in two ways: in one way by a natural light, and then good or bad angels are more illumined than humans souls. In the second way by the light of grace, and in this way bad angels are less capable of such illuminations because of an impediment to grace that remains in them permanently." Cf. DM 3.1 ad 8.

147. *In Ioh.* 12.6 §1685.

148. Ibid.: "Similarly, in the very things in which erring heretics believe they merit the light of truth and grace is the source of their being deprived of it."

149. *Ad Rom.* 8.6 §704.

will see both Christ's glorified body as it exists after the resurrection and the glory of his divine nature.[151] In fact, at the day of judgment even the wicked will see the glory of Christ's body, but will lose even that after judgment, while the saints will see the glory of his divine nature eternally.[152] Only by clinging to Christ are we ourselves able to shine.

The liberating power of Christ's light is demonstrated in Christ's descent into hell after his crucifixion. Aquinas argues that Christ's soul was in hell for the entire time his body was in the tomb and yet even while his soul was in hell it was able to deliver the saints from hell, not by leading them out of hell immediately but rather by "illuminating them with the light of glory."[153] Wherever the glorified body of Christ goes, it seems that the light of glory shines forth.

150. ST III 22.5 ad 1.

151. *In Ioh.* 17.6 §2260. "This can be understood to refer to the glory of his human nature after the resurrection . . . or to the glory of his divine nature, for he is the radiance of the Father's glory and the image of his substance . . . the saints in glory will see both of these glories."

152. Ibid.: "But the sight of this [his human body] glory will be taken away from them [the reprobate] after the judgment."

153. ST III 52.4 ad 1: "When Christ descended into hell He delivered the saints who were there, not by leading them out at once from the confines of hell, but by enlightening them with the light of glory in hell itself." In ST III.52.2, Aquinas differentiates between three levels of hell: the hell of the just, which was populated by Old Testament saints who had only the penalty of original sin, the hell of purgatory, and the hell of the lost. Christ's soul only resided in the first, but the effects of his illumination reached the other two levels.

5

Creation and the Light of God

In the last chapter we investigated what it means for God to be understood as light, both as an essential attribute and as one that is appropriated to the different Persons, primarily the Son. This chapter will focus on the variety of ways in which God expresses his light in creation and how it is found most intimately in the form of intelligible light in angels and humans. For Aquinas, a God who is light in his essence will manifest that light in a multitude of ways. The nature of corporeal light is to diffuse itself over as much area as possible; likewise, God expresses goodness and light throughout creation.

Creation and Corporeal Light

If "God is light and there is no darkness in him," as we have just argued and as the writer of 1 John claimed, then we would expect God's creation to be resplendent with his light. Indeed, creation itself reveals great truths to us about God in the same way that any piece of art or careful craftsmanship reveals something about its maker. By being attentive to the created world we have one basic means to understand something about God, so that

> we know God in this life, inasmuch as we know the invisible things of God through creatures, as it says in Romans (1:20). And so all creation is a mirror for us; because from the order and goodness and multitude which are caused in things by God, we come to a knowledge of His power, goodness and eminence. And this knowledge is called seeing in a mirror.[1]

Mirrors, of course, need light for us to see in them, and in this sense the corporeal light that God provides is a gift that makes all of creation manifest

1. *In I Cor.* 13.4 §800.

to us; without the ability of telescopes to collect in their mirrors light from all over the known universe we would know much less of the beauty and diversity of creation. A mirror, however, does not give one a perfect vision of what is seen, and this was especially true in Aquinas's day, where the mirrors lacked the clarity that ours have. So while creation can reveal important truths about God to us, as Aquinas sees it, that still leaves many important truths unknown to us, for creation can only reveal to us what is true about God inasmuch as God is "the principle of all existing things."[2] Nevertheless, we can see in Aquinas's account of creation that there are a variety of ways that light appears—in the distinction between good and evil, in the very act of the creation of light in the production of corporeal creatures, in the absence of a creation of darkness, in our participation in the light, in God's providential governance of creation, in miracles, and even in the light of heaven and the darkness of hell. We will look at each of these in turn.

Light in the Distinction between Good and Evil

After giving a thorough account of the mystery of the Trinity at the end of the treatise on God in the *Summa*, Aquinas turns his attention to the creation of the universe by God. He begins this section of the *Prima Pars* with a general description of creation and then turns to the distinction of things, that is, how we come to have diverse objects in this world, and he divides those distinctions into two sets: 1) the distinction between good and evil (QQ. 48–49), and 2) the distinction between spiritual beings (QQ. 50–64) and corporeal beings (QQ. 65–74).

The distinction between good and evil might seem like an odd way to begin with the distinctions in creation, when the distinction between spiritual and corporeal beings would seem to be more fundamental to us. Yet again Aquinas seems to have the Cathar heresy fully in his sights in organizing this section, since by Cathar teaching, the creation of corporeal things was caused by an evil principle. As Aquinas understands it,

> the Manicheans misunderstood this [John 18:36], and said that there were two gods and two kingdoms; there was a good god, who had his kingdom in a region of light, and an evil god, who had his

2. ST I 32.1: "Humans cannot obtain the knowledge of God by natural reason except from creatures. Now creatures lead us to the knowledge of God, as effects do to their cause. Accordingly, by natural reason we can know of God that only which of necessity belongs to Him as the principle of all existing things."

> kingdom in a region of darkness, and this darkness was this world, because all material things, they said, were darkness.[3]

Aquinas, then, must show from the beginning that there is no such thing as an evil nature, either one created by God or one that somehow creates the rest of the corporeal world. In making his argument he again relies on the physics of light to make his explanation. His operative principle is that we know opposites through each other, so that we know darkness by light and likewise evil by good. Just as darkness is no "thing" but just the absence of light, so evil is no "thing" with a nature, but rather just something that is deprived of the good of its nature.[4] Because evil is in some sense parasitic upon the good, evil cannot "wholly consume" the good, though Aquinas offers three different ways to understand this. In the first sense evil can destroy the good where the two are actually opposed, just as "the light can destroy the darkness." Second, where the good is the subject of evil, the good cannot be totally destroyed any more than the air is destroyed by the presence of darkness. Third, where something has aptitude to exist in a certain way, or to be actualized in a certain way, to use Aristotelian language, good can be diminished, but "not wholly taken away."[5]

It is the latter two kinds of evil that Aquinas thinks are unable to consume our good. Here he is primarily interested in what sin does to us. Sin has progressively deleterious effects on us, but it cannot totally destroy the good of our nature. Sin can put an obstacle between us and the reception of God's grace, but even

> if opaque bodies were interposed to infinity between the sun and the air, the aptitude of the air to light would be infinitely diminished, but still it would never be wholly removed while the air remained, which in its very nature is transparent. Likewise, addition in sin can be made to infinitude, whereby the aptitude of the soul to grace is more and more lessened; and these sins, indeed, are like obstacles

3. *In Ioh.* 18.6 §2350.

4. ST I 48.1: "One opposite is known through the other, as darkness is known through light. Hence also what evil is must be known from the nature of good. . . . Hence it cannot be that evil signifies being, or any form or nature. Therefore it must be that by the name of evil is signified the absence of good."

5. ST I 48.4: "Evil cannot wholly consume good. To prove this we must consider that good is threefold. One kind of good is wholly destroyed by evil, and this is the good opposed to evil, as light is wholly destroyed by darkness, and sight by blindness. Another kind of good is neither wholly destroyed nor diminished by evil, and that is the good which is the subject of evil; for by darkness the substance of the air is not injured. And there is also a kind of good which is diminished by evil, but is not wholly taken away; and this good is the aptitude of a subject to some actuality."

> interposed between us and God, according to Is. 59:2: "Our sins have divided between us and God." Yet the aforesaid aptitude of the soul is not wholly taken away, for it belongs to its very nature.[6]

That darkness is not itself a nature, but only the absence of a nature (light) in the appropriate context (air), points to Aquinas's conception of the purpose of creation, which is to express God's goodness. God makes creation not because God needs creation or to add anything to himself, but because the nature of the good is to share and make itself manifest. In this sense all of creation is a witness to God and a manifestation of God.[7] The natural question with regard to light and dark is why a God whose creation manifests his goodness would create a world that appears to be imperfect. Surely, one might say, we could conceive of a world without darkness. Aquinas offers an interesting response to this concern. In his mind, the imperfection of creation is a part of its goodness and represents no imperfection in God as a cause, for it was not "owing to imperfection in the active cause that the air was created without light, but through its wisdom that so orders things that they are brought from imperfection to perfection."[8] For Aquinas, it would be an odd creation where all of the creatures were made perfect, for there would be no purpose to their actions. Creatures that were formed perfectly would have no goal, no *telos*, to which their natures and lives would aim; with their purpose already achieved their existence would be, in fact, purposeless. Creatures who must strive for their perfection have a real purpose in their existence—to try and fulfill their very nature.

For Aquinas, it is the metaphysically simple goodnesses found in God, "life, light, and such,"[9] that are the cause of the same goodnesses found in creation, albeit imperfectly. These basic goodnesses are shared with all of creation universally. Aquinas compares God's sharing to the light of the sun, though while the sun is required by its nature to share its goodness, God does so

6. Ibid.

7. *In Ioh.* 1.4 §116: "Here it should be remarked that God makes men, and everything else he makes, for himself . . . not, indeed, to add anything to himself, since he has no need of our good, but so that his goodness might be made manifest in all of the things made by him."

8. DP 3.6 ad 16.

9. *De Causis* 16, 97: "Now, having established the order of things with regard to the infinite, [the author] continues in a similar vein with respect to the other things and says that all the other 'simple goodnesses,' namely, 'life, light, and the like are the causes of things that have such goodnesses.' For just as the first cause is the infinite itself, and all other things have infinity from it, so also is the first cause life itself and light itself, and from it the first created [being], namely, an intelligence, has life and intellectual light." The main quote is from the text of Proclus.

by willing creation, so that there is no necessity for creation.[10] The universal sharing of these simple goods does not, however, preclude God from sharing particular goods through grace and election.[11]

The Creation of Light

Indeed, the creation of corporeal light is at once a sign of God's spiritual light, a treasure, and a manifestation of God's goodness.[12] Corporeal light, which divides the day from the night, is by nature "a delight" to humans and "darkness signifies a certain sadness."[13] It should be no surprise to us that God's first act of creation, God's first self-manifestation outside of God, was to create light and separate it from the darkness. The theological error, however, is to mistake corporeal light for spiritual light, because

> physical light is not the supreme light, which is the intelligible light proper to the rational creature . . . sensible light is an image of the intelligible light, since sensible things are particular and intellectual things are universal. So as physical light has an effect on the thing seen by making colors actually visible and by making the eye able

10. DP 3.15 ad 1: "The comparison of Dionysius must be understood to refer to the universality of diffusion: as the sun sheds its rays on all bodies without differentiating one from another, so likewise is it with God's goodness: but it does not apply to the absence of will." That this means there is no necessity that causes God to create is made clear through the objection to which this statement is a response: "Dionysius (*De Div. Nom.* iv) says: 'As our sun neither by reason nor by Pre-election, but by its very being illumines all things that can participate in its light, so the divine good by its very essence pours the rays of its goodness upon all things according to their capacity.' Seeing then that the sun enlightens without reason or pre-election, it does so of natural necessity. Therefore God also produces creatures by communicating his goodness to them of natural necessity."

11. ST I 23.4 ad 1: "But if we consider the communication of this or that particular good, He does not allot it without election; since He gives certain goods to some men, which He does not give to others. Thus in the conferring of grace and glory election is implied."

12. *In Iob* 37, lines 30–32: "One must remember that sensible things are a kind of sign of intelligible things, and so we come to the knowledge of intelligibles through sensible effects. Among all the sensible effects the most spiritual is light. So light leads more efficiently to knowledge of intelligibles, inasmuch as sight, whose experience of knowing is perfected by light aids intellectual knowledge most. Since, then, that sensible light is hidden from men and communicated to them by the power of God, Job gives us to understand by this that in him there is a more excellent kind of light, i.e. a spiritual light, which God reserves as a reward for men for virtue. So he says, 'He announces it,' the light which is metaphorically represented by physical light, 'to his friend,' the virtuous man, whom God loves, 'that it is his possession,' that this spiritual light is a treasure which God reserves for his friends as a reward, 'and he can ascend to it, when he merits it by the works of virtue and prepares himself to possess it."

13. *In Iob* 3, lines 156–61.

> to see, so intelligible light makes the intellect to know because it is derived from the supreme light.[14]

In discussing the creation of corporeal light on the first day, Aquinas begins by discussing the nature of light, which we addressed in the second chapter, and then takes up the question of whether it was fitting for God to make light first. Here Aquinas is working from a substantial history of commentary on Genesis, from Augustine's various attempts to sort out the first few days to the abundant Hexaemeral literature that developed after Basil produced his *Hexaemeron.*[15] One way to think of Aquinas's account of creation is as a *Hexaemeron* embedded inside of the *Summa*, and taken independently it can be considered in its own right as a contribution to Hexaemeral literature. As such, Aquinas in ST I 67.4 deals with commentaries by Augustine, Chrysostom, and Basil in discussing the fittingness of the first act of creation being the creation of light, and Aquinas splits the responses into two groups. The question is whether or not Moses, as the assumed author of Genesis, should have first mentioned the creation of spiritual beings rather than corporeal light. Aquinas reports that one group thought that Moses did refer to the creation of spiritual things when he mentioned "heaven," and that "earth" referred to corporeal creation. Specifically, the production of light, according to this interpretation by Augustine, represented the creation of spiritual creatures, because "a spiritual nature receives its form by the illumination whereby it is led to adhere to the Word of God."[16] The second group of interpreters thought that Moses intentionally left out the production of spiritual creatures either because the account was intended for sensible beings (Basil) or because Moses was trying to avoid encouraging additional idolatry among the Israelites (Chrysostom).

Without necessarily correcting either group, Aquinas offers two different reasons why the production of corporeal light was fitting for the first day. First, as Aquinas had mentioned in ST I 67.3 and we have discussed previously, light is a quality of a heavenly body. Heavenly bodies are the first agents of corporeal change producing forms in other bodies, so by their production other things would receive their forms. Second, for Aquinas, things that are more universal should precede things that are less so, and since light is a common quality to both celestial and earthly bodies, that is, it appears in the sun, moon, and

14. *In Ioh.* 8.2 §1142.

15. For a detailed account of Hexaemeral literature, with an emphasis on Basil and Augustine's works, see Frank Egleston Robbins, *The Hexaemeral Literature: A Study of the Greek and Latin Commentaries on Genesis* (Chicago: University of Chicago Press, 1912).

16. ST I 67.4.

stars, as well as in fire, candles, and certain animals, it is fitting that a universal being be created before less universal beings. Aquinas adds two final reasons, one of which he picks up from Basil, that light makes everything else manifest, implying that without light we would know nothing else that was created. The final reason, which he gets from one of the objections (actually the *sed contra*), is that quite simply, without light being separated from the dark, there could be no way to demarcate one day from the next.

Aquinas deals with several other interesting objections to the creation of light on the first day. Aquinas rejects one suggestion—that the creation of light involved some kind of "luminous cloud"[17] that sufficed to illumine things, but which then went away or existed invisibly around the sun after the sun was created (or was turned into the sun) on the fourth day. Aquinas rejects the idea that the nebula went away because he sees the act of creation at the beginning as creating things that would endure, and for God to create something only to do away with it right away would seem to be unfitting for God, a waste of creative effort. Instead, Aquinas suggests that the substance of the sun was created on the first day, which includes its general illuminative power, and that later (implicitly the fourth day), it received additional powers that allowed it to produce specific effects.

The distinction between light and darkness results in distinctions of cause, place, and time:

> First, as to the cause, forasmuch as in the substance of the sun we have the cause of light, and in the opaque nature of the earth the cause of darkness. Secondly, as to place, for in one hemisphere there was light, in the other darkness. Thirdly, as to time; because there was light for one and darkness for another in the same hemisphere.[18]

Returning to the question of the creation of spiritual creatures, Aquinas argues that spiritual creatures were created on the first day, because they were not created in their final perfection of glory, but with the perfection of grace, from which they could (and did) fall.[19]

Aquinas's overall outline of the creation account in Genesis 1 is that there was first the general creation of heaven and earth without form, then the works

17. ST I 67.4 ad 2.

18. Ibid.

19. Ibid., ad 4: "And so we must understand the production of light to signify the formation of spiritual creatures, not, indeed, with the perfection of glory, in which they were not created, but with the perfection of grace, which they possessed from their creation."

of distinction that took place on days one through three, followed by the works of adornment in days four through six. Paralleling the work of distinction of light and dark on the first day is the work of adorning the light on the fourth day. Here Aquinas sees two possibilities, either that "heaven and earth were perfected by adding substantial form to formless matter, as Augustine holds, or by giving them the order and beauty due to them, as other holy writers suppose."[20] The lights of the sun, the moon, and the stars are given to humans for their usefulness, to serve our sight, so that we can perceive other objects, to provide a change of seasons that allows us to have food and health, and to give us signs of changes in the weather.[21]

Finally, Aquinas deals with the question of whether the lights of heaven are living beings, of which there was a great variety of opinion. There were basically two camps among both philosophers and theologians, those who held that the lights were living beings and those who thought they were inanimate objects. Aquinas deals with this question by first explaining the purpose of a soul in living beings, including plants and humans, since for anything to be a living being it needs a soul of some kind (an animating principle), and argues that with regard to heavenly bodies, they really only need something approximating a soul to account for their motion. Aquinas follows Aristotle here in suggesting that the heavenly bodies are actually moved by spiritual substances, that is, angels, and so "it is clear that the heavenly bodies are not living beings in the same sense as plants and animals, and that if they are called so, it can only be equivocally."[22]

Participation in the Light

In the creation of light, God also gives life, for life and light go together in the natural order of things and as a result we participate in the light.[23] This recurring theme of participation with regard to light indicates that for Aquinas we relate to the light in two ways. First, we see light as an object, that is, we see the corporeal light with our eyes as an object of our senses. Second, we see light

20. ST I 70.1.

21. ST I 70.2: "First, the lights are of service to man, in regard to sight, which directs him in his works, and is most useful for perceiving objects . . . secondly, as regards the changes of the seasons, which prevent weariness, preserve health, and provide for the necessities of food; all of which things could not be secured if it were always summer or winter . . . thirdly, as regards the convenience of business and work, in so far as the lights are set in the heavens to indicate fair or foul weather, as favorable to various occupations."

22. ST I 70.3.

23. *In Ioh.* 1.3 §100: "And, according to Origen, he fittingly attributes light to life because light can be attributed only to the living."

only by participating in an inner intelligible light, which God gives.[24] Here our inner light, that intelligible light by which we come to knowledge of the world around us, is able to actually understand the light that our eyes see. In this way, by participating in God's light, we come to see as God sees, even if in a severely limited and more compound way.

At one level, of course, God communicates both spiritual and corporeal light universally, so that we all receive the gifts of his goodness. We can, however, put obstacles in the way of this gift, both corporeally and spiritually, that hinder our reception of the gift. We may construct buildings without windows to block corporeal light, so that we live in the dark, or we may construct lives of sin so that we live in a spiritual darkness that prevents us from receiving God's light. But this only means that we "turn away from the light that does not turn away."[25]

Participation, metaphysically speaking, means that we become like the thing in which we participate, where the rule is that "whatever abundantly participates in a characteristic proper to some thing becomes like it not only in form but also in its action."[26] The concept here is that when one agent acts upon another, it impresses its form on it. As the stove heats the tea kettle, the water in the kettle progressively takes on the form of heat, so that it becomes more like the stove heating it. So if we then put our hand on the tea kettle, we would be burned by the tea kettle because it would then have the power to heat other things; it would be able to act like the stove. With regard to light, we are seen by others by participating in the light of the sun or by reflecting the light of the sun, as the moon does. Taken in a spiritual sense, when through the light of grace we participate in God's spiritual and intelligible light, we are able to know and act more like God.[27]

Governance

The gift of God's creation and our participation in both divine and corporeal light comes with a promise of God's providence, governance, and conservation

24. Ibid., §101: "We should note that light can be related in two ways to what is living: as an object and as something in which they participate, as is clear in external sight. For the eyes know external light as an object, but if they are to see it, they must participate in an inner light by which the eyes are adapted and disposed for seeing the external light." Aquinas uses this model to explain why Christ makes the beatific vision possible, both as the object of that vision and the means by which it is made possible.

25. DM 3.1 ad 8.

26. *De Causis* 23, 118.

27. ST I-II 109.4: "Hence, Augustine (*De Correptione et Gratia* 2) having stated that 'without grace men can do no good whatever,' adds: 'Not only do they know by grace what to do, but by its help they do lovingly what they know.'"

of all that God has created. God's providence is "a light shining by itself,"[28] and reflects a divine order to the universe. Indeed, the very intelligibility of the universe seems to be a reflection of God's providential ordering of creation for our benefit, so that we can both flourish and come to know God. God, through the bestowal of forms and their ongoing preservation, causes the actions of creatures in the sense of giving them natures that allow them to act independently in the world, just as "the sun is the cause and manifestation of colors, since it gives and preserves the light by which colors are made manifest."[29] God's creation, as both a source of light and a reflection of God's light, leads us back to God. In this sense, God comes to us through the light of creation and "when he bestows benefits upon man, either by illuminating his intelligence, inflaming his affection, or bestowing any kind of good on him."[30]

At the same time, those benefits can be withdrawn from humans, since they are not given by any necessity, but as pure gift. When God's operation is withdrawn from us, we are cast into a darkness of a perpetual night, a night that can only be overcome by a new influx of light.[31] This operation of God in us goes down to the deepest levels of our being, so that God, as Being Itself, makes all creatures to exist from moment to moment, preserving their being.[32] Thus if God were to withdraw his action by which he gives us existence, we would instantly be annihilated.[33] Just as the influx of light of the sun illumines the air and preserves the illumination, its withdrawal plunges the world into oblivion.[34]

At the heart of Aquinas's account of creation is a deep concern for creation's goodness and sufficiency. Aquinas's argument against the need for humans to receive new illumination with each new thing they know points to this concern. The argument, offered at the beginning of his commentary on Boethius's *De Trinitate*, suggests that we do not need a new illumination beyond

28. *In Iob* 18 lines 84–86.

29. ST I 105.5.

30. *In Iob* 9 lines 303–7.

31. ST I 102.3: "God placed man in paradise that He might Himself work in man and keep him, by sanctifying him, for if this work cease, man at once relapses into darkness, as the air grows dark when the light ceases to shine."

32. DP 3.3 ad 6: "Yet even as the air as long as it is light is illuminated by the sun, so may we say with Augustine (*Gen. ad lit.* 8.12) that the creature, as long as it is in being, is made by God."

33. DP 5.3 ad 2: "If God were to annihilate a thing, there would be no need for any action, and it would suffice if God were to withdraw the action whereby he gives things existence, just as the absence of the sun's action in illumining the air causes the absence of light in the air."

34. ST I 104.1: "All creatures need to be preserved by God. For the being of every creature depends on God, so that not for a moment could it subsist, but would fall into nothingness were it not kept in being by the operation of the Divine power." Cf. ad 1 and ad 4.

that of our natural light to know the truth of (presumably, natural) things. The argument, of course, does not say that we do not need *any* illumination to know truth, but only that we do not need a *new* illumination, so it presumes that there is some source of light that is already there and sufficient.[35] Further, Aquinas argues that if our existing light were insufficient, and this light is given by God, then there is no way that an additional light would suffice as well.[36] What Aquinas seems to be pointing to is that God gives us a fully functioning ability by nature to know creation in ways that are fitting to our mode of knowing. That is, we can know the truth about material objects, since we are material beings. If our natural light were to fail to be able to do this most basic task, it would represent a failure and creative insufficiency on God's part. This is not to say that we cannot diminish the strength of that light through our own choices, as Aquinas thinks is clearly the case through our acts of sin. Rather, God's creation of our world, including the intimate world of our mind, represents the sufficiency of creation for our flourishing. The goodness and sufficiency of God's creation and natural illumination would be yet another theological move against any position that would deny the goodness of the created world.

Miraculous Illumination

The sufficiency of creation, however, does not preclude God from working in it in ways that appear special to us, through both miracles and the gift of grace. With regard to grace, God can give us new illuminations that strengthen our intellects to teach us truths that are above our natural light,[37] in the same way that a telescope augments the power of our eyes to collect light that allows us to see faraway stars. The case of miracles, especially those of illuminating the blind and raising the dead, which are reserved to God and those acting as

35. For a discussion of the way that our natural light is illumination, but not a new illumination, see Matthew Cuddeback, "Thomas Aquinas on Divine Illumination and the Authority of the First Truth," *Nova et Vetera (English Edition)* 7 (2009): 579–602.

36. *De Trin.* I.1 sc: "Thus, therefore, if this created light is not sufficient for the knowledge of truth, but there is required a new illumination, according to the same reasoning this superadded light would not suffice either, but would require still another light, and so on to infinity, which cannot be encompassed; and so it would be impossible to know any truth. Therefore one must stand firm in reliance upon the first light, namely, that the mind by its natural light, without the superaddition of any other, can see the truth." Cf. ST I-II 109.1.

37. ST I-II 109.1: "Hence we must say that for the knowledge of any truth whatsoever man needs Divine help, that the intellect may be moved by God to its act. But he does not need a new light added to his natural light, in order to know the truth in all things, but only in some that surpass his natural knowledge."

instruments of God's power, provides both an example of how God can work in the world and an example of how Aquinas construes nature. In responding to an argument that when God does miracles he acts against nature, Aquinas argues that

> [w]hat God does is not against nature, it is natural in the fullest sense. For we call that natural which is caused by an agent to which the patient is naturally subject, even if it is not in keeping with the specific nature of the patient; for just as the ebb and flow of the sea is natural, because it is produced by the motion of the moon, to which the water is naturally subject, although it is not natural to the form of water: so, too, since every creature is naturally subject to God, whatever God does in creatures is natural in the full sense, although it is not natural to the proper and particular nature of the thing in which it is done, say when a blind man has sight restored or a dead man is revived.[38]

Aquinas sees nature in this sense as belonging to a type of agent, so that different agents act differently depending upon powers that result from their natures. It would be unnatural for my dog to start talking or to start solving math problems, but not unnatural for my son to do so. It would be unnatural for a human being by her own power to rise from the dead after a few days or to suddenly start seeing after a lifetime of blindness, but not unnatural for God to make this happen. For Aquinas, because God created everything and acts to sustain it, it is perfectly within the nature of God to act in creation. It may appear to us to be unnatural or even against the laws of nature, but for Aquinas what determines the naturalness of an action is the agent who performs it, not the one who receives it, as the universe is specifically set up to allow superior causes to act upon inferior ones. By nature, a piece of wood is unable to transform itself into a home, but because nature is set up so that superior causes can act on inferior ones, there is nothing against nature that prevents humans from acting on a piece of wood to turn it into a piece of a home. Wood is naturally inclined to receive changes made by superior forces and humans are naturally inclined to use tools for their benefit.

By working in the blind to provide light for their vision, God demonstrates his natural power over creation, a power that here is demonstrated in the most intimate and intellectual of ways. It is a miracle only to us, but for God there is nothing miraculous or unnatural to it, nor is it even a violation of the laws of

38. *Ad Rom.* 11.3 §910.

nature, unless one presumes from the outset that it would be unnatural for God to work in the world, or that somehow God set up the universe so he could not work in it. The universe is not some hermetically sealed box in which God could not enter, because of logical restrictions, lack of power, or some choice of his own. From a Christian perspective, the Incarnation puts those possibilities aside.

The Darkness of Hell and the Light of the Heavens

With regard to the creation of the universe there is also an eschatological aspect to the creation of light, as there are luminous aspects to heaven and dark aspects to hell. Hell is described by Aquinas as a shadowy land that "lacks the clarity of the divine vision and is said to be 'covered with the mist of death,' because of original sin which is the mist leading to death";[39] hell is so disordered that fire burns in it "without giving light."[40] There would be, one would think, perhaps some glimmer of the faintest light, just because the continued existence of the beings in hell would represent some good, but one wonders if that small glimmer in the land of shadows would be just a further mark of despair for its residents.

While Aquinas does not spend a lot of time talking about hell, perhaps because there is not much to know or talk about a place that suffers from the privation of light, he happily engages in speculation about the corporeal heavens, which all have "in common sublimity and some degree of luminosity."[41] He describes "heaven," which has multiple layers, as

> that body on high which is luminous actually or potentially, and incorruptible by nature. In this body there are three heavens; the first is the empyrean, which is wholly luminous; the second is the aqueous or crystalline, wholly transparent; and the third is called the starry heaven, in part transparent, and in part actually luminous, and divided into eight spheres. One of these is the sphere of the fixed stars; the other seven, which may be called the seven heavens, are the spheres of the planets.[42]

39. *In Iob* 10 lines 444–48.

40. Ibid., lines 454–58.

41. ST I 68.4 ad 3.

42. Ibid., corpus.

In this description of the corporeal heavens we again see hints of a threefold hierarchy of luminosity, with a perfectly luminous region in the empyrean heaven that parallels the light of glory, a second region of a perfectly transparent region that is disposed to receive the light, as are those who are infused with the light of grace, and finally a region that is partially receptive to the light, and contains bodies, including our own. Nowadays all of this medieval cosmology is largely ignored, since we know so much about the universe now, but nevertheless it gives us insight into how Aquinas sees the kingdom of light over which God rules. The corporeal light always points to the spiritual and intellectual light for which we are designed, so the corporeal heavens give us some sense of the spiritual heaven made possible through the light of the Son. In fact, applying the term heaven, meant in a corporeal sense, metaphorically, Aquinas says the very term points us to God, as "the Blessed Trinity, Who is the Light and the Most High Spirit."[43]

Christ the Light of Creation

The source of the lights of creation is found in the one who is sent to illumine us. As we have discussed, God creates and preserves all of creation in the same way that light is preserved in the air: only in the presence of an illuminative source. There is, however, a particular role appropriated to the Word, since "just as he accomplished the first production of things through the Word, so also their conservation."[44] So for Christ to be "the light of the world" (John 8:12) implies that Christ was "not the sun which was made, but the one who made the sun."[45] In this way the Son is both the "primordial principle" of all creation and the "primordial exemplar that all creatures imitate as the true and perfect image of the Father."[46] In this role all of creation finds its fulfillment in its ability to attain its natural perfection as measured by the image of the Father and the life of the Son, who is also the exemplar of the spiritual graces. It would be most fitting, then, for the one who created the world to come and teach us about God and the source of creation. Aquinas quotes Augustine, saying, "the Light which made the sun was himself made under the sun and covered with a cloud of flesh, not in order to hide but to be moderated [to our weakness]."[47] In this sense, the

43. Ibid.

44. *In Ioh.* 5.2 §740.

45. *In Ioh.* 8.2 §1142.

46. *In I Cor.* 11.1 §583.

47. *In Ioh.* 8.2 §1142.

creator of light came as light, taking on a body that allowed us to sense him, yet without completely obscuring the light.

Creation and Intelligible Light: Angels, Demons, and Humans

The creation of light in the corporeal world is mirrored in the creation of an intelligible light in angels and humans. This intellectual light

> makes the intellect to know because whatever light is in the rational creature is all derived from that supreme light "which enlightens every man coming into the world" [i.e., Christ]. Furthermore, it makes all things to be actually intelligible inasmuch as all forms are derived from it, forms which give things the capability of being known, just as all the forms of artifacts are derived from the art and reason of the artisan.[48]

The Word creates not only the corporeal lights that decorate the heavens, but also the inner light that illumines our minds.

In this section we will look at the intelligible light as it is given to those creatures who have that light by nature, angels and humans. In looking at the intellectual light of these two creatures independently it will be helpful to compare and contrast the light in each of them. One can find frequent references to the light of the intellect in humans in studies of Aquinas's theory of mind or epistemology, but this is rarely done in conversation with understandings of angelic intellects. Yet human knowing is part of a continuum that begins with God, runs through angels, and finds its way to humans. To strip human knowing out of its hierarchy and context leaves us without some useful ways of thinking about how humans come to know, in addition to removing human knowing from its proper theological context.

There appear to be two reasons that angelic knowing is often removed from discussion of human knowing. First, the treatise on human nature in the *Prima Pars* can appear to be easily extracted from the rest of the *Summa* and treated as an independent piece of philosophizing, one that is especially dependent upon Aristotle's *De Anima*. There appears to be little in it that requires revelation or scriptural support, so the section is particularly appealing to philosophers who have minimal interest in Aquinas's faith commitments. Second, on the theological side there seems to be a real reluctance to discuss

48. Ibid.

the possibility and theology of angels. One is hard pressed to find substantial treatments of Aquinas's theological understanding of angels in spite of the detailed attention that Aquinas gives to them, and the frequent appearance of angels in scripture.[49] Whether theologians are embarrassed by Aquinas's speculative angelology or just do not seem to think it important, our neglect of his understanding of angels can diminish our understanding of ourselves.

With regard to the first point, to remove Aquinas's discussion of human nature from its broader theological context is to misunderstand the work that he has done earlier in the *Summa*, and to mistake the proximate ends of human knowing for the ultimate ends of human knowing, particularly as expressed in ST I 12. Since the final cause of any existent is the cause of all the other causes, to know that the final cause of human and angelic knowing is the beatific vision is to better understand why the human soul must be immaterial, why we seek to know causes and essences, and why our actions are oriented toward the good. When we strip Aquinas's account of human knowing from its theological context, we miss the broader teleological account of human life that helps the whole treatise cohere.

In neglecting the role of angelic knowing and teaching, we also ignore Aquinas's overall theory of the perfection and gradation of creation. For Aquinas, it is the entire universe that expresses the goodness of God's creation, with the full range of creatures each representing some aspect of God's being. Theologically, angels play an important role in illumining and teaching humans, so that they are crucial secondary causes of our knowledge of God. While they are immaterial, they are our closest relatives intellectually (rather than, say, apes), and so we can learn important truths about ourselves by learning about angels. Additionally, our knowledge of the fallen angels, the demons, gives us helpful insight into how intellectual creatures operate when they have placed obstacles between themselves and God through sin. Humans are not the only fallen intellectual creatures in the universe.

Aquinas, however, does not ignore the broader context of human knowing, and he uses human and divine knowing as a way of framing the way angels know about God. He thereby reveals his broader understanding of knowledge, in which

49. Some notable exceptions include James Daniel Collins, *The Thomistic Philosophy of the Angels* (Washington, DC: Catholic University of America Press, 1947); Howard P. Kainz, *Active and Passive Potency in Thomistic Angelology* (The Hague: Martinus Nijhoff, 1972); Edward J. Montano, *The Sin of the Angels: Some Aspects of the Teaching of St. Thomas* (Washington, DC: Catholic University of America Press, 1955); Jacques Maritain, *The Sin of the Angel: An Essay on a Re-Interpretation of Some Thomistic Positions* (Westminster, MD: Newman, 1959).

> a thing is known in three ways: first, by the presence of its essence in the knower, as light can be seen in the eye; and so we have said that an angel knows himself—secondly, by the presence of its similitude in the power which knows it, as a stone is seen by the eye from its image being in the eye—thirdly, when the image of the object known is not drawn directly from the object itself, but from something else in which it is made to appear, as when we behold a man in a mirror.[50]

Aquinas goes on to argue that the first way of knowing about God is available only to God, who knows things through his own essence, which is natural only to God. The third way of knowing, as in a mirror, is the human mode, and by our nature we can only know about God through the knowledge of material things. It requires a gift above nature to know more than that. The second way is that of the angels, who by their nature know God because they have an image of God (their own *imago Dei*) impressed on their natures, and they understand things through immaterial species without the need to abstract them from sensible knowledge. Even with these immaterial species, an angel "does not behold God's essence; because no created likeness is sufficient to represent the Divine essence. Such knowledge then approaches rather to the specular kind; because the angelic nature is itself a kind of mirror representing the Divine image."[51]

Aquinas has placed ways of knowing, at least in an immaterial and abstract way, in a hierarchy that begins with God, runs through angels, and ends with humans. God's knowledge, of course, is entirely simple and God knows the essences of things simply by knowing himself. We should, however, look more closely at the illumination of angels and their knowing, as well as that of their fallen brethren, the demons.

Angels, the Messengers of Light

The height of angelic theology and speculation was accomplished in the medieval period, where virtually all theologians gave careful consideration to the nature of angels.[52] Aquinas's appellation of the "Angelic Doctor" points to his particular attentiveness to and mastery of the topic, revealed in his treatise on the angels in QQ. 50–64 of the *Prima Pars*.

50. ST I 56.3.

51. Ibid.

52. David Keck, *Angels and Angelology in the Middle Ages* (New York: Oxford University Press, 1998).

Angels are immaterial beings who represent one of the ways that God's perfection is manifest in creation, since the creation of purely intellectual creatures reflects the fact that God creates by means of "intellect and will," and consequently, "the perfection of the universe requires the existence of an incorporeal creature."[53] As Robert Pasnau comments, "on this slender reed, [Aquinas] bases all of" his angelology,[54] for once one can posit the necessity of immaterial creatures, one can work through the metaphysical implications of their existence. This may be a bit of an overstatement on Pasnau's part, as Aquinas bases his belief in the existence of angels on the revelation of scripture, citing Ps. 103:4 in the *sed contra* of this opening question,[55] but in Aquinas's attempt to pursue a deeper understanding of the faith he points to reasons why the existence of angels is necessary for the full goodness of creation.

In spite of their immateriality, angels are unlike God in that they are in potentiality to know some things, while God has no potentiality but is perfectly in act. This is a necessary corollary to the idea that only in God are essence and existence the same thing, while for all creatures there is a difference between their essence and their existence.[56] This potentiality, however, is different from human potentiality, for angels are able to know natural things without the need to abstract their forms from sensible impressions. In this way, angels know all things that they "naturally understand"[57] and are not in potential for any knowledge of this kind. For Aquinas, true knowledge of things comes when they exist immaterially in our souls, which are themselves immaterial. Only by grasping objects at this conceptual level are they actually understandable. Angels are given this way of knowing by nature, so they have no need for an agent intellect to make things available for a possible intellect, as humans do.

Forms are a way that knowledge is mediated to created intellectual beings, since "it is by the form that the agent acts,"[58] and so the process of knowing comes from these intelligible forms existing in the intellect. According to

53. ST I 50.1.

54. Robert Pasnau, *Thomas Aquinas on Human Nature: A Philosophical Study of Summa Theologiae 1a, 75-89* (New York: Cambridge University Press, 2002), 359.

55. ST I 50.1 sc.

56. ST I 54.1: "For an action is properly the actuality of a power; just as existence is the actuality of a substance or of an essence. Now it is impossible for anything which is not a pure act, but which has some admixture of potentiality, to be its own actuality: because actuality is opposed to potentiality. But God alone is pure act. Hence only in God is His substance the same as His existence and His action."

57. ST I 54.4: "They are neither sometimes understanding only in potentiality, with regard to such things as they naturally understand; nor, again, are they intelligible in potentiality, but they are actually such."

58. ST I 55.1.

Aquinas, the fewer and simpler the forms as they exist in the intellect, the higher the intellect. Thus God knows all forms through one simple form, his own essence, while successive hierarchies of angels receive more and more forms and ideas as they are ontologically further from God.[59] An angel that is higher up on the hierarchy will know things through just a few simple forms, angels that are closer to humans will know through more forms, while humans must spend their lives accumulating the forms of things to grow in their knowledge.

If angels know all natural things by God's impression of forms upon their intellect at their creation, then we might wonder why they are in potential for any kind of knowledge. If they know everything they can know by nature from the beginning, whereas humans have to accumulate knowledge over the course of their lives, in what way are angels in potential? The key here is the difference between natural knowledge and supernatural knowledge. Angels have by nature the ability to know through the innate ideas given to them, but these do not include truths that are a part of "the mysteries of grace," which "depend upon the pure will of God."[60] In explaining this, Aquinas says that an angel "cannot learn the thoughts of another angel, which depends upon the will of such angel, much less can he ascertain what depends entirely upon God's will."[61] To use a human comparison, Aquinas seems to be saying that certain truths require an act of the will to be communicated, especially among beings that are equal (one angel to another) or between a superior being and an inferior one (God to angels or humans, though not the reverse). There are certain truths that someone could know about me through their senses, about my physical attributes, my actions, or my words, but there are other truths about me, mainly interior dispositions, which can only be known by my willing that they be known. Since God's knowledge is natural only to God and can only be made known to others by an act of God's will, for those receiving this knowledge it will be experienced as above their own nature, that is, supernatural, and it is this kind of knowledge that angels are in potential to receive. For "with regard to things divinely revealed to them, there is nothing to hinder them from being in potentiality."[62] The term "supernatural," for Aquinas, always means what is above the nature of the creature in question, but since there is no being with a

59. ST I 55.3: "Thus the higher the angel is, by so much the fewer species will he be able to apprehend the whole mass of intelligible objects. Therefore his forms must be more universal; each one of them, as it were, extending to more things." Cf. ST I 55.2.

60. ST I 57.5.

61. Ibid.

62. ST I 58.1.

nature above God, there are no acts of God that are supernatural for God—we just experience them as above our own nature.[63]

One other aspect of angelic knowledge worth noting is that the purpose of angelic knowledge of other creatures is the praise of God. Angels know about creation only so that they can use this knowledge to "refer this back to the praise of God."[64] As we have argued earlier, illumination in its proper sense is knowledge that is ordered to God, so angels of light know natural truths not for their own sake, but as they reveal the goodness and perfection of God and God's praiseworthiness.

Because angelic knowledge is properly ordered to God, one of the roles of angels in creation is to serve as illuminating agents. Aquinas takes up the question of how this works in his overall discussion of God's governance. Beyond God's continual conservation in existence of all of creation, God is able to move bodies, intellects, and wills in creatures.[65] Yet God also gives creatures the ability to move themselves and other creatures in ways that are appropriate to their natures. One of the first ways this is accomplished is through illumination. It is interesting to note that with regard to the actions of angels on angels and of angels on humans, the first question Aquinas asks in each case is whether angels can illumine other angels or humans.[66] Aquinas does not explain why this is the first question he addresses, but we can surmise that since both angels and humans are intellectual creatures, as Aquinas has described in the treatise on angels and the treatise on human nature, it is through our intellects that we are first moved, by seeing, to know the truth of things. Since illumination is the manifestation of truth, the first step in moving another intellectual being is the presentation of the truth.

The first level of illumination takes place among the angels, who can illumine each other, where to illumine means "nothing else but to communicate to others the manifestation of the known truth; according to the Apostle (Eph. 3:8): 'To me the least of all the saints is given this grace . . . to illumine all men, that they may see what is the dispensation of the mystery which has been hidden from eternity in God.'"[67] The context of the verse from Ephesians again indicates that illumination in its proper sense is ordered to knowledge about God, whether it is God's works of "nature, grace, or glory."[68] Aquinas is quite

63. See ST I 105.7–8.

64. ST I 58.6 ad 2.

65. ST I 105.

66. ST I 106.1 and 111.1.

67. ST I 106.1.

68. ST I 106.1 ad 2.

explicit that one angel does not give another angel the "light of nature, grace, or glory,"[69] but instead illumines another angel either by strengthening its power, in the same way that the presence of something hot makes something less hot able to heat other things, or by presenting things that the superior angel knows more universally in a more particular way that the lesser angel understands.[70]

This illumination takes place in a hierarchical chain, beginning with God, since "illumination, which depends on the principle which is God, is conveyed only by the superior angels to the inferior."[71] This takes place in a created context where superior agents can act upon inferior ones, but not the other way around. This is especially true among the angels, because "one order is under another, as cause is under cause; and hence as cause is ordered to cause, so is order to order . . . thus the order which belongs to spiritual substances is never passed over by God; so that the inferiors are always moved by the superior, and not conversely."[72] With regard to humans, God can skip the order of angels and illumine us directly, as he does through grace and through the Incarnation.

God does not always skip the angelic orders when illuminating humans, for they also have an important role in illumining us. Again, the operative principle is that "the order of Divine Providence disposes that lower things be subject to the actions of higher . . . as the inferior angels are illumined by the superior, so men, who are inferior to the angels, are illumined by them."[73] Angels illumine humans in two ways that are similar, but not equivalent, to how angels illumine other angels. First, angels illumine humans by the strengthening of the light of the intellect, which is the same process in both angels and humans. Second, whereas angels can present to other angels the "universal concept" of the truth albeit in a divided way, "the human intellect, however,

69. Ibid.

70. Ibid., corpus: "Now since two things concur in the intellectual operation, as we have said, namely, the intellectual power, and the likeness of the thing understood; in both of these one angel can notify the known truth to another. First, by strengthening his intellectual power; for just as the power of an imperfect body is strengthened by the neighborhood of a more perfect body—for instance, the less hot is made hotter by the presence of what is hotter; so the intellectual power of an inferior angel is strengthened by the superior angel turning to him: since in spiritual things, for one thing to turn to another, corresponds to neighborhood in corporeal things. Secondly, one angel manifests the truth to another as regards the likeness of the thing understood. For the superior angel receives the knowledge of truth by a kind of universal conception, to receive which the inferior angel's intellect is not sufficiently powerful, for it is natural to him to receive truth in a more particular manner. Therefore the superior angel distinguishes, in a way, the truth which he conceives universally, so that it can be grasped by the inferior angel; and thus he proposes it to his knowledge."

71. ST I 107.2.

72. ST I 106.3.

73. ST I 111.1.

cannot grasp the universal truth itself unveiled; because its nature requires it to understand by turning to the phantasms." Consequently, when angels illumine humans, they do so by presenting our minds with "the likeness of sensible things."[74] This illumination, however, can happen without our knowledge, so that an angel can either strengthen our intellect or present things to our mind without us knowing that such knowledge is caused by an angel.[75] This illumination by angels of light, which makes known to us truths about God, serves as one way that God governs creation through his creatures.

All angels, however, are not angels of light.

The Nonillumination of Demons

Perhaps even less discussed than Aquinas's view of the angels is his discussion of demons, but demons may also help us understand light and illumination in Aquinas's theology, even if it is only by means of a negative example. In discussing the punishment of the demons, Aquinas asks whether part of their punishment is to have their "intellect darkened by being deprived of the knowledge of all truth."[76] In response, Aquinas distinguishes between three kinds of knowledge:

> The knowledge of truth is twofold: one which comes of nature, and one which comes of grace. The knowledge which comes of grace is likewise twofold: the first is purely speculative, as when Divine secrets are imparted to an individual; the other is affective, and produces love for God; which knowledge properly belongs to the gift of wisdom.[77]

Regarding the knowledge that comes by nature, Aquinas denies that such knowledge can be withdrawn from angels because as simple substances there is nothing that can be withdrawn from them that would not diminish their nature; they have no "parts," so there is no "part" of their intellectual knowledge that can be withdrawn and have them still retain their natures. The second kind of knowledge, which is speculative knowledge of the divine secrets, is partially withdrawn from them, so that

74. Ibid.

75. Ibid., ad 3: "In like manner not everyone who is illumined by an angel, knows that he is illumined by him."

76. ST I 64.1 ob 1.

77. Ibid., corpus.

> only so much is revealed to them as is necessary; and that is done either by means of the angels, or "through some temporal workings of Divine power," as Augustine says; but not in the same degree as to the holy angels, to whom many more things are revealed, and more fully, in the Word Himself.[78]

Thus demons may be told some truths about God's works, but this is not the kind of knowledge that inflames their affections; they do not know and love, but rather know and hate. Consequently they do not have the most important kind of knowledge, the third kind of knowledge, wisdom, which consists in the knowledge of love that brings them into friendship and union with God.

Without this knowledge that is ordered to God, demons are both unable and unwilling to fulfill the good of their nature by illumining other angels or humans. The knowledge that demons have is perverse and "does not lead one to order another to God, but rather to lead away from the Divine order."[79] Consequently, "not every kind of manifestation of the truth is illumination,"[80] a principle that would apply not just to demonic communication, but to any communication, demonic or human, that leads one away from God or places an obstacle between the creature and God.

This is not to say that God is unable to use even wicked angels to accomplish his purposes, for some of the Divine mysteries are revealed even to demons for the purpose of punishing wicked humans or testing the saints, so demons do know some truths about God, "but it is not an illumination on the part of the demons, for these do not direct it to God; but to the fulfilment of their own wickedness."[81] So while the demons may have a role in the divine justice, they do not act out of accord with justice, but out of a deep malice not just for God but for all that God has created to be ordered to God.

Human Nature and Light

God bookends the six days of creation by bringing into being intellectual creatures, angels on the first day and humans on the sixth, providing from the very beginning creatures who could appreciate the inherent goodness in God's creative act and creatures who would become the locus of his greatest work, the redemption of all that God had created. Humans, while akin to angels in their intellectual nature, are profoundly different than angels due to their material

78. Ibid.
79. ST I 109.3.
80. Ibid., ad 1.
81. ST I 109.4 ad 1.

nature. How to understand the link between our intellectual and material nature was a matter of some dispute for Aquinas and his contemporaries.

Aquinas's hylomorphism, where the soul serves as the form of the material body and acts as its first animating principle, is well known. The soul itself is immaterial, which is less a metaphysical necessity than a theological one, as our final end, the beatific vision of the immaterial and noncomprehensible God, requires that our mode of knowing be receptive to immaterial things. What is of interest here with respect to light is how the body and soul are united. For Aquinas, if the soul is truly the form of the body, there can be no body that serves as a medium between the body and the soul, since forms make things to be what they are in their particular material instantiations, and if there were another body intervening between the body and the soul we would lack a necessary unity at the deepest level of our natures.

Aquinas rejects several possible ways that the body and the soul could be united by some other body. The basic idea common to these possibilities is that the body that unites the body and soul must be naturally incorruptible, as the problem appears to be how to unite something immaterial, and thus naturally incorruptible, with something material, and thus naturally corruptible. What is required to link these two incompatible entities is a materially incorruptible body, like a corporeal spirit. One possible option was that the soul and body were linked by means of light

> which, they say, is a body and of the nature of the fifth essence; so that the vegetative soul would be united to the body by means of the light of the sidereal heaven; the sensible soul, by means of the light of the crystal heaven; and the intellectual soul by means of the light of the empyrean heaven.[82]

This fifth essence, which we know by the term "quintessence," was derived from an ancient Pythagorean theory that held that the four elements of earth, air, water, and fire were all united by a luminous fifth element. Bonaventure, among others, was a contemporary who argued that the quintessence is what united the body and soul.[83]

In a rare display of ridicule, Aquinas mocks this idea, calling it "fictitious and risible," both because light is not a body and because the quintessence "does not enter materially into the composition of a mixed body, since it

82. ST I 76.7.

83. See Bonaventure *II Sent.* 17.2.2. For a brief overview of quintessence, see Pasnau, *Thomas Aquinas on Human Nature: A Philosophical Study of Summa Theologiae 1a, 75–89*, 137.

is unchangeable."[84] Aquinas does not necessarily deny the existence of a quintessence, he just says that it does not apply here. As Pasnau points out, there is a place for a quintessence in his larger cosmology.[85]

His rejection of the union of the body and soul by light does not mean that Aquinas has no role for light in his understanding of human nature. As should be clear by now, the life of the human being, at least as God intended it, is a life of light, but one that reaches its perfection at the immaterial level rather than the material level, if for no other reason than material things are opaque and not receptive to light.

Taking place at the level of our intellect, Aquinas develops a detailed account of the origin and operation of the natural light that has already featured heavily in our discussions and bears greater scrutiny here. It is worth noting from the outset, however, that Aquinas locates his description of our natural light in its ideal state, prior to the Fall. That is, his description of our natural illumination takes place just after his description of creation and prior even to the creation of the first man's body or to the fall of man and all the intellectual consequences that derive from that fall. We would be mistaken if we take Aquinas's account of the function of our natural light to be the way we actually find it in our day-to-day operation, as sin has had an impact upon it. This is not to say that sin has destroyed our intellectual abilities, but rather it has limited them. By nature we can know many truths, but not the most important truth, that the First Truth is our final end.

Human Knowing and the Light of the Agent Intellect

To be human means to be an "intelligent being,"[86] capable of understanding the surrounding world and capable of acting not only by instinct but also through careful consideration of the options and choices presented to us. In describing how human beings come to know, Aquinas uses the concept of light to explain the distinction between our "possible intellect" and our "agent intellect."[87]

First, however, in order to understand the agent intellect we should situate it in Aquinas's overall description of human nature. While the intellect and the will are powers of the soul, rather than its essence, they share the soul's

84. ST I 76.7.

85. Pasnau, *Thomas Aquinas on Human Nature: A Philosophical Study of Summa Theologiae 1a, 75–89*, 137.

86. ST I-II, prologue: "Man is said to be made in God's image, in so far as the image implies 'an intelligent being endowed with free-will and self-movement.'"

87. Also known as the "passive" intellect and the "active" intellect respectively.

immateriality. This allows the intellect to understand universals, which are immaterial—though not in the Platonic sense of existing independently, since forms do not exist without matter in Aristotelian philosophy. The key principle here is that "the object of cognition is proportioned to the cognitive power,"[88] a principle mentioned several times in question twelve of the *Prima Pars*. Thus if our intellect were not itself immaterial, it would be unable to apprehend immaterial objects, most importantly God. Indeed, given what Aquinas believes about the immateriality of God,[89] the need for cognitive proportionality, and the final end of humans as the attainment of a vision of this immaterial divinity, Aquinas must argue for the immateriality of the intellect. Since we are compound beings with a soul united to a body as its form, our intellect cannot immediately comprehend immaterial objects. Instead all knowledge must be accumulated through the senses. This leaves Aquinas with the problem of how to account for the intellectual operation of a creature that takes in information via the senses but must be able to, ultimately, understand things immaterially; taken in context of ST I 12, this is the central concern of ST I 75–89, the Treatise on Human Nature.

In turning to Aquinas's account of the intellect, it will once again be useful to look at his commentary on *De Anima* before we turn to his work in the *Summa*. Aristotle, according to Aquinas, gives his account of how humans come to know by developing the distinction between the possible intellect and the agent intellect. In his account of intellectual cognition, Aristotle conjectures that there is a distinct similarity between sensing things and "intellectively cognizing" them, where "sometimes we sense potentially, sometimes actually, so also intellectively cognizing is a kind of cognizing, and sometimes we have intellective cognition potentially, sometimes actually."[90] That is, just as my eyes have the potential to see the snow on the roofs outside and that potential is actualized by light, the diaphanous medium, the white color, and the presence of snow, so my intellect has the potential to know many different truths—it can know math, theology, colors, morality, and other intellectual concepts, but only in potential. This is the possible intellect, the part of our cognitive abilities that has the potential to know things and is something of a blank slate. By itself, however, the possible intellect is insufficient, for it requires an agent to bring it from potency to act, just as the diaphanous medium requires light to bring it from potency to act.

88. ST I 85.1.

89. See ST I 3.2.

90. DA III.1 429a13 (Leonine) (DA 3.7.675 in Marietti version).

The cognitive function that produces the change from potential to act, according to Aristotle, is the agent intellect. In describing Aristotle's conception of the agent intellect, Aquinas points out that the work of the agent intellect continues the similarity with light:

> That is why Aristotle says that it [the agent intellect] is a "condition like light," which "in a way makes colors that are in potentiality" become "actual colors." He says "in a way" because it was shown earlier that color is visible in its own right. Light makes it become actual color only insofar as it actualizes the diaphanous medium so that it can be moved by color; in this way color is seen. Agent intellect, however, actualizes the intelligibles that previously were in potentiality by abstracting them from matter, for in that abstracted condition they are intelligibles in actuality, as was said.[91]

So in the Aristotelian model the agent intellect operates on the possible intellect in the same way that light operates on the diaphanous medium in making it possible for the colors to be received. The agent intellect activates the possible intellect, making merely potential knowledge actual by abstracting ideas from physical realities, which allows them to be known at the intellectual level.

Aquinas further develops these ideas from the *De Anima* commentary in his Treatise on Man in the *Prima Pars*. In the second article of his discussion of the intellectual powers of humans in ST I 79.2, he describes the possible (passive) intellect by comparing the human intellect to the Divine intellect. Whereas the Divine intellect is in perfect act, without potentiality, and thus knows everything there is to know, created intellects cannot possibly be perfectly actualized or we would also be gods. In fact, humans start from the opposite position, as blank slates that are only potential; the "human intellect, which is the lowest in the order of intelligence and most remote from the perfection of the Divine intellect, is in potentiality with regard to things intelligible."[92] This possible intellect is dependent upon sense data being received by the body, but there are three problems here. First, the intellect is immaterial and so can only understand immaterial things, such as intelligible species, while the sense data are physical (even a spiritual impression is a physical impression of a specific type and resides in a bodily organ). Second, and closely related to the first, the senses only detect particulars, while the intellect exists to deal with universals, their being, and their truth. Third, as a passive capacity, the possible intellect

91. DA III.4 430a10 (DA III.10.730 in Marietti).

92. ST I 79.2.

needs an agent to actualize it, operating under the principle that anything in potency must be actualized by something else already in act. Without a link between the material and the immaterial, the particular and the universal, and a means of actualizing the possible intellect, Aquinas's account of the operation of the intellect would seem to be at an impasse.

The solution to this threefold problem is the agent intellect. The agent intellect abstracts the form from the matter of a material thing, and since forms are immaterial the intellect can now work with it.[93] In doing so the agent intellect takes the actual likeness of particular things (phantasms) produced by impressions on the sense organs and abstracts away its particular features so that it may observe its universal features. Phantasms are unable on their own to make impressions on the possible intellect, as they belong to the bodily organs (remembering the principle mentioned above, that there must be proportionality between the object and the cognizing capacity) and are thus part of the body/soul compound rather than of the intellect alone; phantasms are only "potentially immaterial."[94] So after abstracting the forms from the particular things, the agent intellect illuminates the phantasms, where illumination is understood as making the phantasms "suitable to have intelligible concepts abstracted from them."[95]

Here we can return back to the question of the sense of sight, since illumination plays an important role in sight and the agent intellect. Aquinas makes the connection explicit in ST I 79.3 ad 2. In order for the eye to see, it has to be touched by the object it is attempting to sense. This is done by light actualizing the diaphanous medium between the object and the eye, so that the object moves the medium and touches the eye and leaves its likeness. Likewise, the agent intellect serves as a kind of medium between the possible intellect and the phantasm of the sense object. By illuminating the phantasm of the original sensible object, the agent intellect allows the sensible object to leave its impression on the possible intellect, but in a completely immaterial way. In making this argument, Aquinas is attempting to overcome the objection that

93. ST I 85.1: "But to know what is in individual matter, not as existing in such matter, is to abstract the form from individual matter which is represented by the phantasms."

94. ST I 79.4 ad 4: "The intellectual soul is indeed actually immaterial, but it is in potentiality to determinate species. On the contrary, phantasms are actual images of certain species, but are immaterial in potentiality."

95. ST I 85.1 ad 4: "Phantasms are illuminated by the agent intellect, and further, by the power of the active intellect, intelligible species are abstracted from the phantasm. They are illuminated because, just as the sensitive part when in conjunction with the intellect receives a greater power, so the phantasms by the power of the active intellect are rendered suitable to have intelligible concepts abstracted from them."

unlike the case of color, there is no medium that needs to be activated in the intellect, and therefore there is no need for an agent intellect. Aquinas responds:

> There are two opinions as to the effect of light. For some say that light is required for sight, in order to make colors actually visible. And according to this the active intellect is required for understanding, in like manner and for the same reason as light is required for seeing. But in the opinion of others, light is required for sight not for the colors to become actually visible, but in order that the medium may become actually luminous, as the Commentator says on *De Anima* II. And according to this, Aristotle's comparison of the active intellect to light is verified in this, that as it is required for understanding, so is light required for seeing; but not for the same reason.[96]

Aquinas presents two alternatives here. The first, which uses an understanding of light different than that of Aquinas, holds that colors are not visible without light. The second holds that colors are visible in themselves, but it is the medium that must be made luminous so that we can actualize the visibility. Aquinas prefers this second option, which, as we have indicated above, puts the agent intellect in the position of serving as a medium between the phantasm and the possible intellect.

The question, however, is where the agent intellect's power to illuminate originates. Aquinas's solution is to suggest that the agent intellect receives this power from a higher intellect, that is, God, by participation.[97] There are two possibilities here. One (which Aquinas rejects) is that of Averroes, who held that there is one agent intellect for all persons which is external to all of us, but in which we participate equally. The other (and Aquinas's preferred option) is that each of us has our own agent intellect and distinct power, but one that is derived from superior powers. Here again, the illuminating power of the agent intellect becomes important, as the illuminating power is derived from and participates in the divine light, "for the intellectual light that is in us is nothing other than a certain participating likeness of the uncreated light in which the eternal natures are contained."[98]

96. ST I 79.3 ad 2.

97. ST I 84.4 ad 1: "The intelligible species which are participated by our intellect are reduced, as to their first cause, to a first principle which is by its essence intelligible—namely, God."

98. ST I 84.5.

Aquinas is more explicit about the divine origin of the principles by which the agent intellect works in DV 11.1:

> We must give a similar explanation of the acquisition of knowledge. For certain seeds of knowledge pre-exist in us, namely, the first concepts of understanding, which by the light of the agent intellect are immediately known through the species abstracted from sensible things. These are either complex, as axioms, or simple, as the notions of being, of the one, and so on, which the understanding grasps immediately. In these general principles, however, all the consequences are included as in certain seminal principles. . . . Now, the light of reason by which such principles are evident to us is implanted in us by God as a kind of reflected likeness in us of the uncreated truth. So, since all human teaching can be effective only in virtue of that light, it is obvious that God alone teaches interiorly and principally, just as nature alone heals interiorly and principally. Nevertheless, a human being is said both to heal and to teach, in the way we have explained.[99]

Thus the preexisting concepts in the agent intellect come from a divine source that knows perfectly the nature of all things.

To summarize, what we have in Aquinas's ideas about the human form of intellectual cognition is directly modeled on the role that light and the diaphanous medium play in human sight. Light here is not a casual metaphor, but rather the key to understanding how Aquinas conceives of the human capacity to learn. We can now compare the key elements of angelic and human cognition.

A Comparison of Angelic and Human Lights

The most obvious difference between angels and humans is that humans must acquire all of their knowledge through material realities, unless they receive some additional power from an intelligent being above them. By taking in sense data and then abstracting it, the human agent intellect prepares a place for immaterial forms to be received by the possible intellect. Angels, on the other hand, receive their knowledge of the nature of things at their creation, and since they are immaterial beings they receive it immaterially. Their knowledge is not

99. DV 11.1. The idea that these principles are "implanted" in us by God seems to have its origin in John Chrysostom's *On the Orthodox Faith*, Book I, Chapter 1.

about particulars, but about more universal realities, which they know through progressively simpler forms as they are higher up on the celestial hierarchy.

Illumination is received by both angels and humans from the one source of light—God—though this illumination is mediated through creatures. Thus one angel can illumine another, one angel can illumine a human, and one human can in a limited sense illumine another, by teaching. Illumination, in this proper sense, is knowledge that is ordered to God and so imparts knowledge of God's mysterious works. Because illumination is ordered to God, the fallen angels cannot illumine other beings; extrapolating from this principle with regard to humans, one would expect that our illumination of one another would also be ordered to God. This does not mean that humans must be free of evil to do this, since God can use humans instrumentally, as he does the demons, to accomplish his works or to reveal the truth (think of Pharaoh or Pontius Pilate),[100] though for the most part illumination that is ordered to God requires sanctifying grace. Without sanctifying grace we would be unable to illumine others.

The differences between angels, demons, and humans also help us understand what Aquinas means with regard to "nature" and our intellectual capacities. Our intellectual nature is determined by what we are able to know under our own power, even as we acknowledge that the natural light we have is derived from God's light and implanted in us by God. The truth of our nature is revealed by what happens to us after sin. Good angels and Adam prior to the fall were able to know God only because they received grace from God that enabled them to know him. Fallen angels and humans have both lost that grace, which removed their ability to love God in the case of the demons, and to both know and to love God in the case of humans. Nevertheless, both demons and fallen humans retain the capacity to know what is natural to their cognitive capacities. In the case of humans, we are still able to know our material world, precisely because our intellect is geared to learn through material realities. What we have lost is the ability to know that the material world is both created by and ordered to God and that God is our final end. We may be morally oriented to pursue happiness, but have lost the ability to locate the source of perpetual happiness. Because our senses are oriented to a material world, we are stuck in the darkness of ignorance and because of our sin we sink deeper into the darkness of sin. Only a being who can teach us materially and rescue us from our sin can save us from the ultimate darkness of condemnation.

100. See ST II-II 172.4.

Christ the Light of Our Intellect

In the face of this darkness of sin and ignorance, humans are left without the resources to come to the light. There are several requirements that must be met in order for humans to receive the light necessary for saving knowledge of God. First, the light that comes must have its light as an essential property rather than an accidental or participated one, for something that has a form perfectly is best able to communicate that form to others. Second, because we have lost our knowledge of God, especially of God as our final end, due to sin, we need someone who can restore our grace and who has perfect knowledge of God. Third, because we are material beings we need someone who can come to us and teach us in our material reality.

Christ, as the "teacher of teachers,"[101] meets all three of these criteria. First, Christ has light by essence, that is, Christ is light and is the source of our light.[102] Second, Christ has perfect knowledge, not just of God, but of all creation.[103] Third, by coming to us in a human body, Christ was able to teach his apostles in a way that was most fitting to their understanding.

Christ the Essential Source of Light

Aquinas provides his longest description of Christ as the source of light, and thus the one who gives us the light, in his commentary on verses 9–10 of the first chapter of the Gospel of John: "He [the Word] was the true light, which enlightens every man coming into this world. He was in the world, and through him the world was made, and the world did not know him."[104] The problem that Aquinas is concerned to address in his commentary is how a true light, that is, a being that has light by essence, could come into the world and remain unknown. One would presume that someone who has light

101. *Rigans Montes.*

102. *In Ioh.* 1.4 §117: "Christ bears witness as the light who comprehends all things, indeed, as the existing light itself."

103. *In Ioh.* 6.2 §868: "Now in Christ there were three kinds of knowledge. First of all, there was sense knowledge. And in this respect he had some similarity to the prophets, insofar as sensible species could be formed in the imagination of Christ to present future or hidden events. This was especially due to his passibility, which was appropriate to his state as a 'wayfarer.' Secondly, Christ had intellectual knowledge; and in this he was not like the prophets, but was even superior to all the angels: for he was a 'comprehensor' in a more excellent way than any creature. Again, Christ had divine knowledge, and in this way he was the one who inspired the prophets and the angels, since all knowledge is caused by a participation in the divine Word."

104. Quoted at the beginning of *In Ioh.* 1.5.

as an essential property would be able to illumine everything or make himself manifest, and yet the gospel writer says that exactly the opposite happened.

In addressing the question, Aquinas first distinguishes different types of illumination: false (philosophical), symbolic (Jewish law), participated (angels and prophets), or essential (Christ).[105] The first three of these all lacked some perfection, but "the Word of God was not a false light, nor a symbolic light, nor a participated light, but the true light (*lux*), i.e. light by his essence."[106] Because of this perfection the Word was capable of illumining everything he came in contact with, so much so that "everything that shines must do so through him, insofar as it participates in him."[107]

Aquinas goes on to distinguish the two kinds of illumination we have previously described, illuminations that come from our natural light and the light of grace. With regard to the natural light, Aquinas confirms that the intellectual nature of humans, who derive their light "from a source external to the world,"[108] requires that the statement, "the true light enlightens every man coming into this world," is correct inasmuch as we are talking about the spiritual nature of our intellects. In this sense, our ability to understand the material world intellectually is dependent upon and derived from the Word, who gives us the light, and this ability is created in us and represents the "world" of the gospel quote.

The deeper problem is how to understand the effectiveness of the light of grace that comes into the world. Here Aquinas understands "world" to mean humans, who lack divine knowledge both by nature and by having an inordinate love of material things due to their sin.[109] This lack of knowledge, however, is not the result of any ineffectiveness or absence of the Word, who has "produced a work in which his likeness is clearly reflected," and made it

105. *In Ioh.* 1.5 §125: "Before the Word came there was in the world a certain light which the philosophers prided themselves on having; but this was a false light . . . there was another light from the teaching of the law which the Jews boasted of having; but this was a symbolic light . . . there was also a certain light in the angels and in holy men in so far as they knew God in a more special way by grace; but this was a participated light."

106. Ibid.

107. Ibid., §127.

108. Ibid., §129.

109. Ibid., §138: "We attribute this lack of divine knowledge either to the nature of man or to his guilt. To his nature, indeed, because although all the aforesaid aids were given to man to lead him to the knowledge of God, human reason in itself lacks this knowledge . . . but if this lack is attributed to man's guilt, then the phrase, 'the world did not know him,' is a kind of reason why God was not known by man; in this sense 'world' is taken for inordinate lovers of the world. It is as though it said, 'The world did not know him,' because they were lovers of the world."

"in order that the light might be manifested in it," so that "the whole world is nothing else than a certain representation of the divine wisdom conceived within the mind of the Father."[110] If humans cannot see the image of God in the world, which is resplendent with light, it is because of the darkness of ignorance and sin; the lack is on our side, not that of the light.

Thus for Aquinas, there are "three reasons why God willed to become incarnate." First, the darkness of our mind through sin meant that "God came in the flesh so that the darkness might apprehend it, i.e. obtain a knowledge of it." Second, the illumination of the prophets and John was insufficient, so "it was necessary that the light itself come and give the world a knowledge of itself." Third, because creatures alone cannot lead us "to a knowledge of the Creator. . . . Thus it was necessary that the Creator himself come into the world in the flesh, and be known through himself."[111]

Christ, then, comes to us both as the one who illumines our natural intellect through creation and as the one who illumines us by grace. By far the more important of the two is the illumination by grace, because it gives us God's own knowledge of himself and so properly orders our knowledge to him. This is possible only because Christ has light by his essence.

The Light of Christ's Perfect Knowledge

We have previously discussed Aquinas's description in ST III 9 of how Christ had perfect knowledge of God's essence, perfect infused knowledge, and the perfect natural knowledge due to a human, that is, how Christ had all three lights of glory, grace, and nature. Because of Christ's perfect knowledge of everything as it relates to God, he was able to come and teach us about God, since he "by descending to us, raised us to things divine."[112]

Christ's ability to teach us is the consequence of two characteristics, his superior knowledge of God and his ability to teach interiorly. With regard to an infusion of natural and graced knowledge, Christ first knew

> whatever can be known by force of a man's active intellect, e.g. whatever pertains to human sciences; secondly, by this knowledge Christ knew all things made known to man by Divine revelation, whether they belong to the gift of wisdom or the gift of prophecy, or

110. Ibid., §136. Note the Trinitarian implications of the last statement.

111. Ibid., §141.

112. DP 6.7.

> any other gift of the Holy Spirit, since the soul of Christ knew these things more fully and completely than others.[113]

Additionally, the soul of Christ also had a more perfect knowledge of God's essence, though still noncomprehensive because of the limitations of the human soul. Therefore "it more fully receives the light in which God is seen by the Word Himself than any other creature. And therefore more perfectly than the rest of creatures it sees the First Truth itself, which is the Essence of God."[114] So with regard to all three kinds of knowledge, Christ in his human nature had all three lights in a way superior to any other person.

The effectiveness of Christ's teaching flows not just from his superior knowledge, but also from his mode of teaching. At one level, Christ taught like any other human, by speaking words, telling parables, and so on, and Aquinas thinks there is nothing quite unique about this. Of course, it is Christ's ability to teach in these most human of ways that is at one level an expression of God's willingness to reach out to us in a way that we understand. The primary difference between Christ and other teachers, however, is that Christ "also instructs within [and] thus he alone gives wisdom,"[115] where wisdom "is the knowledge of divine things, and science is the knowledge of created things."[116] This power to reach us interiorly is natural to God, who is present to each of us, especially because we are made in his image.

What Christ offers to us through the light of his perfect knowledge are the deep treasures of God's self-knowledge, which are all found in Christ, since

> whatever can be known about God, which pertains to wisdom, God knows in himself, and exhaustively. And likewise, whatever can be known about created things, God knows in himself, and in a super-eminent way. Now whatever is in the wisdom of God is in his single Word, because he knows all things by one simple act of his intellect, for in God knowledge is neither in potency nor in a habitual state. And thus in this Word are all the treasures of wisdom and knowledge.[117]

Because all knowledge of God and natural things, that is, all wisdom and knowledge, can be found in Christ, the Incarnate Word, we need only to know

113. ST III 11.1.

114. ST III 10.4.

115. *In Ioh.* 3.1 §428.

116. *In Col.* 2.1 §81.

117. Ibid.

Christ to begin to know these things. By turning to Christ in faith we avoid the threefold darkness of "ignorance, of unbelief, and eternal damnation."[118] We avoid ignorance by knowing that other things are ordered to him and by judging all "other things in the light of Christ . . . [by] setting one's mind on things that are above, when one governs one's life according to heavenly ideas, and judges all things by such ideas."[119] Now this overcoming of ignorance of the created world does not mean that by knowing Christ, one automatically knows all the secrets of the human body or quantum physics or other important aspects of creation. Rather, what one comes to know is how those things are created by and ordered to God. In this way, the created world is seen under a new aspect as an expression of God's natural willingness to share his goodness with creation. Humans come to know that their final end comes not at the point of burial, but through union with a spiritual reality that is greater and more satisfying than any material reality. By seeing things in the light of Christ we are able to more accurately judge the reality we are in.

The darkness of sin is overcome by the establishment of Christ's kingdom, a kingdom of truth, since "to the extent that I manifest myself, the Truth, to that extent I establish my kingdom. For this cannot be done without manifesting the truth, which can only be done fittingly by me, who am the light."[120] We will discuss in more depth the relationship between light and darkness with regard to sin in the next chapter, but the establishment of God's true kingdom, one where our minds are fully conformed to the reality of things as they are, means that our actions will be led by a true identification of the good and a willingness to act toward that good. We will both know the truth and be able to act upon it.

Finally, the light of Christ's perfect knowledge will preserve us from the darkness of condemnation. Since the created soul of Christ sees the divine essence as perfectly as humanly possible by its union to the Word, and the blessed see the Divine essence "by a partaking of the Divine light which is shed upon them from the fountain of the Word of God,"[121] it is by being conformed to Christ that humans can come to see the Divine essence, rather than the total darkness of condemnation.

118. *In Ioh.* 12.8 §1714.

119. *In Col.* 3.1 §139.

120. *In Ioh.* 18.6 §2359.

121. ST III 10.4.

Christ's Light as the Fulfillment of Our Intellect

Our intellect, which is an intelligible light, is created to seek out truth, most especially the First Truth, and so when we attain that goal our intellect has fulfilled its purpose and is finally able to rest. This is possible only through belief in Christ, primarily because his soul's power with regard to both nature and grace served as an instrument of the Word, and so

> if we speak of the soul of Christ in its proper nature and with its power of nature or of grace, it had power to cause those effects proper to a soul (e.g. to rule the body and direct human acts, and also, by the fulness of grace and knowledge to illumine all rational creatures falling short of its perfection), in a manner befitting a rational creature.[122]

In this way, Christ serves as a guide to life with God, who leads us by his light out of the darkness into the true light. Commenting upon John, Aquinas compares those who do not follow Christ to those who walk in darkness and so do not know where they are going. Only through "perfect belief" in Christ can we know our final goal, and that perfect belief provides an interior light that directs our will toward that goal.[123] Christ leads us away from all three forms of darkness, because, "Whoever follows me will not walk in darkness: the darkness of ignorance, because I am the truth; nor the darkness of sin, because I am the way; nor the darkness of eternal damnation, because I am the life."[124]

Christ's instrumental power to illumine and his guidance on the path toward God can be received in no other way than by entering into the life of Christ. Christ is the door to our beatitude because he has the fullness of truth, which humans cannot have on their own. Instead, we must participate in the "true and uncreated light. Consequently, we have to enter by the truth which is Christ."[125] Perfect light is the fulfillment of our intellect, and we only achieve that fulfillment by following the one who has the perfect power to illumine because he has the fullness of the light of truth, and no darkness in him.

122. ST III 13.2.

123. *In Ioh.* 12.6 §1685: "For light, whether exterior or interior, directs man. Exterior light directs him as to external bodily acts, while the interior light directs his will. One, therefore, who does not walk in the light, not perfectly believing in Christ, 'but walks in the darkness, does not know where he goes,' that is, to what goal he is being led."

124. *In Ioh.* 8.2 §1144.

125. *In Ioh.* 10.1 §1370.

6

Light and Morality

Aquinas uses language of light and dark throughout his discussion of morality and sin, so much so that someone not acquainted with his thought might label him a dualist in the Manichean tradition. A world divided into light and dark would seem to lack an appreciation for the difficulty in making sharp judgments about the morality of our actions; surely, one might argue, this is just an old divisive mode of ethics that lacks subtlety and has too much confidence in its own moral reasoning. In fact, the whole metaphysical basis of Aquinas's ethics is decidedly nondualistic. He is always aware of the Manichean heresy that manifested itself in the lives of the Cathars.

As we approach Aquinas's ethics, we will begin with those metaphysical assumptions about privation that maintain the unity of creation, goodness, and light and dark, then turn to Aquinas's account of the darkness of sin and its consequences, investigate his understanding of human nature, look at the role of conversion in his ethics, and finally turn to how Aquinas's use of illumination language can help us make sense of the role played by reason, law, and the virtues in his moral theology.

Metaphysical Assumptions

As we discussed in chapter 2 and the last chapter, darkness is a privation—it is no "thing" in itself, with "no form or nature of its own,"[1] but strictly a privation or absence of light. Darkness has no substance or being, while light exists as a quality of an illuminating object. Aquinas maintains this stance when he talks about light and darkness with respect to good and evil in moral acts. Again, the goal here is to avoid any account of evil that makes God responsible for creating evil, while maintaining that God created everything. At the same time, we must

1. ST I 48.1.

in no way deny our experience of evil, for without the evil of sin there is no need for Christ to heal us of the darkness of sin.

Aquinas thinks there are two kinds of privation, a privation where a substance has been fully deprived of its reality in some aspect, and a privation where a substance is in the process of being deprived. It is the difference between being bald and balding, where both are privations of hair, but one is complete and one is in process. Aquinas uses a different example: of death, which is a complete privation of life, versus being sick, in which one still has some health, but is deprived of perfect health. He claims that this latter kind of privation is the kind of privation that we understand as evil.[2] There is a problem here, however, with regard to the discussion of light and dark. As we have seen in previous chapters, Aquinas sees darkness as occurring instantaneously, and resulting in a complete privation, but here he sees evil as a process. Perhaps, however, the experience of evil he is talking about here is more like the setting sun, which slowly deprives the air of the light it needs, so that eventually the total dark takes over. Part of what is going on here is based on Aquinas's idea of the convertibility of being and good, where to exist is a good and to have goodness is (at least) to exist.[3] No rational being, including the devil, can be completely evil, for complete evil would be a complete privation of existence.

Aquinas takes up the same issue from a different angle in his discussion of whether all sins are equal. In making the case that all sins are not equal and some are worse than others, Aquinas makes the same distinction between privations of being, which in this article he calls a "simple or pure privation,"[4] and privations of becoming. The former, he says, do not admit of more or less, so that a pure privation is not capable of being any more deprived. Aquinas gives the example that if a house is already dark, covering a window will not make it any more dark. Privations of becoming are explained here as a matter of corruption; they thus admit a scale of being. Here Aquinas draws in a discussion of the vices and sin. Sins are privations of the "due commensuration of reason,

2. ST I-II 18.8 ad 1: "The other privation consists in becoming deprived, thus sickness is privation of health; not that it takes health away altogether, but that it is a kind of road to the entire loss of health, occasioned by death. And since this sort of privation leaves something, it is not always the immediate contrary of the opposite habit. In this way evil is a privation of good . . . because it does not take away all good, but leaves some."

3. ST I 5.1: "But everything is perfect so far as it is actual. Therefore it is clear that a thing is perfect so far as it exists, for it is existence that makes all things actual, as is clear from the foregoing. Hence it is clear that goodness and being are the same really. But goodness presents the aspect of desirableness, which being does not present."

4. ST I-II 73.2: "For there is a simple and pure privation, which consists, so to speak, in 'being' corrupted; thus death is privation of life, as darkness is privation of light."

but not in a way that totally takes away the order of reason."[5] The gravity of the sin, then, depends on how far "it recedes from the rightness of reason."[6] In this sense, sin maintains some order of reason, so that those who sin are perhaps using their rational capacities to decide how to lie, cheat, or steal, yet they also lose the order of reason inasmuch as the use of reason is not ordered to God and, in particular, to the eternal law (variously manifested as natural law and divine law). This loss of properly ordered reason makes sin a privation, and the degree of loss determines the gravity of the sin.

This discussion so far has used sin and evil as roughly interchangeable, though this does not always seem to be the case with Aquinas. We might think of evil as any kind of privation of the good that belongs to us by nature, such as being blind instead of seeing or being dead instead of alive. The key here is that the evil of privation is dependent upon the nature of the creature. We do not say that a dog suffers evil because it cannot speak, but we would say the dog suffers evil if it cannot eat. A human who cannot speak, however, would be suffering evil, since speaking is a good of human nature. The loss of a good can be the result of something beyond our control, like losing a leg in a car accident, or it can be the result of one of our own actions, such as causing that car accident by driving drunk. This latter situation is what Aquinas tends to think of as the evil that comes from sin. A sin is a moral act that lacks the due order of reason and is voluntarily committed by a person,[7] but as privations of becoming they do not destroy all of our nature, especially the part of our nature that can receive grace. Instead, sins provide an obstacle to our reception of grace.[8]

Aquinas clarifies the distinction between evil and sin, arguing that evil can be anything that is a privation of good, such as blindness, while sin requires a willful act that lacks the correct order to the end, which is measured by human reason proximately and eternal reason ultimately. So what we would think of as natural evils are evils that result from some natural power doing what comes naturally to it, whereas what we think of as moral evils are sins because they deviate from the eternal law which is the measure of our actions, so that "every voluntary action that turns aside from the order of reason and of the Eternal

5. Ibid.

6. Ibid.

7. ST I-II 71.6: "A human act is evil through lacking conformity with its due measure: and conformity of measure in a thing depends on a rule, from which if that thing depart, it is incommensurate. Now there are two rules of the human will: one is proximate and homogeneous, namely the human reason, and the other is the first rule, namely the eternal law, which is God's reason, so to speak."

8. DM 2.12 ad 3: "A privation that takes away acts does not take away aptitude, and the privation of grace is such a privation, as is darkness, which deprives air of light. And sin is an obstacle to grace that prevents grace, not the very privation of grace."

Law, is evil, and . . . every good action is in accord with reason and the Eternal Law. Hence it follows that a human action is right or sinful by reason of its being good or evil."[9]

Sin, in fact, has a threefold darkness to it, as Aquinas explains in his commentary on Romans. First, it has the aforementioned lack of the light of reason in it. Second, sins are often performed in the dark, such as the sin of adultery. Third, sins bring people to eternal darkness.[10] But the first one, the lack of the light of reason, is the primary darkness that leads to the others, and is actually the result of rejecting two kinds of light. Sin is a rejection, first, of the light of reason, and second, of "refulgence of the Divine light."[11] Yet we should not draw too sharp a line between the two, recalling that the light of reason implanted in our natures is put there by God and is a participation in the divine light. The "refulgence of the Divine light" is actually the light of wisdom and grace.[12] This light perfects our intellect for its final end, so by rejecting it we end up with the darkness of damnation. In rejecting both the lights of nature and of grace, we condemn ourselves to darkness.

Sin and Anthropology

One might wonder why Aquinas consistently says that sin is an error of reason or a misuse of the light of reason. Is this too cognitive an account of sin? There is an additional puzzle here, which is how to account for the role of the will in sin, since Aquinas says that the act of the will is the form of a sin, and the exterior act itself is the matter, just as light is the form and color is the matter of vision.[13] Understanding his emphasis on the role of reason, or the lack thereof,

9. ST I-II 21.1.

10. *Ad Rom.* 13.3 §1071: "Here the works of sin are called works of darkness: first, because in themselves they lack the light of reason with which man's works should be illumined . . . second, they are performed in the dark . . . third, because by them a person is brought to darkness."

11. ST I-II 86.1: "Now man's soul has a twofold comeliness; one from the refulgence of the natural light of reason, whereby he is directed in his actions; the other, from the refulgence of the Divine light, viz. of wisdom and grace, whereby man is also perfected for the purpose of doing good and fitting actions."

12. Ibid.

13. DM 2.2 ad 5: "In acts of vision we see color by means of light, and color is something material in relation to light, which can be seen even apart from color, although color cannot be seen apart from light. And similarly, in acts of the will, ends are the reason why one wills means. . . . Therefore, since acts of the will are the reason why external acts are culpable, acts of the will are, with respect to there being culpable sins, something formal in relation to external acts, and external acts are something material, not accidental, in relation to such sins."

in sin, requires us to go back both to his understanding of the beatific vision and to his resulting anthropology. Our final end is the beatific vision which is made possible through the light of glory, so any act that keeps us from achieving that final end is a rejection of that light as well as the light of reason. Aquinas, in his discussion of beatitude and happiness at the beginning of the *Prima Secundae*, is clear that any proximate end or goal that does not have God as the final end ultimately misunderstands the source of true happiness. To reason wrongly about our end is to end up reasoning wrongly about a whole host of proximate goals that we think, falsely, are important.

With regard to his anthropology, what makes us human and different from other animals is our ability to reason both speculatively and practically, that is, morally.[14] Unlike other animals who act by instinct, we have the ability to reason morally by thinking through a host of considerations, such as the rightness or wrongness of an action, the intention we have, the possible consequences, the mitigating circumstances, and so on. When we sin there must be an error in the use of reason, or worse, a lack of the use of reason, which reduces the sinner to a position no better than other animals, and certainly not one commensurate with the image of God.

In fact, error in the use of the light of reason is grounded precisely in the idea of humans as made in the image of God and in the threefold hierarchy of light. For Aquinas, it is not only the use of reason that differentiates us from other animals—humans as "rational animals," to use the Aristotelian terminology he adapts—but reason is also what makes us to be in the image of God. Our immaterial intellect is a sign that we are made in the image of God, and we "are most perfectly like God according to that in which we can best imitate God in his intellectual nature. Now the intellectual nature imitates God chiefly in this, that God understands and loves Himself."[15] So we are most like God when we know and love God in the same way that God knows and loves himself, and as we have mentioned, this is made possible to us through the mission of the Son with regard to knowledge and the mission of the Spirit with regard to love.[16]

The image of God is found in humans in the three-level hierarchy of lights of reason, grace, and glory. By nature we have an aptitude, a natural capacity, for understanding and loving God. When that capacity is realized by having actual knowledge and love, even imperfectly, we have the image of God by

14. *In Ioh.* 11.7 §1577: "For a human being is what is the chief thing in him, but this is the intellect and reason. Thus a human being is what he is because of reason."

15. ST I 93.4.

16. ST I 43.5 ad 2.

"the conformity of grace," which is not possible to attain by nature, but only through God. And, finally, when we come to know and love God perfectly, through the light of glory, we have the image of God "in the likeness of glory." Aquinas calls these the "three-fold image of creation, of re-creation, and of likeness."[17] Sin removes the second and third images, but the capacity of the first image remains.[18]

The relation between the proper use of the light of reason and the will is understood by Aquinas to be a function of what principles the will chooses to attend to. The lack of the light of reason which causes sin can itself be a sin, as Aquinas argues in his discussion of whether blindness of the mind is a sin. As he does consistently, Aquinas argues that there is never a privation of the light of natural reason from the soul, but that it can be impeded from its proper use by the lower powers of the soul. This is one form of blindness of the mind. Another source of blindness is the removal of grace that comes as a punishment for sin. The third principle, and the most interesting one here, is what Aquinas calls an "intelligible principle" to which we can pay attention or not.[19] The intelligible principle to which he refers is God, who is the intelligible principle of all that exists (recall his description of God as the intelligible light from his commentary on *The Divine Names* 4.4). In calling God an "intelligible principle," Aquinas is implying both that God is intelligible in himself and that by knowing God we come to know better all that is, including how we should act morally. Aquinas gives two reasons why we might ignore this important principle. First, we might by our own will turn away from consideration of this principle, and second, we might be so consumed with other things "we love more" that we neglect this intelligible principle.[20] In both cases, by deliberately turning from God or by loving something else more, this blindness is itself a sin, and not just a punishment for sin. In this sense our moral acts not only lack the light of reason, but are already suffering from blindness due to a prior act of our will to turn from God.

17. ST I 93.4.

18. Recall from ST III 9 that Christ has all three lights perfectly, which means he is able to impart their perfections to us.

19. ST II-II 15.1: "A third principle of intellectual sight is an intelligible principle, through which a man understands other things; to which principle a man may attend or not attend. That he does not attend thereto happens in two ways. Sometimes it is due to the fact that a man's will is deliberately turned away from the consideration of that principle . . . whereas sometimes it is due to the mind being more busy about things which it loves more, so as to be hindered thereby from considering this principle. . . . In either of these ways blindness of mind is a sin."

20. Ibid.

Aquinas describes this movement away from God as a "preference for darkness"[21] in which sinners willfully turn away from God (in this passage, he is specifically referring to those who turned away from the teaching of Christ). Those who persistently practice evil, rather than repentance, "hate the light, not because it reveals truth, but because it reveals a person's sins."[22] Thus the lack of the light of reason in a sinful act can be the consequence not only of bad moral reasoning that comes from ignoring or not knowing one's proper end, but also from explicitly hating the light that is cast upon one's sin. At the core of this idea is Aquinas's acute psychological understanding of humans, which recognizes the intellectual pretzels we often tie ourselves in as we conduct elaborate intellectual justifications for acts that we simply know to be wrong. Lost behind all of the structure and conflict of the *disputatio* method is Aquinas's keen understanding of why we come to prefer the darkness to the light.

It is important to underline the relationship between sin, human nature, and the consequences of sin. As we have mentioned in the threefold image of God, the use of the light of natural reason remains as a capacity in the face of sin, though even here in a diminished capacity with regard to moral reasoning. But one of the key consequences of our sin is what Aquinas consistently describes as an "obstacle imposed between the soul and God" or "an obstacle that prevents the reception of grace."[23] Here again Aquinas uses a light model to explain his idea. In corporeal illumination, an area can become darkened when there is an obstacle between the sun and our eyes—think of a lunar eclipse, an especially dark thunderstorm, the floor of a rainforest, or even (to use Plato's analogy) a cave. Aquinas argues that an obstacle between our eye and the sun does not diminish the capacity of the sun to illumine us, nor does the obstacle stop making the sun a universal cause of goodness. Likewise, sin does not diminish our natural capacity to know corporeal things. One can be deeply darkened by mortal sin and still know all sorts of truths about the corporeal world. For Aquinas, however, not to know all of these truths as ordered to God is to not know them in their deepest being.

Moral reasoning, however, seems to be different than reasoning about the nature of the world, since it tends to go in the opposite direction from speculative reason, that is, from universal truths, such as that we should not kill, to more practical and particular situations. This is not to claim Aquinas as some kind of medieval situational ethicist, but rather to point out that for him the question of what to do always involves reasoning about something specific

21. *In Ioh.* 3.3 §491.

22. Ibid., §494.

23. DM 2.11.

rather than only about the universal, about something practical rather than speculative, about something contingent rather than necessary. Even when, however, we get the moral reasoning right in the midst of our darkness, this still does not mean we are actually able to do the right thing, which requires an infusion of grace, and it is in regard to the reception of grace that our sin becomes an obstacle.

Aquinas notes that there are two kinds of darkness, understood as "night." One is our separation from "the Sun of Justice" due to mortal sin, which causes the loss of actual grace and the ability to do works that merit eternal life, and the second is the darkness of eternal damnation.[24] The key is that this darkness is our own fault, not the fault of the light. Aquinas deals with the objection that if we must believe in God to be saved, but only God can give us that belief, then we cannot be held culpable for our damnation. Instead, Aquinas argues that we are always the cause of our unbelief. If we close our eyes to the sun, this in no way diminishes the illuminative power of the sun—we cannot see because of our own action of closing our eyes, and both original and actual sin are the moral equivalent of closing one's eyes to God.[25] Thus, sin is an obstacle to grace, and yet it is only grace that can open our eyes.

From Darkness to Light: The Role of Conversion in Aquinas's Ethics

In this regard Aquinas sees a twofold movement in the human journey away from, and back toward, the light. In several places he talks of our aversion or rebellion against the light.[26] In DM 3.1 ad 8 he says that a sinner *avertitur* himself "from the light that does not turn away," and in his commentary on Psalm 6 he explicitly uses the aversion/conversion language, suggesting that "the human turns away (*avertit*) from him [God], so it is necessary that God converts (*convertat*) them inasmuch as by first turning (*convertitur*) to them he

24. *In Ioh.* 9.1 §1307: "And so night in this passage refers to that night which comes from the spiritual separation from the Sun of Justice, that is, by the separation from grace. This night is of two kinds. One is by the loss of actual grace through mortal sin . . . when this night comes, no one can perform works that merit eternal life. The other night is total, when one is deprived not only of actual grace by mortal sin, but even of the ability of obtaining grace because of an eternal damnation in hell."

25. *In Ioh.* 10.5 §1447: "Thus, I cannot see the light unless I am illumined by the sun. Yet if I were to close my eyes, I would not see the light; but this is not due to the sun but to me, because by closing my eyes I am the cause of my not being illumined. Now sin, for example, original sin, and in some persons actual sin, is the cause of why we are not illumined by God through faith. This cause is in everyone."

26. See *In Ioh.* 1.4 §121 and 11.2 §1491.

converts (*convertendo*) them to him."[27] In fact, this is one of the things that sinners must like least about God—that he is always present as a light that exposes our sins. We turn our backs on God and avert our gaze from his light, and as a result we live in the darkness of our own thoughts and sin.

The need for this conversion in which God appears to turn (given what Aquinas says elsewhere, I am ruling out any kind of turning that suggests change in God) to us so that we turn to him is because sin diminishes our capacity to receive grace. Aquinas argues that because the capacity for grace is in our nature, that capacity cannot be completely erased due to sin,[28] which has the happy implication that no human, no matter how severe the sin, is beyond the salvation offered and effected by God. That capacity, however, whether severely diminished or just marginally diminished (and Aquinas clearly recognizes that there is a gradation of the impact of sin on different people) means that we cannot turn back to God on our own, so as the Psalm commentary suggests, God has to turn us back to him. In fact, it is not enough just to stop sinning in order to move out of the darkness and into the light, for if a sinner were to stop sinning he would still be stuck in the dark. Aquinas argues that what is needed is for God to move our will in the other direction.[29] This movement is often referred to by Aquinas as a transference from light to dark, implying that God moves us from one state to the other.

There is, as one would expect, a Christological and sacramental element to this as well. In his commentary on 2 Corinthians, Aquinas paraphrases Paul's epistle by explaining that

> before being converted to Christ we [the apostles] were darkness . . . but now, after Christ has called us to himself by his grace, that darkness has been taken away from us and now the power of the glory of Christ's brightness shines in us, and it shines in us in such a way that not only are we illumined so that we can see, but we illumine others.[30]

27. *In Psalmos* 6, 164b.

28. DM 2.11 ad 3: "Therefore sin does not diminish the aptitude for grace regarding what is rooted in the substance of the soul—for then the contraries would belong to one common existing substance—but regarding what is ordained to the contrary as different from grace."

29. ST I-II 86.2: "And therefore so long as man remains out of this light, the stain of sin remains in him: but as soon as, moved by grace, he returns to the Divine light and to the light of reason, the stain is removed. For although the act of sin ceases, whereby man withdrew from the light of reason and of the Divine law, man does not at once return to the state in which he was before, and it is necessary that his will should have a movement contrary to the previous movement."

30. *In II Cor.* 1.4 §129.

There is, then, not just a return to the light, but a return to the light that by participating in the light of Christ allows us to illumine others, primarily through good works. There is a threefold set of actions that encompasses this transference to good works—we must stop sinning, repent, and then do good works, and Aquinas is clear that this "is all from God,"[31] since "two things are requisite for the justification of a sinner, namely, a free decision cooperating in the act of rising [from sin] and grace itself. And certainly the free decision itself is had from prevenient grace, while the meritorious actions that follow are from subsequent grace."[32] The good works that we do reflect God's light back onto God, so that we become beacons of light that attest to God's goodness, not our own.[33]

One of the ways we participate in this process is through the act of confession, which allows evil "to be brought into the light."[34] The moral stance that makes confession possible (always within the context of God's grace) is that of humility. In his Johannine commentary, Aquinas summarizes and accepts Augustine's understanding of John 9:39[35] by arguing, as usual, that inasmuch as we are in sin, we are blind: "[T]hus, the one who does not recognize his own sins regards himself as seeing; while one who recognizes himself as a sinner regards himself as not seeing. The first is the characteristic of the proud; the second, of the humble."[36] One of the marks of spiritual blindness, then, is to proudly claim that one is able to see, which in Aquinas's understanding of vision, means that one claims the light for oneself, while the mark of true humility and real vision is to be able to acknowledge one's sinfulness. Indeed, as we have seen, the very nature of the divine light brings to light our sin, which is precisely what sinners dislike about it. In our pride we not only claim the light for ourselves, which is a sin of its own, but we also end up underestimating the depths of our predicament. The process of confession acts to make our sins manifest, and manifestation is what light does.

31. *In Ioh.* 3.3 §496: "Such a person 'comes to the light to make clear that his deeds are done in God,' that is, according to God's commandment or through the grace of God. For whatever good we do, whether it be avoiding sin, repenting of what has been done, or doing good works, it is all from God."

32. *In Eph.* 5.5 §300.

33. *In Ioh.* 3.3 §496: "Yet, holy persons desire that their good works be known to men for the sake of God's honor and for the good of the faith."

34. *In Eph.* 5.5 §299: "'For all evil that is made manifest' through confession, 'is light,' that is, is turned into light."

35. "Jesus said, 'I came into this world for judgment so that those who do not see may see, and those who do see may become blind.'"

36. *In Ioh.* 9.4 §1360.

The Light of Reason in Moral Action

So far we have discussed Aquinas's moral theology primarily from a negative perspective, attending to the darkness that comes from sin, the consequences of sin, and the process by which God moves us from the darkness to the light. Under its proper function, whether by nature or grace, our moral capacity is one filled with light in our use of reason, the role of the law, and the powers of the soul that make possible the virtues. At the core of this illuminationist approach to moral theology is Aquinas's anthropology, which is made clear with respect to morality in his reflection on sin. In discussing the stain of sin, Aquinas mentions that the soul has a twofold brightness (*nitorem*) to it, the first being from the "refulgence of the natural light of reason, which directs his actions . . . and the second from the refulgence of the divine light, namely wisdom and grace, through which he is perfected to do good and pleasing works."[37] The natural light of reason, as we have stressed, derives its own light from God,[38] so our intentional actions, which all have a moral component to them inasmuch as they are freely chosen, must accord with right reason.

A discussion of "right reason" must begin with Aquinas's concept of law, which is an important, though sometimes overemphasized, aspect of Aquinas's moral theology. Aquinas holds that the purpose of the law is instruction by God to lead us toward the good,[39] and that the essence of law is that it is "a rule and measure of acts"; and since "the measure and rule of human acts is the reason, which is the first principle of human acts . . . it follows that law is something pertaining to reason."[40] Aquinas neatly defines law as "nothing else than an ordinance of reason for the common good, made by him who has care of the community, and promulgated."[41] Aquinas deals with four kinds of laws, three of which (as we would now expect) have illuminating elements to them.

The first is the eternal law, which is a function of God's providence and governance over the universe, and is "not distinct from himself."[42] Here Aquinas is not specific about how the eternal law illumines us, but we can argue for it in two ways. First, in the context of what we have said about God as having

37. ST I-II 86.1.

38. ST I-II 68.1 ad 2: "The vices are opposed to the virtues, in so far as they are opposed to the good as appointed by reason; but they are opposed to the gifts, in as much as they are opposed to the Divine instinct. For the same thing is opposed both to God and to reason, whose light flows from God."

39. ST I-II 90 prooemium: "But the extrinsic principle moving to good is God, Who both instructs us by means of His Law, and assists us by His Grace."

40. ST I-II 90.

41. ST I-II 90.4.

42. ST I-II 91.1 ad 3.

light in his essence, we can surmise that anything not distinct from him must by nature illumine. Second, as we will see from our discussion of natural law, since the natural law is a function of our own light, which is just a participation in the eternal light, the eternal law must be illuminating as well.

The second, then, is the natural law, which is one of the most heavily contested aspects of Aquinas's moral theology. In a much-cited article, Vernon Bourke argues that the very idea of natural law is understood to mean a variety of things, so that we are often not speaking of the same thing when we discuss natural law, and he simplifies the possibilities into two streams of thought. The first is the idea of natural law as "a code of moral precepts divinely implanted in man's nature, or mind, and issuing from the legislative Will of God," which he calls "a type of theological approbative ethics."[43] Bourke is mainly talking about the voluntarist moral theology of Ockham here, but he claims that while aspects of this can be found in Aquinas, this is not what makes Aquinas's understanding of natural law "distinctive."[44] The second idea of natural law "stresses the rational discernment of norms of human conduct," which Bourke sees "as a rational appraising of the fitting character of some human actions, as seen empirically in terms of man's natural experiences."[45] This second theory, which is the one that Bourke sees as applying to Aquinas, does not require someone "to have a special communication from God to know that *some* kinds of actions are fitting and others unfitting."[46] Bourke argues that "what is good for man, and what is evil, must be determined by the use of human reasoning."[47] Bourke thinks that this emphasis of right reason is what makes Aquinas's moral theology distinctive.

Bourke's emphasis on right reason as distinctive of Aquinas's ethics has much to offer, but it overlooks the importance of the relationship between right reason and the reason of God. There is no doubt that for Aquinas all perfect moral actions must necessarily be the result of right reasoning, and for Aquinas any action that is imperfect leads to sin.[48] But the rule and measure of this is ultimately the eternal law of God. As we have seen, the key verse for Aquinas's reflection on this, and that of many other medieval theologians, is Ps. 4:7—"the light of your countenance is signed over us." Aquinas uses this verse quite often

43. Vernon J. Bourke, "Is Thomas Aquinas a Natural Law Ethicist?," *The Monist* 58, no. 1 (1974): 53.

44. Ibid.

45. Ibid.

46. Ibid. My emphasis.

47. Ibid., 58.

48. ST I-II 18.4 ad 3: "However, an action is not good simply, unless it is good in all those ways: since 'evil results from any single defect, but good from the complete cause,' as Dionysius says (Div. Nom. iv)."

in describing how humans come to know rightly the difference between good and evil, and he turns to it in his initial discussion of the existence of natural law. After quoting Ps. 4:7, he comments:

> thus implying that the light of natural reason, whereby we discern what is good and what is evil, which is the function of the natural law, is nothing else than an imprint on us of the Divine light. It is therefore evident that the natural law is nothing else than the rational creature's participation of the eternal law.[49]

Our ability to discern the difference between good and evil is based upon, and thereby measured by, God's own ability to know the difference between the two. Aquinas again makes explicit the relationship between the eternal law and all other laws, arguing that "all laws, insofar as they partake of right reason, are derived from the eternal law."[50] It is difficult, given all of this, to see how Bourke can so easily dismiss what he calls a "theological approbative ethics,"[51] as being an important part of Aquinas's understanding of natural law. Whether it is distinctive of Aquinas is beside the point. The question is how, in Aquinas's understanding, we come to have the ability to reason rightly in the first place.

Nor does this make Aquinas a voluntarist in the vein of Ockham, where something is good just because God has commanded it and those precepts are infused into our soul as part of our nature. For Bourke is also correct that we can make these assessments based on the empirical realities "of man's natural experiences."[52] This is made possible because all of creation, including that of human nature, is itself a reflection of God's right reason. Humans are made good by God and are made to seek the good that is God, so by observing how we are made and how we act in our environment inasmuch as we seek out the good for which we were made, we can make assessments about our actions based on those ends. Those goods are twofold—temporal and spiritual, and only the former is available to us by nature, as our spiritual goods are only possible for us to know by means of revelation.[53] Inasmuch as our own nature

49. ST I-II 91.2.

50. I-II 93.3. Additionally, Aquinas argues that the goodness of the human will with respect to moral acts is also dependent upon the light of the eternal law, once again using Ps. 4:7 as a basis for his conclusion. See ST I-II 19.4.

51. Bourke, "Is Thomas Aquinas a Natural Law Ethicist?," 53.

52. Ibid.

53. *In I Cor.* 2.3 §113: "Secondly, we should note why such men cannot perceive the things of the Spirit of God, whether they are sensual in perception or in their manner of life. For the things about which the Holy Spirit illumines the mind transcend sense and human reason . . . consequently, they

is a reflection of the eternal law, we can use the light of reason instilled in our nature in discerning good from evil.

In understanding this, there are two matters to which we should pay attention—what Aquinas means by "nature," and the content of the natural law. With respect to nature, Aquinas does not mean that the natural law is to be found in our experiences of other animals, so that, for example, we look to other primates to understand our sexual norms. All of nature is not the measure of the moral natural law. Instead, Aquinas draws on Aristotle's discussion of the varieties of meanings of nature in the *Metaphysics*, where he describes the evolution of our understanding of the term "nature" from our experiences of generation to a more proper understanding of nature as substance; he distinguishes between the order in which we name nature from the order of being in which nature actually is understood in its proper sense.[54] In this account of nature, which Aquinas defines as "the form of those things which have within themselves as such the source of their own motion,"[55] Aquinas points to the idea that whatever is the nature of something is what provides its source of motion and rest.

For the purpose of understanding his moral theology, the more relevant text is ST I-II 10.1, which is a discussion of how the will is moved. Here Aquinas distinguishes between two main meanings of "nature." The first functions as "the intrinsic principle in movable things,"[56] and is understood as the matter or material form of a thing. For instance, a stone has an intrinsic principle of mass that causes it to drop, and fire has the intrinsic principle of heat that moves it upwards. This idea of nature pertains to inanimate objects, which cannot move themselves.

The second way nature is understood is as the substance of a thing, "and in this sense, that is said to be natural to a thing which befits it in respect of its substance. And this is that which of itself is in a thing."[57] This definition

cannot be grasped by a person who relies solely on sense perception. Again, the Holy Spirit inflames the affections to love spiritual goods and despise sensible goods. Hence, a person whose manner of life is sensual cannot grasp spiritual goods of this sort."

54. *Meta.* 5.5. Cf. *Phys.* 2.1.

55. Ibid., §826.

56. ST I-II 10.1. In I-II 31.7, Aquinas describes human nature: "Now, in man, nature can be taken in two ways. First, inasmuch as intellect and reason is the principal part of man's nature, since in respect thereof he has his own specific nature. . . . Secondly, nature in man may be taken as contrasted with reason, and as denoting that which is common to man and other animals, especially that part of man which does not obey reason." What makes a human being a human being, and different from other creatures, is the human activities of intellection and reason.

57. Ibid.

of nature, which takes place in a discussion of the human will, points to the nature of intellectual creatures, which are the sources of their own actions. Thus the nature of a thing is that which makes it what it is and it is in this way that Aquinas understands the term "nature" with respect to natural law. This is important in understanding how the will is moved by nature toward the good, since the implication is that along with the truth, which is the natural object of the intellect, at the deepest level of human nature is a desire for the good. This means not just that we seek out the good, but that we are made to be good and that our nature will be perfected only when we become perfectly good. Thus, nature is not entirely understood just as what we do naturally, but by what we are like when we are perfected. We can observe empirically a whole host of human actions, but as Aquinas consistently notes, when we see effects we have to work backwards to understand their causes, so the natural law ultimately points us back to the fact that we are made to be good, and this is only possible inasmuch as we participate in the Ultimate Goodness, who also is the Eternal Law.

Light and the Law

The content of the natural law begins with our ability to discern good and evil. The first precept of the natural law, "good is to be done and pursued, and evil is to be avoided,"[58] indicates that natural law has two illuminating elements to it. First, as based on the first principle of practical reason, "that good is what all things seek after,"[59] this first precept is a self-evident proposition, which for Aquinas means that it is self-illuminating. Fundamental propositions of any science, such as the principle of noncontradiction in metaphysics, as self-evident propositions, are intrinsically knowable and manifest to those who understand the terms.[60] One might object that this is a false principle, as we can see from the many people who commit acts harmful to themselves. Aquinas would reply that even when we seek false goods that end up being harmful for us, we do so because we have identified the object of our action as some good that should be sought. Even a horrendous evil such as genocide could be viewed as a group identifying that the world would be better—more good—if the other group was eliminated. Our more-than-occasional inability to identify the good does not

58. I-II 94.2.

59. Ibid.

60. Ibid.: "Any proposition is said to be self-evident in itself if its predicate is contained in the notion of the subject: although, to one who is ignorant of the definition of the subject, it happens that such a proposition is not self-evident."

negate the basic principle, but rather points to the consequences of sin on our intellect and its ability to identify the good correctly.

This first precept is illuminating in a second way: when functioning properly, it leads us toward the good. In this sense it serves as a kind of light on our path, illuminating the actions we should take and those we should avoid. The basic function of the light of natural reason is to illuminate our actions with respect to practical reason and our understanding with respect to speculative reason. This light of reason, which contains the first precept of the natural law, is a basic part of our human nature and continues to operate even when we are darkened by sin, though its ability to choose actual goods over imagined goods is severely hampered.

From this basic precept, others follow, but they are all dependent upon this first one. These precepts, which Aquinas breaks into three main categories, are derived from what he calls our "natural inclinations." Howard Kainz helpfully summarizes these as "living, sensing, and reasoning,"[61] and connects them back to the organization of the *De Anima*. These three sets of subprecepts are: 1) self-preservation, 2) preservation of the species through sexual reproduction and education of our children, and 3) an inclination to know the truth.[62] Again, Aquinas's concept of nature is in play here, as natural inclinations are not necessarily physical or material drives, but inclinations that are based on the metaphysics of being human. We can recall the definition of a human as a "rational animal" and see how all three of these natural inclinations come into play. With regard to self-preservation, a definition of anything assumes its basic existence, so a human is an existing rational animal; a definition presumes the existence or life of a thing, and it is because humans exist that it is possible for us to define them.[63] The "animal" part of the definition aligns with the second

61. Howard P. Kainz, *Natural Law: An Introduction and Re-Examination* (Chicago: Open Court, 2004), 21.

62. ST I-II 94.2: "Because in man there is first of all an inclination to good in accordance with the nature which he has in common with all substances: inasmuch as every substance seeks the preservation of its own being, according to its nature: and by reason of this inclination, whatever is a means of preserving human life, and of warding off its obstacles, belongs to the natural law. Secondly, there is in man an inclination to things that pertain to him more specially, according to that nature which he has in common with other animals: and in virtue of this inclination, those things are said to belong to the natural law, 'which nature has taught to all animals' such as sexual intercourse, education of offspring and so forth. Thirdly, there is in man an inclination to good, according to the nature of his reason, which nature is proper to him: thus man has a natural inclination to know the truth about God, and to live in society: and in this respect, whatever pertains to this inclination belongs to the natural law; for instance, to shun ignorance, to avoid offending those among whom one has to live, and other such things regarding the above inclination."

subprecept of reproduction, since the preservation of the species is common to humans and animals, while the "rational" part of the definition points to the third subprecept of our desire to know the truth. Further, this definition differentiates us from both angels and other animals on the hierarchy of being, as the rational part differentiates us from other animals but indicates something common with angels, while the animal part differentiates us from angels and indicates what we have in common with other animals in our ability to receive information via the senses.

These three subprecepts, when taken together, point to only one kind of creature—the human being. The progression from existing thing, to an animal nature, to a rational nature eliminates all other creatures from having the same natural law as humans. As a result, for Aquinas it would make no sense to look at either dogs or angels for how humans are supposed to act in totality. The fact that many animals are nonmonogamous would mean nothing to Aquinas's concept of matrimony, other, perhaps, than to indicate that what differentiates humans from animals is our ability to use our reason to overcome our sensible desires, so to suggest we should look to animals as models for our moral behavior is a serious category mistake. While we may share some similarities with different creatures, the natural law for humans is unique to our species. Our ability to use our reason, as we have mentioned, is derived from and a participation in the eternal law. Knowing what we are supposed to do, however, is not enough. While Bourke argues that we do not need a special revelation in order "to know that some kinds of actions are fitting and others unfitting,"[64] this would seem to hold true in theory only if our reason were unaffected by sin. We might, however, look at what Aquinas sees as an actual case of natural law under sin in his description of the state of the Gentiles under the natural law.

63. See PA II.6–8 for Aquinas's understanding of the limits and possibilities of definitions. Since "being" is not in any genus, it is not part of a definition. So properly speaking, we cannot have a definition of a unicorn, but can understand what the word signifies. Every true definition, then, presumes existence. At the same time, we are unable to know what a thing is unless we first are made aware of its existence, but this is easier with composite substances, such as humans, than it is with simple substances. So, "A person who knows some thing to be must know it through something of that thing, namely, something outside the essence of the thing or something pertaining to its essence. And he clarifies this with the example of knowing thunder to be, because we perceive a sound in the clouds—which of course pertains to the essence of thunder, albeit not the entire essence, because not every sound in the clouds is thunder—or of knowing a defect, i.e., an eclipse, of the sun or moon to be, because there is a failure of light—although not every failure of light is an eclipse. And the same applies if someone perceives a man to be, because there is an animal; or a soul to be, because something is moving itself" (PA II.7 93a21).

64. Bourke, "Is Thomas Aquinas a Natural Law Ethicist?," 53.

There are two important places in his scripture commentaries where Aquinas deals with the status of the natural law among the Gentiles before they were converted to Christ. In these cases it is clear that Aquinas cannot be talking about their moral status in any other way than in reference to the natural law, since before their conversion they would have not received the grace found in the New Law, nor have received the precepts of the Old Law as had the Jews. This is not, of course, to say that they were not responsible for their behavior, since the natural law, as an imprint of the divine law, is in its proper function enough to guide our moral actions.[65] And yet, it did not. The problem, primarily, is that knowing what one should do and actually doing it are not the same thing. In his lectures on Romans, Aquinas argues that the Law (and here he understands that Paul is primarily referring to the natural law) does not justify. While

> the Law is given that man might know what to do and what to avoid . . . from the fact that man knows a sin he should avoid as being forbidden, it does not at once follow that he avoids it, as justice requires, because concupiscence *subverts the judgment of reason*, when it bears on a particular moral action as performable.[66]

Aquinas's moral theory requires not only that we identify the proper action by our intellect, but also that we will it. Natural law, taken in both its personal instantiations and in the discourse on metaethics, can at best only tell us what humans are supposed to do, but it cannot make us will it. As Aquinas explains in his commentary on Ephesians, the problem is even worse than he makes it appear in *Ad Romanos*. In order to "walk justly and make spiritual progress,"[67] he says that there are actually three things we need, and which are found in humans. The first is the reasoning about what we are to do in particular instances, the second is the understanding of synderesis (which is a habit), and the third is the divine law, so that the "action is in accord with the judgment of reason, and this reason judges according to true understanding, or synderesis; and this synderesis is, in turn, directed by the divine law."[68] According to Aquinas, the Gentiles prior to their conversion were missing all three of these.[69]

65. ST I-II 100.1.

66. *Ad Rom.* 3.2 §298. My emphasis. See also ST I-II 98.6, where Aquinas describes the state of humanity before the advent of the Mosaic law, where "the natural law began to be obscured on account of the exuberance of sin."

67. *In Eph.* 4.6 §232.

68. Ibid.

With regard to the proper reason that is indicative of the natural law, the Gentiles, and anyone else who has not been converted by Christ, suffered from a darkened understanding that led to erroneous moral thinking, which Aquinas sees as the natural consequence of not sharing in the divine light. The implication is that even if the natural law is in us, under the regime of sin we cannot properly use it without first knowing the divine law.[70] Natural law and the proper understanding of its precepts requires participation in the divine light. In fact, one question that merits discussion is whether one can even know that the natural law exists without some form of divine revelation.[71]

Aquinas hints at an answer to this in his discussion of the gift of understanding, which is a supernatural gift given by the Holy Spirit that accompanies the gift of faith. In discussing whether the gift of understanding is speculative or practical, Aquinas offers an objection that since the gift of understanding illumines our mind to things that are above our natural reason while the practical intellect deals with regular human activities that do not surpass natural reason, the gift of understanding is not practical, and thus, implicitly, is speculative and metaphysical.[72] At stake here is the question of whether the gifts of the Holy Spirit are only oriented to the life to come and to deep understanding of God, or whether this gift has a practical application to our present moral acts. In response to this objection, Aquinas argues that the rule of human actions is both human reason and the eternal law, and that the eternal law exceeds human reason, "so that knowledge of human actions as ruled by the eternal law exceeds our natural reason and needs a gift of the supernatural light of the Holy Spirit."[73] This is a typically compact statement by

69. Ibid.: "But the life of the Gentiles was not like this, but rather was lacking of these three. First, rational judgment was deficient, because they walked in the vanity of their senses."

70. In ST I-II 99.2 ad 2, Aquinas argues, "It was fitting that the Divine law should come to man's assistance not only in those things for which reason is insufficient, but also in those things in which human reason may happen to be impeded. Now human reason could not go astray in the abstract, as to the universal principles of the natural law; but through being habituated to sin, it became obscured in the point of things to be done in detail. But with regard to the other moral precepts, which are like conclusions drawn from the universal principles of the natural law, the reason of many men went astray, to the extent of judging to be lawful, things that are evil in themselves. Hence there was need for the authority of the Divine law to rescue man from both these defects."

71. One might point to Cicero's development of natural law as an easy response to this question, but perhaps the ability to know the natural law is similar to our naturally acquired knowledge of God, something rare, difficult to achieve, and only with an admixture of errors.

72. ST II-II 8.3 ob 3: "Further, the gift of understanding illumines the mind in matters which surpass natural reason. Now human activities, with which the practical intellect is concerned, do not surpass natural reason, which is the directing principle in matters of action, as was made clear above. Therefore the gift of understanding is not practical."

Aquinas, but taken in context with his overall response to this question, which extends the gift of understanding to both speculative and practical questions and which requires us to "contemplate and consult"[74] with the eternal law, I take him to mean that the gift of understanding deals with speculative matters of God and his eternal law. As a supernatural gift, the gift of understanding provides the revelation necessary for one to know that the natural law, which is a participation in the divine law, is ordered to our beatitude.

If so, this would seem to shift the direction of the debate over natural law. First, the natural law is often used as a way to bridge the secular/religious gap in ethics, so that Christians can have a conversation with non-Christians on ethics that is based on reason alone, rather than revelation, a move that is particularly important in a post-Enlightenment pluralistic society. But if natural law is a participation in eternal reason, and is available only through revelation or is unavailable to those whose minds are darkened by sin and are not converted to the light by Christ, then one wonders if this gap is bridgeable after all.[75] Perhaps Christians could serve as witnesses of the natural law by reflecting the divine light and teaching non-Christians about natural law, but one wonders if it is really a coherent system outside of a relationship to a divine lawgiver. Some, like Finnis, have attempted to divest natural law of revelation, but this seems to create a whole set of additional problems. Second, one wonders if an understanding of natural law that focuses only on natural goods can really do the work Christians might want it to do, since ultimately humans are not made for natural goods alone, especially if we think that the goods of our nature are only material. The gift of understanding is required to help humans identify the true end that should orient their actions, and Aquinas at the very beginning of the *Prima Secundae* carefully eliminates any end as constituting true happiness that is not eternal.

The fundamental problem with a theory of natural law that stops at the natural goods to which we are oriented—those of living, sensing, and knowing—is that these goods are, from Aquinas's perspective, bound to fail. Aquinas outlines four reasons why the natural law is insufficient for our moral lives. First, as we have just said, we are, under our own power, incapable of knowing our final end, which is required for us to know how our actions should be oriented. So while we have a natural inclination to the good, if we

73. Ibid., ad 3.

74. Ibid., corpus. Quoting Augustine.

75. In this interpretation, humans could act under the natural law without actually knowing its source. Knowing the source of the natural law would require illumination so that we could know that the natural law is given to us by God to bring us to our final end.

limit this to only natural goods, we will end up, wrongly, focusing only on the attainment of those goods as the end of worldly human morality. Instead, a properly Christian morality requires that actions seeking to attain those natural goods must do so within the perspective of our supernatural end: attaining the eternal good. Second, just as with knowledge of God, our knowledge of what it is right to do based on the principles of our nature is severely limited. We are unable to know all the possible consequences of our actions, and given the variety of contexts in which we operate we are likely to come to different judgments about what the goods we seek are in actuality. Thirdly, we are unable to judge the motivations and interior dispositions of persons, yet for Aquinas the interior disposition and motivation is just as important to the morality of the human act as the outward act itself. Fourth, human law that attempted to restrict all evil actions would also tend to restrict our ability to achieve a number of goods, so human law must by nature leave some potential evils unaddressed.[76]

In response to these four limitations on natural law, Aquinas argues that humans must have access to divine law, which directs us to our final end, gives us specific directions with regard to critical acts that can contribute to our merit, forms our inner dispositions and not just our exterior acts, and provides a means by which all evil is addressed.[77] The gift of the divine law allows us to "participate more perfectly in the eternal law."[78] So while the natural law allows us to know some basic things that we should do by the light of our own reason, the divine law provides substantially more specificity in directing our exterior and interior actions. To make his case for the need of divine law in the *Summa*, Aquinas uses two different scriptural texts that rely on illuminative language,

76. ST I-II 91.4: "First, because it is by law that man is directed how to perform his proper acts in view of his last end . . . secondly, because, on account of the uncertainty of human judgment, especially on contingent and particular matters . . . thirdly, because man can make laws in those matters of which he is competent to judge. But man is not competent to judge of interior movements, that are hidden, but only of exterior acts which are apparent . . . fourthly, because, as Augustine says (*De Lib. Arb.* i, 5,6), human law cannot punish or forbid all evil deeds: since while aiming at doing away with all evils, it would do away with many good things, and would hinder the advance of the common good, which is necessary for human intercourse."

77. Ibid.: "Therefore it was necessary that, besides the natural and the human law, man should be directed to his end by a law given by God . . . in order, therefore, that man may know without any doubt what he ought to do and what he ought to avoid, it was necessary for man to be directed in his proper acts by a law given by God, for it is certain that such a law cannot err . . . consequently human law could not sufficiently curb and direct interior acts; and it was necessary for this purpose that a Divine law should supervene . . . in order, therefore, that no evil might remain unforbidden and unpunished, it was necessary for the Divine law to supervene, whereby all sins are forbidden."

78. Ibid., ad 1.

that of Ps. 18:9, "the commandment of the Lord is lucid, illumining the eyes," with respect to the Old Testament precepts,[79] and John 12:36, "Believe in the light that you may be the children of light," with regard to New Testament precepts.[80] In seeking to show the continuity of the divine law, even as he shows the need for a new law, Aquinas maintains the illumining nature of the divine law from beginning to end. To treat Aquinas as only a natural law theologian is to miss how limited he thinks natural law is in its application, just as our light of natural reason with respect to knowledge of God is limited. In both cases we require divine illumination and revelation, to know who God is and to know how we are to act so that we may attend to our final end; focusing our efforts to understand Aquinas's moral theology on ST I-II QQ. 91 and 94 is akin to treating ST I QQ. 2–26 as the whole of his doctrine of God—both leave out so much of the overall picture that we can go badly wrong in understanding him. Both the law of the Old Testament and the New Law written on our hearts provide illumination for our moral acts, illumination that will not lead us in the wrong direction; both represent an increased participation on the part of humans in the divine light.

The Light of the Virtues

The increase in participation in the divine light has the consequence of leading us to living lives of virtue, and it is to Aquinas's account of the virtues that we now briefly turn. The basic, inherited structure of the virtues is well known—there are four cardinal virtues of prudence, justice, courage, and temperance, and three theological virtues of faith, hope, and charity. The former are products of the light of natural reason and so are available to all humans,[81] while the latter are given by the infusion of grace, which is an illumination that strengthens the human mind for the acts proper to the theological virtues. Aquinas is quite careful to distinguish, with respect to the theological virtues, the difference between virtues and grace. Virtues, as he understands them, are powers of the soul that allow us to act well, whether by the light of natural reason or the infusion of grace;[82] in both cases the light we receive by nature or grace is from God. Aquinas sometimes speaks of the cardinal virtues as illuminating, but more often speaks of the theological virtues this way.

79. ST I-II 102.1 sc.

80. ST I-II 108.1 sc.

81. Normally, the cardinal virtues are acquired, but may also be infused through grace. See ST I-II 63.3–4.

82. See ST I-II 55.4 ob1 and corpus.

In his commentary on Rom. 13, Aquinas tells us that in exhorting the Romans to live an honorable life, Paul is ordering them to turn away from works of darkness that lack the light of reason and instead assume the virtues by putting on "the armor of light" (Rom. 13:12). Putting on the armor of light is a way of saying that the virtues are a means of dressing for the day—a Thomistic trope based on the idea that we act and dress differently in day and night, which he extends to our moral acts. The virtues, as armor, protect us because they "are decorated and perfected by the light of reason, tested by light, and illumine others by virtuous actions."[83] Here it is unclear whether Aquinas is referring to virtues in general, just the cardinal virtues, or just the theological virtues. It is most likely that he is referring to the virtues in general, since they all accord with the light of reason, though clearly in a gradation based on the infusion of divine light.

It is this infusion of light by God that makes both virtue and knowledge possible. Aquinas compares the process to the way that the air takes on the form of light in the presence of the sun, so that just as the sun is the cause of the form of light, so God is the cause of our virtue and knowledge.[84] Of the infused virtues, Aquinas makes reference to illumination with respect to both faith and charity, where with respect to faith, "the light of faith makes us see what is believed,"[85] so that we know what it is that we assent to in faith. In this sense, the light of faith, as a means of grace, enhances our natural powers so that we can see and understand those things that are above our natural ability to know. We begin to see the things of faith more clearly in this light, which makes their truth more evident to us.

Charity, however, is not given as a means of illuminating our intellect, but rather as a means of "illumining human actions."[86] One might wonder how charity, which Aquinas defines as "the friendship of man with God,"[87] might illumine human actions, and the idea seems to be that when we have charity, our love and friendship with God causes us to love others as well and to seek out their good. Works of charity are particularly illuminating because they are

83. *Ad Rom.* 13.3 §1072.

84. ST II-II 52.3: "When the mover is cause not only of the movement, but also of the form to which the movement tends, then the action of the mover does not cease even after the form has been attained: thus the sun illumines the air even after it is illumined. In this way, then, God causes in us virtue and knowledge, not only when we first acquire them, but also as long as we persevere in them: and it is thus that God causes in the blessed a knowledge of what is to be done, not as though they were ignorant, but by continuing that knowledge in them."

85. ST II-II 1.4 ad 3.

86. *In Eph.* prooemium.

87. ST II-II 23.1.

in accord with the right reason that leads us to our ultimate end, and because our greater participation in the divine light becomes evident in the quality of our actions. Aquinas gives an example of this in his description of why John the Baptist was called "a lamp, blazing and burning brightly" (John 5:35). John was not a light in himself, Aquinas argues, but rather a lamp because he was illumined to bring humans to Christ. A lamp, however, only gives light if there is a fire blazing inside of it, and this is the fire of love.[88] John's ministry of illumination was made possible by the love enkindled in him by the Holy Spirit, and only because he loved God was he able to do his work of illumining others. Charity, then, as a gift of the Spirit, allows us to love God in a way that illumines others.

Christ the Light of Morality

Christ is ultimately the one whose two natures, human and divine, make possible the moral life for all of us. One might not know this from reading just the *Summa*, but in his commentary on John, Aquinas is clear that it is Christ in his divinity who both converts us and allows us to participate in the divine goodness. There are two main passages in the Johannine commentary where Aquinas talks about Christ's role in morality. In the first, Aquinas speaks of the effect of Christ's teaching, which is "to drive away the darkness of sin," since Christ "is light."[89] Since the effect of the light is to expel the darkness, Aquinas outlines three ways that the light of Christ does so, where the three kinds of darkness parallel the three lights that we have discussed. Christ overcomes the darkness of ignorance, which is a part of our nature as created beings who do not have light by essence; he overcomes the darkness of sin which is the result of our inordinate desires; and he overcomes the darkness of eternal damnation that follows from the first two. Aquinas concludes by saying that we will not walk in "the darkness of ignorance, because 'I am the truth'; nor the darkness of sin, because 'I am the way'; nor the darkness of eternal damnation, because 'I am the life.'"[90] Through his illuminating mission Christ brings light to the darkness of our ignorance and sin, thus making a moral life possible.

In the second passage, Aquinas calls Christ the "Sun of Justice," and says that only when this Sun "is present to us, the works of God can be one in us, for

88. *In Ioh.* 5.6 §812: "For as a lamp cannot give light unless there is a fire blazing within it, so a spiritual lamp does not give any light unless it is first set ablaze and burns with the fire of love. Therefore, to be ablaze comes first, and the giving of light depends on it, because knowledge of the truth is given due to the blazing of love."

89. *In Ioh.* 8.2 §1141. See all of sections 1140–44.

90. Ibid., §1144.

us, and by us."[91] Aquinas speaks of two ways that Christ is present to us, through his physical presence and through grace, both of which effect good works in us. When he was with us physically during his earthly ministry, it was daytime and thus fitting to do good works, while when he is with us in the "day of grace," it is also fitting to do good works.[92]

In comparing Christ and the sun to those who are illuminated by them, Aquinas makes the distinction between the perpetual illumination and daytime that is natural to them and the partial illumination that is available to their recipients. For the sun it is always daytime, while those of us on earth experience the sun as being

> sometimes present and at other times absent, [so] it is not always acting and illuminating. In the same way for Christ, the Sun of Justice, it is always day and the time for acting, but not with respect to us, because we are not always able to receive his grace due to some obstacle on our part.[93]

Our inability to receive the illuminating grace that makes good works possible is never due to some insufficient power in Christ, but rather to our sin, which places an obstacle in the way of receiving his grace and places us into the nighttime. To do good works, which is the goal of the moral life that will lead to our final end of the beatific vision, requires the illuminating grace of Christ.

Aquinas describes how we come to receive this grace in his commentary on Romans, where he discusses the process of "putting on the armor of light" (Rom. 13:12). One must first cast aside the works of darkness, "because in themselves they lack the light of reason with which man's works should be illumined . . . they are performed in the dark . . . and because by them a person is brought to darkness."[94] Once again we see the threefold darkness that parallels the threefold light. Once we have turned from darkness, a move that we have already seen requires God to change our will, then we can put on the virtues, which Aquinas sees as the "armor of light" that Paul is discussing, for three reasons: "they are decorated and perfected by the light of reason . . . they are tested by light . . . and because others are illumined by virtuous acts."[95] Thus the virtues counter the threefold darkness in these three distinct ways, with the

91. *In Ioh.* 9.1 §1305. See all of sections 1293–1311.

92. Ibid.

93. Ibid., §1306.

94. *Ad Rom.* 13.3 §1071.

95. Ibid., §1072.

ultimate purpose of sharing the illumination with others—acts that accord with and are made possible by the divine reason seem to have their own luminous quality to them.

We take up this armor of light by "putting on the Lord Jesus Christ" (Rom. 13:14), who has all of the virtues "most abundantly."[96] Putting on Christ is first accomplished by being baptized, and then by imitating him, "for a person who imitates Christ is said to put on Christ, because, just as a man is covered by a garment and is seen under its color, so in one who imitates Christ the works of Christ appear. Therefore, we put on the armor of light when we put on Christ."[97]

Aquinas's moral theology, then, finds both its exemplar and its very possibility in the person of Christ. Christ demonstrates the right reason of the moral life in his acts, which we should imitate; Christ illuminates our minds about the final end which properly orients our acts; Christ takes on our human nature in order to heal it and so that we can, in some sense, take on the nature of Christ through baptism and do the works of Christ; Christ converts us to the light and cures our hatred of the darkness; Christ reveals the existence and proper relation between natural law and the divine law; it is Christ who we put on when we live lives of virtue. In the end, Aquinas's moral theology is centered on the person of Christ, who brings the light to us.

96. Ibid., §1079.

97. Ibid.

7

Christ the Light

Throughout this book we have incorporated Christological elements within each of the chapters, with the exception of the chapter on the nature of light. We have seen how Christ makes holy teaching possible through his illuminative teaching, how he expands our capacity to talk about God, how his splendor is a reflection of God's glory, how he both creates and re-creates our intellectual capacities, and how he makes it possible for us to turn from the dark to the light in our moral acts. All of these outcomes are the result of what Aquinas sees as the effects of grace that are the purpose of the mission of the Son, to illumine our minds so that the Spirit may kindle our affections.[1] This chapter will expand upon this theme and fill in a few gaps where the full illuminative mission of the Son has not been discussed.

Light the Work of Love

Without the mission of the Son, who takes up human nature in the Incarnation, humans through the darkness of ignorance and sin would be trapped in darkness,[2] so Christ comes to illumine all humans in a mission to rescue us from the darkness and restore us to the light. Aquinas argues that the Incarnate Son accomplishes three excellent works, those of creation, illumination, and justification.[3] Yet, as we have seen, there are aspects of a theology of light in each of these works, not just in the work of illumination. Christ creates the

1. ST I 43.5 ad 3.

2. *In Col.* 2.4 §128: "They were not holding fast to the head, that is, Christ, by faith. Such people are deceived, because without Christ they are in the dark."

3. *In Heb. prooemium* §3: "Here it should be noted that the matchless work of Christ is threefold: one extends to every creature, namely, the work of creation: 'All things were made through Him' (Jn. 1:3); a second extends to the rational creature, who is illumined by Christ, namely, the work of illumination: 'He was the true light which illumines every man that comes into the world' (Jn. 1:9); the third extends

light, illumines us, and returns us to the light by making us just. All of this, however, is a work of love in which Christ creates us for, illumines us about, and restores us to friendship with God.

Aquinas makes the connection between light and love explicit in his commentary on Christ's miracle of walking on the water, explaining that

> [i]n the mystical sense, the "dark" signifies the absence of love; for light is love, according to: "He who loves his brother dwells in the light" (1 Jn 2:10). Accordingly, there is darkness in us when Jesus, "the true light" (Jn 1:9) does not come to us, because his presence repels all darkness.[4]

This light and love come in a way that reveals the deep secrets of God, since those that draw closer to Christ for illumination receive "the secrets of divine wisdom," which are "especially revealed to those who are joined to God by love."[5]

Ultimately, to know Christ is to know God's love, since Christ's work is itself an act of love:

> For whatever occurred in the mystery of human redemption and Christ's incarnation was the work of love. He was born out of charity . . . That he died also sprang from charity. . . . It follows that to know Christ's love is to know all the mysteries of Christ's Incarnation and our Redemption. These have poured out from the immense charity of God; a charity exceeding every created intelligence and the [combined] knowledge of all of them because it cannot be grasped in thought. Thus he says "which surpasses all natural knowledge" and every created intellect. . . . For the charity of Christ is [the manifestation of] what God the Father has accomplished through Christ.[6]

We must only "believe and love" Christ to reap the rewards of his charity, and by following his light we receive the reward of eternal light.[7]

The remainder of this chapter will explore the additional ways that Christ's illuminating love for us is expressed through his healing and redemptive work

to justification, which pertains only to the saints, who are vivified and sanctified by Him, i.e., by life-giving grace."

4. *In Ioh.* 6.2 §877.

5. *In Ioh.* 13.4 §1807.

6. *In Eph.* 3.5 §178.

on the cross, which enables our adoption as children of light; how his grace makes possible our illumination, which allows for our mission to others; and finally, how his headship of the church illumines the work of the church, most especially in the sacramental gifts of baptism, penance, and Eucharist, which all contribute to our journey toward our final end and the light of glory. Before we turn to these topics, however, we must begin by looking at the prime example of a person living fully illumined by the infusion of grace; we must begin with the example of Mary.

Mary, the Star of the Sea

There was a substantial medieval tradition of calling the Blessed Virgin Mary the Stella Maris, the Star of the Sea, a tradition that reached Aquinas through Bede and Bernard of Clairvaux.[8] In this capacity Mary was both the source of light in the extended sense of bringing Christ into the world and a guide for our own lives as an example of a person who was completely infused with grace according to her nature. In particular, Aquinas sees Mary as being prefigured in the Old Testament as the source of light. In the *Summa* he mentions that she is prefigured in the Old Testament feast of the New Moon in whom "appeared the first rays of the sun, i.e. Christ, by the fullness of grace."[9] This fullness of grace was given to Mary before she was born, so that she was cleansed from "the night of original sin" so as to make room for the light to come.[10]

By far the longest reflection that Aquinas gives on the illumination provided by Mary is in his sermon, *Lux Orta*, which is a reflection on Ps. 97:11: "A light has gone up for the just, and joy for the upright of heart." In this

7. *In Ioh.* 8.2 §1145: "He says, Whoever follows me, because just as one who does not want to stumble in the dark has to follow the one who is carrying the light, so one who wants to be saved must, by believing and loving, follow Christ, who is the light."

8. Aquinas quotes Bede in his *Catena Aureas* on Matthew (ch. 1, lect. 9): "Mary is interpreted, 'Star of the Sea,' after the Hebrew; 'Mistress,' after the Syriac; as she bore into the world the Light of salvation, and the Lord"; Luke (ch. 1, lect. 8): "Maria, in Hebrew, is the star of the sea; but in Syriac it is interpreted Mistress, and well, because Mary was thought worthy to be the mother of the Lord of the whole world, and the light of endless ages"; and John (ch. 20, lect. 2): "Mystically, Mary, which name signifies, mistress, illumined, illuminer, star of the sea, stands for the Church, which is also Magdalene, i.e. towered, (Magdalene being Greek for tower) as we read in Psalm 60:4, 'you have been a strong tower for me.' In that she announced Christ's resurrection to the disciples, all, especially those to whom the office of preaching is committed are admonished to be zealous in setting forth to others whatever is revealed from above." For the influence of Bernard, see below.

9. ST I-II 103.4 ad 4.

10. ST III 27.2 ad 2.

sermon, which was given on the Feast of the Birth of the Blessed Virgin Mary, Aquinas again sees Mary as being prefigured in this Old Testament passage, specifically through her sanctification, which is represented by the ascent of the dawn, and through the integrity of her virginity, which is represented by the rising of the morning star.[11] Before Mary was born, the world was in deep darkness, but her birth represents the dawning of a new day, one where "the night of guilt has ended and the day of grace has begun."[12] In comparing her virginity to the morning star, Aquinas points out that stars are incorruptible and share their light without losing it and likewise Mary was able to bring forth Christ without losing her virginity.[13]

Aquinas finds a myriad of ways to compare Mary to light and to show how it is a fitting comparison. While both angels and the apostles are called light in scripture, Aquinas points out that Mary is also suitably called light because she "transcends the companies of the apostles and angels because of her excellence," and because she gave birth to the light in a form of univocal generation (where like begets like).[14] He goes on to offer even more reasons why Mary is suitably called light, since

> we see that physical light is a source of joys, the leader of travelers and of those who are on the way, the expeller of darkness, the spreader of its likeness, the mother of the heavens' graces, the most splendid of creatures, and a delight as well as a consolation to the eyes.[15]

All of these good things, which corporeal light brings to us, are found in Mary in a spiritual way. She brings the joy of a new light because she has no "darkness of sin and ignorance";[16] like a light or lantern that lights our path in the darkness

11. *Lux Orta* 2, 243: "We read that the birth of the Blessed Virgin is shown beforehand by many figures in the Old Testament. Among other figures it is pointed to by three figures in particular, namely, in the ascent of the dawn, in the rising of the morning star, and in the sprouting of a twig from the root. In the dawn her birth is designated insofar as her sanctification is concerned. In the rising of the star we find a prefiguration insofar as it concerns the integrity of her virginity."

12. Ibid., 244.

13. Ibid.: "Now the rising of her star is compared to the integrity of her virginity, because, just as a star shines without being corrupted and without diminution or loss of light, thus the Blessed Virgin brought forth her Son, without a violent opening of the flesh and without the loss of her virginity." Aquinas picks this up from Bernard of Clairvaux's *Homilies on Mary*, Homily II.17, which can be found in Bernard of Clairvaux and Amadeus of Lausanne, *Magnificat: Homilies in Praise of the Blessed Virgin Mary*, trans. Marie-Bernard Saïd and Grace Perigo (Kalamazoo, MI: Cistercian, 1979), 30–31.

14. Ibid., 245.

15. Ibid., 247.

16. Ibid.

she "directs us on this way"[17] and as a shining light "she proceeds from what is good to what is better and increases until full day, that is, until the joy of eternity";[18] by the power of her light she expels the darkness of sin and helps eliminate vices, which she accomplishes by "fleeing from the darkness of sin and introducing the light of grace";[19] her light shines on all persons, so that we receive an abundant grace from "the bosom of her mercy";[20] she is the "mother of virtues" in the same way that light is "the gracious mother of colors";[21] light is "the most splendid of creatures" just as Mary is, who shines greater than all of the "just in the church militant . . . or the saints in the church triumphant";[22] and finally, as light is a "delight and consolation to humans," so Mary is a delight and consolation to us, whose light is good for both our "intellect that is made healthy by faith, and for our affections that are made healthy by love."[23]

Aquinas here is very much in conversation with Bernard of Clairvaux's homilies on Mary, quoting Bernard in almost every section, but this kind of hymn to the goodness and grace of Mary might seem very odd in a post-Reformation ecclesial setting; yet there is some subtle language that both circumvents typical Protestant concerns and is instructive on both the role of Mary and of Christ in bringing the light to us. As we have already discussed, Christ has light as an essential attribute and all other lights participate in his light. Aquinas never claims that Mary has light as an essential property, but rather follows scripture and claims that she is "full of grace." While she "illumines all humans, her son illumines the whole world,"[24] so her light must be a participation in the divine light. He is also careful to call her a creature, even if she is a creature who is superior to all of the angels and saints due to the perfection of her grace.

Yet it is this fullness of grace that allows her to accomplish all that Aquinas says she does. As Aquinas argues elsewhere, things that have a form perfectly are most capable of communicating that form to others; fire, which has the perfect form of heat, can communicate heat to other objects. Mary's grace, which is infused perfectly, means that she can communicate the blessings of that grace to others. The nature of the good is to share itself with others, and the perfect

17. Ibid., 248.

18. Ibid.

19. Ibid., 249.

20. Ibid., 250.

21. Ibid.

22. Ibid., 251.

23. Ibid.

24. Ibid., 248. Note that the implication is that the effect of Mary's light is limited just to her fellow humans, while Christ's light is more universal. Cf. ST III 27.5.

goodness that comes through the perfection of grace will by nature share itself. Mary's lovingly obedient "yes" to the Incarnation signals the dawning of a new day.

In this sense Mary serves as the model for what a deified human looks like in this life. Through "the introduction of the light of grace"[25] she is able to lead others to Christ, expel darkness, and help us on the path away from vice and toward virtue. We can look to her not just as a model for the grace-filled life, but as a secondary and efficient cause of that grace.[26] The intimation is that she does this as an instrument of God, thus maintaining God's ultimate causality while having the dignity of her own causality. This suggests that all of those who claim to have received grace can, as we can with Mary, measure their claim by how they are able to help cause grace in others as participants in the Divine life.

The Light of Christ's Healing, Redemption, and Adoption

If Mary provides the model of the deified life, Christians come to that life through the work of Christ, whose mission it is to illumine us. He redeems us from our sins and transfers us from dark to light, heals our minds and bodies from the effects of sin, and adopts us into the spiritual life of God, which is a life of light. All of this is an effect of grace and takes place through his entire life's work and teaching, but most especially upon the cross.

The Redemption of the Healing Light

One of the works of salvation is our redemption from sin. Christ effects in us a transference from darkness to light, where we come into "possession of the light."[27] Our humanity is repressed due to the slavery of sin and because we are due to be punished for turning away from God. Christ, however, "as man, became a sacrifice for us and redeemed us in his blood . . . and as God, we have the forgiveness of sins through him, because he took away the punishment of

25. Ibid., 249.

26. Ibid.: "Fourth, the light of its rays is wide and expansive. In a similar way the Blessed Virgin lets the rays of her grace shine on all and gives all a share in it." While the specific language of secondary and efficient causality is not directly mentioned here and in the previous note, the acts of introduction, diffusion, and communication are all acts of causal efficacy; because grace must originate in God, she must be a secondary cause of grace.

27. *In Col.* 1.3 §25.

sin."[28] Christ, then, redeems us from the darkness by entering into the darkness and ultimately conquering it.

Aquinas accounts for four effects of sin and points to how Christ heals us from each one of them:

> [I]n sin is involved, first of all, a transgression of the eternal law and of God's rights, since all sin is an iniquity which transgresses the law. . . . Therefore, since the eternal law and divine right stem from the eternal Word, it is clear that cleansing from sins is Christ's prerogative, inasmuch as He is the Word. . . . Secondly, sin involves a loss of the light of reason and, consequently, of God's wisdom in man, since such a light is a participation of divine wisdom. . . . Furthermore, according to the Philosopher, all evil is ignorance. Therefore, to set aright according to divine wisdom belongs to the One who is divine wisdom. But this is Christ. . . . Thirdly, in sin is a deformity of the likeness of God in man. . . . Therefore, it belongs to the Son to correct this deformity, because He is the image of the Father. . . . Fourthly, there is a loss of the eternal inheritance, the sign of which was man's expulsion from Paradise. . . . Therefore, it is obvious that it belongs to Christ to purge sins both by reason of His human nature and by reason of the divine.[29]

Of these four elements of sin, the last three deal specifically with nature, grace, and glory, with all three of them having illuminative aspects, either explicitly or implicitly. The second aspect of sin, the loss of the light of reason, is explicit in its illuminative aspect, and in Aquinas's insistence that Christ comes to heal our natural light. The third aspect, the deformation of the likeness of God, is another way of saying that sin causes the loss of the light of grace, which is restored to us when we become conformed to Christ. The final aspect, the loss of the eternal inheritance, points to the loss of the light of glory, which is restored to us when we become the adopted sons of God through the redemption offered by Christ.

Following a line of thought developed by Augustine,[30] Aquinas likens this healing to that of the blind man healed by Christ in John 9:6. As the blind man was unable to see the light, Christ as both human and divine (represented by the clay and saliva of the miracle), comes to heal our eyes, which allows us to see

28. Ibid., §28.

29. *In Heb.* 1.2 §39. Note that this is a fragment of a *reportatio* by Remigio Nanni.

30. See the *Catena Aurea* on John 9.

God's glory.[31] He does so by healing the concupiscible part of our soul from its deviations and by illumining our rational intellect.[32] In short, the justification of humans involves a healing of our rational capacities by the light of wisdom that Christ brings,[33] because it is our rational capacities that are what distinguish us from other animals. When our concupiscent appetite, which is in the sensible part of the human soul, drives our moral lives instead of our reason, we need real healing from spiritual blindness.

Christ's illuminative healing and its power to reach everywhere can be found most emphatically in the harrowing of hell, in which Christ was said to manifest his power by "visiting it [hell] and illuminating it."[34] While the journey into hell was a spiritual journey, accomplished in a manner similar to angelic motion rather than local motion (or, perhaps like the motion of light in the air in Aristotelian physics), Christ brought his light into all levels of hell (there were four levels for Aquinas, the hell for the damned, limbo, purgatory, and the hell of the patriarchs).[35] In hell, Christ's illumination was there as an effect of his power without his actual physical presence. His illumination especially affected those who were justified through faith prior to the Incarnation, as those patriarchs received an infusion of "the light eternal of glory" which overcame their original sin.[36] In Christ's illumination of hell we see how the effects of his illumination extend to the darkest levels of existence, whether well received or not.

31. *In Ioh.* 1.8 §182: "Hence in order that the divine light might be seen by us, he healed our eyes, making an eye salve of his flesh, so that with the salve of his flesh the Word might heal our eyes, weakened by the concupiscence of the flesh. And this is why just after saying, 'the Word was made flesh,' he says, 'we have seen his glory.' To indicate this the Lord made clay from his saliva and spread the clay upon the eyes of the man born blind. For clay is from the earth, but saliva comes from the head. Similarly, in the person of Christ, his human nature was assumed from the earth; but the incarnate Word is from the head, i.e., from God the Father. So, when this clay was spread on the eyes of men, 'we saw his glory.'"

32. *In Gal.* 4.2 §202: "God, therefore, sent His Son to heal the errantry of the concupiscible part and to illumine the ignorance of the rational creature."

33. ST III 44.3 ad 1: "Now the end for which Christ's miracles were worked was the health of the rational part, which is healed by the illumination of wisdom, and the justification of man."

34. ST III 52.1.

35. See all of III 52 for descriptions of Christ's effects in the various levels of hell, which are initially mentioned in III 52.2.

36. ST III 52.2.

Adoption as Children of Light

A key effect of the healing offered to humans by Christ is that we become adopted as children of light. In a number of places Aquinas explores this biblical image of Christians who become adopted children of God through the work of Christ, where we participate in his inheritance. Adoption, according to Aquinas, "is nothing more than conformity, because a person adopted into the sonship of God is conformed to his true Son," which allows us to be heirs of God.[37] One of the effects of this adoption is that we come to share in Christ's splendor, which means that just as Christ is a reflection of God's light, so we too become reflections of God's light. Christ gives us this light through the illumination of "wisdom and grace, [which] makes them be conformed to himself."[38] By the illumination that comes from Christ we come to believe in Christ and are "reborn into the truth,"[39] which again suggests that illumination properly understood is knowledge of truth as it is ordered to God. Consequently, this infusion of grace makes possible the perfection of our actions and finally the gift of the light of glory that illumines our mind and glorifies our body.[40]

What Aquinas seems to suggest here is that when we are adopted as children of light, we enter into the very light and life of God. We take on light that illumines our mind and our actions, so that we come to do works similar to those of Christ. As we saw with regard to the Blessed Virgin Mary, when we receive this illumination that brings us into the life of God, by being conformed to Christ, we begin to be deified so that we live a life of grace here and a life of glory in heaven.

The Light of Grace

As we have suggested in a number of places, it is the light of grace that makes our life with God possible, and here we will look at several aspects of this light that we have not yet addressed. Grace is a gift of God that allows us to know and act in ways that are above our natural capacities. By nature we can only know through our senses and only act in accord with the goods of our physical and

37. *Ad Rom.* 8.6 §704.

38. Ibid.

39. *In Ioh.* 12.6 §1686.

40. *In Ioh.* 1.6 §150: "Men are sons of God according to a threefold likeness to God. First, by the infusion of grace; hence anyone having sanctifying grace is made a son of God. . . . Secondly, we are like God by the perfection of our actions, because one who acts justly is a son. . . . Thirdly, we are made like God by the attainment of glory and by a certain quantity of the light of glory in the soul."

intellectual nature. We can know the truth of particulars, think about universal truths that we get from abstracting from particulars, and act in ways that lead to our physical and intellectual flourishing based on our material limitations. But the limits of human knowing and acting bump up against any possibility of knowing a completely immaterial reality and acting in a way that orients our lives to that reality. Sin, of course, makes the problem even worse, as we come to look to material realities as the whole of human good.

Grace, according to Aquinas, is a gift from God that is a quality of the essence of the human soul, and whose form allows us to know and act in a way above our nature. Grace is not opposed to our nature, as we are created with the capacity to receive it, as is any creature with an intellectual soul, but rather represents an additional gift that perfects our intellectual and moral abilities. Humans were given grace at their creation, which allowed them to know God, but lost this grace through sin. Consequently, all of humanity is in a disordered state with regard to God because of the stain of sin that infects us all. Only God can restore us to grace, "for since the lustre of grace springs from the shedding of Divine light, this lustre cannot be brought back, except God sheds His light anew: hence a habitual gift is necessary, and this is the light of grace."[41]

By describing grace as a habit, Aquinas is thinking of it within the larger context of humans acts where habits are qualities of the soul, "dispositions whereby that which is disposed, is well or ill disposed either in regard to itself, that is, to its nature, or in regard to something else, that is, to the end."[42] In this definition Aquinas is already making a substantial adjustment to the Aristotelian idea of habit, as suggesting that a habit can be a disposition to either nature or a final end leaves room for a final end that might be above nature. The payoff for this subtle move comes when Aquinas argues that habits can be infused in humans by God, which is a most non-Aristotelian idea. Since the ultimate perfection of humans is found in the beatific vision, an end that is above our nature, and because "habits need to be in proportion with that to which man is disposed by them, therefore it is necessary that those habits, which dispose to this end, exceed the proportion of human nature."[43] A gift of habitual grace, then, disposes us to act toward that final end which brings us our perfect happiness.

The gift of habitual grace differs from acquired habits in another way, which is that it is infused. Whereas we must practice a certain sort of action over time in order to acquire a habit, as in the case of temperance among

41. ST I-II 109.7.

42. ST I-II 49.3.

43. ST I-II 51.4.

the positive habits or virtues, grace is given instantaneously. Here again an understanding of light, darkness, and privation can help us see how this works. When our minds are turned toward the dark there is a privation of the proper form of the mind, which is to be full of light. The darkness in the air is not the contrary of corporeal light, but rather its absence, which means that there is nothing to resist the light when it comes, assuming there are no opaque obstacles that prevent its reception. Likewise, grace can come in an instant and give us the habits, which are the theological virtues, that allow us to be justified instantaneously, but in this case the obstacle of sin, which is itself a privation, is also removed.[44]

Christ comes to institute the time of grace, where Aquinas compares the time of grace to "a day, in that it is illuminated by the sun of justice."[45] The Sun of Justice, of course,

> is Christ, our God . . . therefore, as long as this Sun is present to us, the works of God can be done in us, for us, and by us. At one time this Sun was physically present to us; and then it was day . . . therefore, it was fitting to do the works of God. He is also present us by grace; and then it is the day of grace, when it is fitting to do the works of God.[46]

In this sense Aquinas thinks that Christ has "delivered us from the power of darkness and brought us into the kingdom of his love."[47]

Christ brought the light of grace in his earthly ministry, where he did the works of God, and just as importantly, he continues to be with us through grace, which allows us to continue to do the works of God that he began. The purpose of the light of grace is not only to justify us and restore our life to its proper order toward God, but also to enable us to continue Christ's mission. The illumination and teaching that Christ provided through his earthly ministry would be useless unless they were passed along, so that "these mysteries would be of no use if they were not imparted to others," which is accomplished through "preaching and miracles."[48] The light of grace provided by Christ has

44. See ST I-II 113.7; ST II-II 4.4 ad 3; *Ad Rom.* 4.2 §349.

45. *In Heb.* 8.2 §395: "Dicit ergo quantum ad temporis opportunitatem ecce dies veniunt, id est tempus gratiae, quod comparatur diei, quod illuminatum est a sole iustitiae."

46. *In Ioh.* 9.1 §1305.

47. *In Ioh.* 18.6 §2351.

48. *In Eph.* 3.2 §150.

a distinctively evangelical aspect to it, which surely would have appealed to the Dominican friar.

Christ makes all of this possible because he has the fullness of grace in his soul and because he serves as the exemplar cause of all the spiritual graces. With regard to the latter, Aquinas links the idea of the person of the Son, who is the primordial principle of all things, with Christ as the exemplar of all the spiritual graces.[49]

The grace that Christ received was, according to Aquinas, predestined from the beginning. The grace he received also makes the grace that we receive manifest to us, and in this way his predestination and reception of grace is an exemplar of ours.[50] The Christian who enters into the life of God through Christ receives habitual grace in the same manner as Christ, through the gift of the Holy Spirit.[51]

The grace of Christ exists in his soul, and in two places Aquinas compares the influx of grace to the light of the sun. The habitual grace of Christ, which was given by the Holy Spirit as a consequence of the grace of union between the human and divine natures of Christ, is likened by Aquinas to light that flows from the sun, where the sun represents the initial grace of union and the habitual grace is the light that flows from it.[52] The grace of Christ is also compared to the sun by means of the infinite power of both. Just as the sun has every possible feature of light, so too Christ is the infinite principle of grace in the sense that he has every feature of grace.[53] What this means for us is that

49. *In I Cor.* 11.1 §583: "Now the primordial principle of the production of things is the Son of God . . . he is, therefore, the primordial exemplar, which all creatures imitate as the true and perfect image of God . . . but in a special way He is the exemplar of spiritual graces, with which spiritual creatures are illumined."

50. ST III 24.3: "Secondly, [predestination may be considered] in respect of the manner of obtaining this good—that is, by grace. This is most manifest in Christ; because human nature in Him, without any antecedent merits, was united to the Son of God: and of the fulness of His grace we all have received."

51. Christ receives grace first in the grace of union of the Divine nature with the human nature and subsequently receives habitual grace from the Holy Spirit. We receive habitual grace from the Holy Spirit as well, but not because of our union with Divine nature.

52. ST III 7.13: "For grace is caused in man by the presence of the Godhead, as light in the air by the presence of the sun . . . but the presence of God in Christ is by the union of human nature with the Divine Person. Hence the habitual grace of Christ is understood to follow this union, as light follows the sun."

53. ST III 7.11: "Secondly [the grace of Christ] may be viewed in its specific nature of grace; and thus the grace of Christ can be termed infinite, since it is not limited, i.e. it has whatsoever can pertain to the nature of grace, and what pertains to the nature of grace is not bestowed on Him in a fixed measure; seeing that according to the purpose of God to Whom it pertains to measure grace, it is bestowed on Christ's soul as on a universal principle for bestowing grace on human nature . . . thus we might say that

Christ's soul has the perfect power "by the fulness of grace and knowledge to illumine all rational creatures falling short of its perfection, in a manner befitting a rational creature."[54]

We participate in the grace of Christ first through participating in his resurrection, for it is his resurrection at the break of the morning that signifies that he will be leading us to the light of glory.[55] This grace not only leads us to the light of glory, but allows us to do the good works that merit our salvation, so that we turn from dead works to works of light.[56] In doing so, we take up Christ's own mission.

The Christian Mission of Light

As we have mentioned, there is a distinctively evangelical aspect to Aquinas's understanding of the Christological shape of the theology of light. We do not possess the light for just our own benefit, but so that we may share it with others. Christ himself carried his cross,

> as a teacher his candelabrum, as a support for the light of his teaching, because for believers the message of the cross is the power of God: "No one after lighting a lamp puts it in a cellar or under a bushel but on a stand, that those who enter may see the light" (Lk 11:33).[57]

While Christ was the first to bear the cross this way, others have followed him and so too bring the light into the world.[58] As the verse from Luke suggests,

the light of the sun is infinite, not indeed in being, but in the nature of light, as having whatever can pertain to the nature of light."

54. ST III 13.2.

55. ST III 53.2 ad 3: "Christ rose early when the day was beginning to dawn, to denote that by His Resurrection He brought us to the light of glory; just as He died when the day was drawing to its close, and nearing to darkness, in order to signify that by His death He would destroy the darkness of sin and its punishment." We will address the role of baptism in illumination later in this chapter.

56. *In Eph.* 5.5 §300: "Hence it must be said that the Apostle is introducing the image found in Isaiah 60:1, 'Arise, be enlightened, O Jerusalem; for your light has come, and the glory of the Lord has risen upon you.' Thus 'wherefore it says' refers to Scripture. 'Rise' from a neglect of good works, 'you who sleep.' 'How long will you sleep, O sluggard?' (Prov. 6:9). 'Shall he that sleepeth rise again no more?' (Ps. 40:9). 'And arise from the dead,' that is, from dead or destructive actions. Christ 'will cleanse our conscience from dead works' (Heb. 9:14). 'Your dead men shall live, my slain shall rise again' (Is. 26:19). Rise therefore 'and Christ shall enlighten you.' 'The Lord is my light and my salvation; whom shall I fear?' (Ps. 26:1). 'Enlighten my eyes that I never sleep in death' (Ps. 12:4)."

57. *In Ioh.* 19.3 §2414.

Christians cannot hide the light that is given to them by grace, since the power of grace allows one's works to shine forth.

To fulfill our mission we receive special gifts, "For God gives special gifts to some, that they may pour them out for the benefit of others; for he does not give light to the sun in order that the sun may shine for itself alone, but for the whole world . . . whether they be riches or power of knowledge or wisdom."[59] Here Aquinas goes on to discuss that these gifts are for the benefit of others, but he discusses this with respect to the comfort we receive and are to pass along to those who are afflicted. In this sense, the grace we receive from Christ is a comfort to us, perhaps by giving us knowledge of our final end and making our afflictions bearable in light of our eternal reward. The grace we receive is one that allows us to see the deep spiritual and material needs of other persons and respond to them by sharing the grace that has been shared with us.

We accomplish this by doing good works for others, which we do by first turning away from works of darkness, "because in themselves they lack the light of reason with which man's works should be illumined."[60] More positively, Aquinas explores what it means to be "children of light" in his commentary on Eph. 5:8. Here he distinguishes two ways that we act like children of the light, in the substance of our acts and in our intentions.[61] The substance of our acts under illumination should bear fruit and requires that our acts be ordered in three ways: first with regard to ourselves, second with regard to others, and third with regard to God [recall that any imperfection in an act renders it sinful]. So we must be good in ourselves, just to others, and "ordered to God through knowledge and a confession of the truth."[62] Only when the substance of our acts is perfect in these three ways will we be accomplishing good works that will bear divine fruit, provided that they are also done with the correct intentions. Here he seems to think of "intention" as more than simply willing the good, which is already implied in the substance of the act; there is right intention when the act is done with full discernment and good judgment and

58. Ibid.: "This does not lack its own mystery: for although Christ was the first to endure the sufferings of the cross, others did so after in imitation of him, especially strangers, that is, the Gentiles."

59. *In II Cor.* 1.2 §15.

60. *Ad Rom.* 13.2 §1071.

61. *In Eph.* 5.4 §290: "However, a person walks as a child of the light in two ways; first in reference to the substance or kind of actions he performs, then in reference to the manner or intention he does them with."

62. Ibid., §291: "Whence it must be recalled that every act of virtue is reduced to three relationships. For it is necessary that the agent be ordered within himself, to his neighbor, and to God. Within himself, that he be good in himself . . . he must be ordered to his fellow man by justice . . . while he is ordered to God through knowledge and a confession of the truth."

with the goal of pleasing God.[63] All of this requires that we be illumined by Christ, or we will end up back in the dark.

A final good work made possible by Christ's light is preaching. The importance of this to Aquinas should be of no surprise to us given his position in an order founded upon good preaching. For Aquinas, there was a certain order to the illuminating preaching of Christ, whom Aquinas believes came to preach first to the Jews so that the apostles could then preach to the Gentiles. Christ first shared his illumination with the Jews, and the apostles and their followers in the church had the mission of spreading that illumination to the Gentiles.[64] This process itself mimics the process of angelic illumination in heaven, where the angels that are closer in the angelic hierarchy illumine those lower in the hierarchy; we might conclude that a similar hierarchy exists between Jews and Gentiles. But the whole point of preaching is to take the light that has illumined us, "so that Christ may be preached among the Gentiles,"[65] that is, so that his light may reach all of the world, just as the light of the sun illumines everything.

Christ the Light of the Church

The influx of grace that is provided by Christ, and our mission to share his light, are centered upon and made possible by the church, whose head is Christ. Aquinas's Christological ecclesiology, which sees Christ as being the spiritual head of the church, and the Spirit as its heart, as we would expect from the divine missions, means that we receive the light of grace by being a part of the body of Christ. Christ through the union of the divine and human natures has the highest grace, the fullness of grace, and consequently the power to infuse grace into all of us.[66] As the divine head of the church he can act upon both our bodies and our souls,[67] and can act across time, so that he is the eternal head of the church.[68] As the head of the church Christ provides "the interior influx

63. Ibid., §292: "You ought to have the intention of doing whatever pleases God."

64. ST III 42.1 ad 1: "Christ was given to be the light and salvation of the Gentiles through His disciples, whom He sent to preach to them."

65. *In II Cor.* 4.2 §130.

66. ST III 8.1: "Now these three things [order, perfection, and power] belong spiritually to Christ. First, on account of His nearness to God His grace is the highest and first, though not in time, since all have received grace on account of His grace . . . secondly, He had perfection as regards the fulness of all graces . . . thirdly, He has the power of bestowing grace on all the members of the Church . . . and thus it is plain that Christ is fittingly called the Head of the Church."

67. ST III 8.2: "Hence the whole manhood of Christ, i.e. according to soul and body, influences all, both in soul and body; but principally the soul, and secondarily the body."

of grace . . . which has the power to justify."[69] Other leaders of the church can only influence the church in an exterior way, through "external persuasion to do works of grace."[70] Christ is not just the head of the church, but is right in the middle of it. Aquinas compares Christ to a lamp that is in the middle of a house and so gives light to the whole house.[71]

Aquinas especially uses the idea of Christ as the light of the church in his allegorical readings of the Old Testament. In a discussion of various ways of reading "Let there be light" in Genesis 1, Aquinas says that if we understand "Let there be light" as meaning "Let Christ be born in the church" we are reading the passage allegorically,[72] with the obvious implications that Christ is the light of the church and that in some sense the church was founded at the very beginning of creation. It is because of this founding of the church at creation that Aquinas can look at the candelabrum in the Holy of Holies and argue that

> inasmuch as Christ was prefigured by them, they are all found in Him: first, as to the holy things, for He is a candlestick of light: "I am the light of the world" (Jn. 8:12). In it are six orders: three on the left, namely, the perfect of the Old Testament; and three on the right, namely, of the New Testament. They are designated in Ezekiel (chap. 14): By Noah, prelates; by Daniel, contemplatives; by Job, the actives. Those branches receive light and impart it: "As every man has received grace, ministering the same one to another" (1 Pt 4:10).[73]

Here Aquinas sees not only Christ as representing the light of the church, but also three Old Testament figures, Noah, Daniel, and Job (based on the description of their righteousness in Ezek. 14:14) as prefiguring the clerical and religious roles of church leadership through their lights on the candelabrum.

68. ST III 8.3: "Hence we must say that if we take the whole time of the world in general, Christ is the Head of all men, but diversely."

69. ST III 8.6.

70. Ibid., ad 2.

71. *In Heb.* 2.3 §132: "Just as a pillar in the midst of a house supports it and a lamp in the midst of a house gives light and the heart in the midst of the body gives life, so Christ is in the midst of the Church."

72. *In Gal.* 4.7 §254: "For when I say, 'Let there be light,' referring literally to corporeal light, it is the literal sense. But if it be taken to mean 'Let Christ be born in the Church,' it pertains to the allegorical sense."

73. *In Heb.* 9.1 §423.

In the *Summa* Aquinas provides a detailed discussion of various ways that articles in the temple could be understood allegorically or as prefiguring Christ, since he takes the tabernacle to prefigure Christ. Again, the candelabrum comes into view as representing "the seven gifts of the Holy Spirit," or "the candlestick and table may signify the Church's teaching, and faith, which also illumines and refreshes."[74] Even Old Testament feasts, such as the Neomenia (Feast of the New Moon), prefigured Christ coming to "illumine the primitive church through preaching and miracles."[75]

While this might strike contemporary biblical exegetes as a wild flight of fancy, for Aquinas, the role of the Son in creation and Christ's headship of the church, which spans time, means that at some level the church has been in existence from the beginning of time. The church existed in some primordial form and was able to be found in the figures of Israel's worship, and this points to the idea that God was in the process of creating a place for the light of Christ from the very beginning.

Perhaps at the root of this idea is the relationship between the celestial and ecclesiastical hierarchies. We have seen how in the celestial hierarchy angels illumine each other with regard to the eternal mysteries of the divine life, with superior angels illumining lesser angels about the works of God. The church is modeled on this celestial order, albeit imperfectly, where members of the church can illumine each other, though in multiple directions rather than just one as in the celestial hierarchy.[76] That is, in the church militant, people that we might think of as having less natural ability can illumine those we would think of as having more, because the light of grace has strengthened their ability to know God and because they have more charity. More importantly, the link between the celestial and ecclesiastical hierarchies is their mutual purpose, which is "the glory of enjoying God. Hence the mystical body of the Church consists not only of men but of angels."[77] If this is the case then it would make sense that the church would have existed from the beginning of time, at the creation of the

74. ST I-II 102.4 ad 6.

75. Ibid., ad 10.

76. ST I 106.3 ad 1: "The ecclesiastical hierarchy imitates the heavenly in some degree, but by a perfect likeness. For in the heavenly hierarchy the perfection of the order is in proportion to its nearness to God; so that those who are the nearer to God are the more sublime in grade, and more clear in knowledge; and on that account the superiors are never enlightened by the inferiors, whereas in the ecclesiastical hierarchy, sometimes those who are the nearer to God in sanctity, are in the lowest grade, and are not conspicuous for science; and some also are eminent in one kind of science, and fail in another; and on that account superiors may be taught by inferiors."

77. ST III 8.4.

angels, and would be evident throughout the Old Testament whenever God is being worshiped, thus providing evidence of Christ.

Just as the existence of angels is necessitated by the perfection of creation in representing all kinds of beings, including purely intellectual substances, so the light of the church made possible by the grace and headship of Christ has within it all manner of diversity. Different members of the church may receive more or less grace depending upon how God has prepared their wills, "who dispenses his gifts of grace variously, in order that the beauty and perfection of the church may result from these various degrees."[78] Thus the perfection of the church is not found in the homogeneity of its members, but from its diversity of grace and gifts, all of which contribute to the light that the church sheds upon the world as a reflection of the glory of Christ.

The Light of Christ in the Sacraments

The mission of the Son is to illumine our intellects so that the Spirit may kindle our affection for God, and we participate in this light by becoming a member of the body of Christ, whose light shines in his church. Our path to sharing in the light of Christ, however, does not end simply with walking into our church, for Christ instituted sacraments that allow us directly to participate in and receive the light of grace. These sacraments provide the link between the light of grace and our mission as instruments of illumination, between the church and its individual members, between our bodies and souls, and between the material and the spiritual.

Aquinas is most explicit about the relationship between Christ, the church, grace, and the sacraments in the prologue to his Johannine commentary:

> The things that are under Christ are the sacraments of his humanity, through which the faithful are filled with the fullness of grace. In this way, then, the things that were under him filled the temple, i.e., the faithful, who are the holy temple of God (1 Cor 3:17) insofar as through the sacraments of his humanity all the faithful of Christ receive from the fullness of his grace.[79]

The grace of Christ is in the sacraments and because, as we have discussed, his grace is perfect it is able to create the form of grace in others. The ecclesial import of this is to clarify the role of the priest in the sacraments, so that

78. ST I-II 112.4.

79. *In Ioh. prooemium* §8.

Aquinas is quite clear that priests are instrumental causes of grace by the power of Christ working in them rather than because of any power intrinsic to the priest. Aquinas notes that "the inward sacramental effect is to cleanse man from sin and illumine him by grace,"[80] but argues that this interior effect is only something that can be accomplished by God. Consequently, priests have a role in illumination, but only through giving the sacraments as instrumental agents, not as the principal agents of grace, which is reserved to God.[81] There are three sacraments where the illumination of Christ is one of the key sacramental effects, namely baptism, penance, and Eucharist, with baptism being the primary illuminating sacrament.

Baptism and the Light of Christ

By the time Aquinas did his work, the link between baptism and illumination was well established in the Christian tradition. The biblical basis of the link comes from a passage in Hebrews that describes both baptism and illumination and eliminates the possibility of rebaptism:

> For it is impossible to restore again to repentance those who have once been illumined, and have tasted the heavenly gift, and have shared in the Holy Spirit, and have tasted the goodness of the word of God and the powers of the age to come, and then have fallen away, since on their own they are crucifying again the Son of God and are holding him up to contempt.[82]

Justin Martyr was among the first church fathers to describe baptism as illumination, saying, "And this washing is called illumination, because they who learn these things are illuminated in their understandings."[83] Augustine inherited this understanding of baptism as illumination, where the theme is especially prominent in his Easter sermons, but is evident throughout his writings. Those who took up the threefold idea of purgation, illumination, and perfection often incorporated baptismal elements into this structure as well.[84]

80. ST III 64.1 ob 1.

81. Ibid., ad 1: "In like manner also priests are said to illumine God's people, not indeed by giving them grace, but by conferring on them the sacraments of grace."

82. Heb. 6:4–6.

83. Justin Martyr, *First Apology*, ch. 61 in Alexander Roberts, James Donaldson, and A. Cleveland Coxe, *The Ante-Nicene Fathers Vol. I* (Peabody, MA: Hendrickson, 1994), 183.

84. E.g., Pseudo-Dionysius, *Ecclesiastical Hierarchy* §2.

Aquinas incorporated this theme into both his scriptural commentaries and his account of baptism in the *Summa*.

In his commentaries on scripture, we can see that for Aquinas, baptism just is illumination, and in his commentary on this verse from Hebrews he describes the present and future goods received through baptism, remarking that "in the present they had spiritual rebirth; in regard to this he says 'illumination,' namely by baptism. And baptism is fittingly called an illumination, because it is the beginning of spiritual rebirth, in which the intellect is illumined by faith."[85]

Aquinas follows one of Augustine's allegorical interpretation of scripture on the healing of the blind man at the pool of Siloam in John 9:1–7, where the pool of Siloam is seen as a type of baptismal font where the blind man was sent "to wash and receive his sight, i.e., to be baptized, and in baptism to receive full illumination. Thus according to Dionysius, baptism is an illumination."[86] In recounting this story, Aquinas sees a fivefold effect in the blind man that is accomplished through his washing, which we can take as indicative of how baptism works in others as well. After his baptism, the blind man was able to identify Jesus correctly as a true man (avoiding a number of Christological heresies), tell the truth, recount the command that led to his healing, become obedient to Christ, and then explain the good effect of his healing, because "it was fitting that he be illumined after obeying."[87]

All of these effects are made possible not just because we are illumined, but primarily because we have put on Christ, and are then illumined. As we mentioned in discussing the light of the virtues, Aquinas thinks we put on Christ, who is an armor of light, by receiving baptism and then imitating Christ.[88] We can see that the five effects of baptism in the blind man all flow from Christ—a perfect knowledge of God, perfection in the truth, an understanding of God's commands, perfect obedience, and a correct understanding of what has happened. By "putting on Christ" in baptism we come to participate in Christ's own illumination and perfection.

Aquinas again links the headship of Christ in the body of the church with baptism when he turns his attention to the sacrament in the *Summa*. Comparing the material head of a body with the spiritual head, Aquinas argues that members of Christ

85. *In Heb.* 6.1 §289.

86. *In Ioh.* 9.1 §1311.

87. *In Ioh.* 9.2 §1318.

88. *Ad Rom.* 13.3 §1079: "For a person who imitates Christ is said to put on Christ, because, just as man is covered by a garment and is seen under its color, so in one who imitates Christ the works of Christ appears. Therefore, we put on the armor of light, when we put on Christ."

> derive a spiritual sense consisting in the knowledge of truth, and spiritual movement which results from the instinct of grace . . . and it follows from this that the baptized are illumined by Christ as to the knowledge of truth, and made fruitful by Him with the fruitfulness of good works by the infusion of grace.[89]

There is a role for humans to participate in this illumination through the preparation that comes in the catechetical teaching of those who are preparing for baptism, but this illumination is an exterior one, whereas God prepares and illumines the one to be baptized interiorly.[90] Given what we have discussed about God's role in teaching, we can surmise that the teaching that happens exteriorly will be limited by the capabilities of the student, whereas the interior teaching of God provides an additional ability to understand that is not available to the person by nature.

One of the reasons that water is the material element of baptism is directly related to its role in transmitting light. Because water has a diaphanous nature it is able to be actualized by light,[91] and so it signifies in the recipient of baptism a receptivity to the lights of grace and glory. Given this, it would seem that the cleansing effect of baptism represented by the cleansing power of water extends to a certain cleansing of the mind as well. Since sin creates obstacles to our life with God, the cleansing from sin would remove the obstacles that prevent our reception of God's light.

Light and Penance

The illuminative effects of the cleansing from sin that take place in baptism provide a link to the second illuminative sacrament, that of penance. Aquinas suggests that there are three main effects from the sacraments, the Dionysian trinity of purgation, illumination, and perfection. Some of the perfections of life are achieved directly, by the addition or strengthening of some power, while sometimes those perfections are achieved by the removal of some accidental property in the same way that our bodies are healed by the removal of disease.[92]

89. ST III 69.5.

90. Ibid., ad 2: "The teacher illumines outwardly and ministerially by catechizing: but God illumines the baptized inwardly, by preparing their hearts for the reception of the doctrines of truth."

91. ST III 66.3: "Because it [water] is diaphanous, it is susceptive of light; hence its correspondence to Baptism as the sacrament of Faith."

92. ST III 65.1: "With respect to himself man is perfected in the life of the body, in two ways; first, directly [per se], i.e. by acquiring some vital perfection; secondly, indirectly [per accidens], i.e. by the removal of impediments to life, such as ailments, or the like."

Baptism allows us to enter into the spiritual life and so we receive the additional perfections we just described, especially that of illumination. Penance, on the other hand, removes the accidental character of sin from our soul and thus removes the obstacles to illumination that follow upon postbaptismal sin. So while purgation and illumination are primarily the effects of baptism, "for him who falls back into sin, they belong secondarily to penance and extreme unction."[93]

While Aquinas gives us a long discussion of the sacrament of penance, we can see how illumination is a secondary effect of the sacrament by how he describes the act of penitence elsewhere, since the internal motion toward God and away from sin is the same in both, while the sacrament adds a material component. Aquinas links the malice of sin with a turning away from "the light of wisdom," but argues that we "come back to wisdom by repentance."[94] Those who hate the spiritual light even come to hate the corporeal light, so much so that many of their evil acts take place in the dark.[95]

The problem for the sinner is that the dark is unable to hide them from the light of God's judgment, since "the Lord coming to judgment, will bring to light the things now hidden in darkness, i.e., will make clear and obvious the things done secretly in darkness; and will disclose the purposes of the heart, i.e., all the secrets of the heart," including both "good things and the evil things that have been committed and not covered over by penance."[96] Part of the function of penance is to make manifest our sins now so as to avoid the light of judgment later. Through penance we turn away from the dark and back into the light of God.

The Light of the Eucharist

Aquinas only discusses the Eucharist and illumination in two places, so it would be overstating the case to suggest that illumination is a key idea with respect to his understanding of the Eucharist. Nevertheless, given the presence of Christ in the Eucharist, and what we have discussed with regard to the light of Christ, it would be odd to think that there was no connection between the Eucharist and light. In one place, Aquinas quotes John of Damascus to the effect that the Eucharist "will consume our sins, and illumine our hearts, so that we shall be

93. Ibid., ad 3.

94. *In Iob* 24:13–18, 136–41.

95. Ibid., 142–44: "As a sign that they oppose the spiritual light of wisdom he says that loving darkness they even hate exterior light."

96. *In I Cor.* 4.1 §196.

inflamed and made deiform."[97] In the other, Aquinas argues that it was fitting for Christ to institute the Eucharist at night, since "the soul is illumined by the power of this sacrament."[98]

Going beyond what Aquinas has said, it should be clear why he makes these statements. Christ has light by his very essence and when we take Christ into our bodies through his gifts of bread and wine, we are in the most real sense taking the divine light into us. Second, the Eucharist is a reflection of Christ's death on the cross and we have seen how Aquinas thinks that the cross represents the greatest teaching of Christ about who God is and about our final end. The cross represents the great sacrifice of obedience, an obedience which itself leads to further light, and so when we participate in this sacrifice we too become capable of illumining others because of our own participation. Indeed, one wonders if the whole metaphysical concept of participation that has appeared throughout this book can be found in its highest form in our participation in the Eucharistic celebration in which we fully participate in Christ's life, death, and resurrection and thus most fully participate in his light.

There can be no more fitting way to end this book than with that final thought about the connection between Christ, the Eucharist, and the light. Holy teaching, as we argued at the very beginning, is an illuminating enterprise that gives us knowledge of our final end and of the means to achieve that end. That teaching reaches its earthly apotheosis in the life, death, and resurrection of Christ, a life that we participate in through the gift of the material and spiritual reality found in the Eucharist, which makes our final end both manifest and possible. Aquinas argues that we will receive perfect illumination at Christ's second coming,[99] and while he was discussing this with regard to the second coming that coincides with the final judgment, we can extend this idea to the coming of Christ every time the Mass is celebrated. The eschatological breakthrough that happens each time the host is elevated means that Christ is not just the light at the center of the church[100] in some attenuated way, but rather that the elevation of the body of Christ on the cross and in the Mass brings light in its most essential character into our lives. When we partake of the body of Christ through the Eucharist, we participate in that light, so that "In his light, we shall see light" (Ps. 4:7).

97. ST 78.8 sc.

98. *In I Cor.* 11.5 §648.

99. ST III 46.9 ad 3: "And since the perfect illumination will come about at Christ's second coming..."

100. *In Heb.* 2.3 §132: "He says, in the midst, because just as a pillar in the midst of a house supports it and a lamp in the midst of a house illumines and the heart in the midst of the body vivifies, so Christ is in the middle of the Church."

Bibliography

Primary Texts and Critical Editions

The Leonine Edition: *Sancti Thomae Aquinatis doctoris angelici Opera omnia iussa Leonis XIII P.M. edita*, cura et studio fratrum ordinis praedicatorum, Rome, 1882–present.

Commentaria in octo libros Physicorum Aristotelis. t.II. Rome, 1884.

Expositio libri Boetii De ebdomadibus. Edited by L.-J. Bataillon and C. A. Grassi. t.L. Rome-Paris: Commissio Leonina – Les Éditions du Cerf, 1992, 267–82.

Expositio libri Posteriorum. Edited by R.-A. Gauthier. t.I*–2. Rome-Paris: Commissio Leonina – Librairie Philosophique J. Vrin, 1989.

Expositio super Iob ad litteram. Edited by A. Dondaine. t. XXVI. Rome: 1965.

In libros Aristotelis De caelo et mundo expositio. t.III. Rome, 1886, 1–257.

Liber Contra errores Graecorum ad preces papae Urbani editus, Edited by H.F. Dondaine. t.XL, Opuscula, vol. I. Rome, 1969, A.69–A.105.

Quaestiones de quolibet. Edited by R.-A. Gauthier. t.XXV.1–2. Rome-Paris: Commissio Leonina – Les Éditions du Cerf, 1996.

Quaestiones disputatae De veritate. Edited by A. Dondaine. t. XXII.1–3. Rome: 1972–76.

Sentencia libri De anima. Edited by R.-A. Gauthier. t. XLV/1. Rome, 1984.

Sentencia libri De sensu et sensato cuius secundus tractatus est De memoria et reminiscencia. Edited by R.-A. Gauthier. t.XLV-2. Rome-Paris: Commissio Leonina – Librairie Philosophique J. Vrin, 1985.

Summa contra Gentiles. t. XIII-XV. Rome, 1918–30.

Summa Theologiae. t. IV-XII. Rome, 1888–1906.

Super Boetium De Trinitate. Edited by P.-M. J. Gils. t.L. Rome-Paris: Commissio Leonina – Cerf, 1992, 75–171.

Parma:

Sancti Thomae Aquinatis Doctoris angelici ordinis predicatorum Opera omnia ad fidem optimarum editionum accurate recognita, Parmae typis Petri Fiaccadori. New York: Musurgia, 1948–50.

In psalmos Davidis expositio. t.14, 148–312

Marietti:

Expositio et Lectura super Epistolas Pauli Apostoli. Edited by R. Cai. 2 vols., Taurini: Marietti, 1953.

In duodecim libros Metaphysicorum Aristotelis exposition. Edited by M. R. Cathala and R.M. Spiazzi. Taurini: Marietti, 1964.

In librum beati Dionysii De divinis nominibus exposition. Edited by C. Pera. Taurini: Marietti, 1950.

Lectura super Ioannem. Edited by R. Cai. Taurini: Marietti, 1952.

Opuscula Theologica. Edited by Raymundi Spiazzi. Vol. II. Taurini: Marietti: 1954.

Quaestiones disputatae. Edited by R. M Spiazzi and P. Bazzi. Taurini: Marietti, 1953.

Rigans Montes de superioribus and Hic est liber mandatorum Dei, in vol. 1 *Opuscula theologica*. Edited by R. A. Verardo and R. M. Spiazzi. Taurini: Marietti, 1954.

Mandonnet-Moos:

Scriptum super libros Sententiarum magistri Petri Lombardi episcopi Parisiensis, 4 vols. Edited by P. Mandonnet (vols. 1–2) and M. F. Moos (vols. 3–4). Paris: P. Lethielleux, 1929–47.

Others:

Lectura Romana in Primum Sententiarum Petri Lombardi. Edited by John F. Boyle and Leonard E. Boyle. Toronto: Pontifical Institute of Mediaeval Studies, 2006.

Super librum De causis expositio, ed. H. D. Saffrey. Textus Philosophici Friburgenses, 4/5. Fribourg, Suisse – Louvain: Societé Philosophique – Éditions de Nauwelaerts, 1954.

Corpus Thomisticum database:

www.corpusthomisticum.org. Fundación Tomás de Aquino (for access to entire corpus electronically; accessed September 30, 2013).

Secondary Texts and Translations

Alexander of Aphrodisias. *Alexander of Aphrodisias: On Aristotle's "On Sense Perception."* Translated by Alan Towey. Ithaca, NY: Cornell University Press, 2000.

Allers, Rudolph. "St. Augustine's Doctrine on Illumination," *Franciscan Studies* 12 (1952): 27–46.

Anselm. *Opera Omnia*. Edited by F. S. Schmitt. Edinburgh: Thomas Nelson & Sons, 1946.

Aristotle. *The Complete Works of Aristotle: The Revised Oxford Translation*. Edited by Jonathan Barnes. Vol. 2. 2 vols. Princeton: Princeton University Press, 1984.

———. *The Complete Works of Aristotle: The Revised Oxford Translation*. Edited by Jonathan Barnes. Vol. 1. 2 vols. Princeton: Princeton University Press, 1995.

Augustine. *Exposition of the Psalms 73-98*. Edited by John E. Rotelle. Translated by Maria Bolding. The Works of St. Augustine: A Translation for the 21st Century 18 of Part III. New York: New City Press, 2002.

———. *Homilies on the Gospel of John 1-40*. Edited by Boniface Ramsey. Translated by Edmund Hill. The Works of St. Augustine: A Translation for the 21st Century 12 of Part III. New York: New City Press, 2009.

———. *On Genesis: A Refutation of the Manichees; Unfinished Literal Commentary on Genesis; The Literal Meaning of Genesis*. Edited by John E. Rotelle. Translated by Edmund Hill. The Works of St. Augustine: A Translation for the 21st Century. Hyde Park, NY: New City Press, 2002.

Bernard of Clairvaux and Amadeus of Lausanne. *Magnificat: Homilies in Praise of the Blessed Virgin Mary*. Translated by Marie-Bernard Saïd and Grace Perigo. Kalamazoo, MI: Cistercian, 1979.

Boland, Vivian. *Ideas in God According to Saint Thomas Aquinas: Sources and Synthesis*. Studies in the History of Christian Thought 69. Leiden; New York: E. J. Brill, 1996.

———. "Truth, Knowledge and Communication: Thomas Aquinas on the Mystery of Teaching," *Studies in Christian Ethics* 19, no. 3 (2006): 287–304.

Bourke, Vernon J. "Is Thomas Aquinas a Natural Law Ethicist?" *The Monist* 58, no. 1 (1974): 52–66.

Boyle, John F. "St. Thomas Aquinas and Sacred Scripture," *Pro Ecclesia* 4, no. 1 (1995): 92–104.

Brown, Peter Robert Lamont. *Augustine of Hippo: A Biography, A New Edition with an Epilogue*. Berkeley: University of California Press, 2000.

Burrell, David B. *Aquinas: God and Action*. Scranton, PA: University of Scranton Press, 2008.

Cessario, Romanus. *A Short History of Thomism*. Washington, DC: Catholic University of America Press, 2005.

———. "A Thomist Interpretation of Faith: The Gifts of Understanding and Knowledge: 'The One Who Does What Is True Comes to the Light' (John 3,24)." In *Novitas et Veritas Vitae*, 67–102. Fribourg, Suisse: Éditions Universitaires, 1991.

Chenu, Marie-Dominique. *Aquinas and His Role in Theology*. Translated by Paul J. Philibert, O.P. Collegeville, MN: Liturgical Press, 2002.

———. *Toward Understanding Saint Thomas*. Translated by A.-M. Landry and D. Hughes. Chicago: Regnery, 1964.

Collins, James Daniel. *The Thomistic Philosophy of the Angels*. Washington, DC: Catholic University of America Press, 1947.

Corrigan, Kevin. "Light and Metaphor in Plotinus and St. Thomas Aquinas," *Thomist* 57 (1993): 187–99.

Cuddeback, Matthew. "Light and Form in St. Thomas Aquinas's Metaphysics of the Knower." Ph.D. dissertation, Catholic University of America, 1998.

———. "Thomas Aquinas on Divine Illumination and the Authority of the First Truth," *Nova et Vetera (English Edition)* 7 (2009): 579–602.

Davies, Brian. "Aquinas and the Academic Life," *New Blackfriars* 83, no. 977–78 (2002): 336–46.

——. *The Thought of Thomas Aquinas*. Oxford: Oxford University Press, 1992.

Dewan, Lawrence. *Wisdom, Law, and Virtue: Essays in Thomistic Ethics*. New York: Fordham University Press, 2008.

DeYoung, Rebecca Konyndyk, Colleen McCluskey, and Christina Van Dyke. *Aquinas's Ethics: Metaphysical Foundations, Moral Theory, and Theological Context*. Notre Dame: University of Notre Dame Press, 2009.

Doherty, Alexander J. "Aquinas on Scriptural Metaphor and Allegory," *American Catholic Philosophical Association Proceedings* 76 (2002): 183–92.

Doherty, Kevin F. "St. Thomas and the Pseudo-Dionysian Symbol of Light," *The New Scholasticism* 34, no. 2 (1960): 170–89.

Dondaine, Antoine. *Liber de Duobus Principiis: Un Traité Néo-manichéen du 13e Siècle*. Rome: Istituto Storico Domenicano, 1939.

Dougherty, M. V. "Aquinas on the Self-Evidence of the Articles of Faith," *Heythrop Journal* 46, no. 2 (2005): 167–80.

Eco, Umberto. *The Aesthetics of Thomas Aquinas*. Cambridge, MA: Harvard University Press, 1988.

Emery, O.P., Gilles. *The Trinitarian Theology of Saint Thomas Aquinas*. Translated by Francesca Aran Murphy. Oxford and New York: Oxford University Press, 2007.

——. *Trinity in Aquinas*. Translated by Matthew Levering. Ann Arbor, MI: Sapientia Press of Ave Maria University, 2006.

——. *Trinity, Church, and the Human Person: Thomistic Essays*. Naples, FL: Sapientia Press of Ave Maria University, 2007.

Feser, Edward. *Aquinas: A Beginner's Guide*. Oxford: Oneworld, 2009.

French, Roger, and Andrew Cunningham. *Before Science: The Invention of the Friars' Natural Philosophy*. Aldershot, UK: Scolar, 1996.

Führer, Markus L. "Albertus Magnus' Theory of Divine Illumination." In *Albertus Magnus zum Gedenken nach 800 Jahren: Neue Zugänge, Aspekte und Perspektiven*, edited by W. Senner, O.P., H. Anzulewicz, M. Burger, R. Meyer, P. Sicouly, O.P., M. Nauert, J. Söder, and K.-B. Springer, 141–55. Berlin: Akademie Verlag, 2001.

———. "Henry of Ghent on Divine Illumination," *Bochumer Philosophisches Jahrbuch für Antike und Mittelalter* 3 (1998): 69–85.

Gasper, Giles E. M. "Towards a Theology of Light in the Twelfth-Century Renaissance." In *Outside Archeology: Material Culture and Poetic Imagination*, edited by Christine Finn and Martin Henig, 21–27. BAR International Series 999. Oxford: Archeopress, 2001.

Gilson, Étienne. "Pourquoi Saint Thomas a critiqué Saint Augustin," *Archives d'Histoire Doctrinale et Littéraire du Moyen Âge* 1 (1926–27): 5–127.

———. *The Christian Philosophy of St. Thomas Aquinas*. Translated by L. K. Shook, C.S.B. Notre Dame: University of Notre Dame Press, 1994.

Gilson, Simon A. *Medieval Optics and Theories of Light in the Works of Dante*. Lewiston, NY: Edwin Mellen, 2000.

Guillet, J. "La Lumière Intellectuelle d'après S. Thomas," *Archives d'Histoire Doctrinale et Littéraire du Moyen Âge* 2 (1927): 79–88.

Hankey, Wayne J. "'Participatio Divini Luminis,'" *Dionysius* 22 (2004): 149–78.

Hedwig, Klaus. *Sphaera Lucis: Studien zur Intelligibilität des Seienden im Kontext der Mittelalterlichen Lichtspekulation*. Beiträge zur Geschichte der Philosophie und Theologie des Mittelalters N.F., Bd. 18. Münster: Aschendorff, 1980.

Higgins, James. "St Thomas's Pedagogy—Ignored, Rediscovered, and Applied," *Heythrop Journal: A Bimonthly Review of Philosophy and Theology* 50, no. 4 (2009): 603–19.

Hittinger, Russell. *The First Grace: Rediscovering the Natural Law in a Post-Christian World*. Wilmington, DE: ISI Books, 2003.

Honecker, Martin. "Der Lichtbegriff in der Abstraktionslehre des Thomas von Aquin," *Philosophisches Jahrbuch* 48 (1935): 268–88.

Hoye, William J. *Actualitas Omnium Actuum: Man's Beatific Vision of God as Apprehended by Thomas Aquinas*. Monographien zur Philosophischen Forschung Bd. 116. Meisenheim (am Glan): Hain, 1975.

Hundersmarck, Lawrence F. "Thomas Aquinas on Beatitude." In *Imagining Heaven in the Middle Ages: A Book of Essays*, 165–83. New York: Garland, 2000.

Jenkins, John I. *Knowledge and Faith in Thomas Aquinas*. Cambridge and New York: Cambridge University Press, 1997.

Jordan, Mark D. *Rewritten Theology: Aquinas After His Readers*. Challenges in Contemporary Theology. Malden, MA and Oxford: Blackwell, 2006.

——. "The Order of Lights: Aquinas on Immateriality as Hierarchy." In *Immateriality*, edited by George F. McLean, 52:112–20. Proceedings of the American Catholic Philosophical Association. Washington, DC: American Catholic Philosophical Association, 1978.

Justin Martyr. *First Apology*. Edited by Alexander Roberts, James Donaldson, and A. Cleveland Coxe. Ante-Nicene Fathers 1. Peabody, MA: Hendrickson, 1994.

Kainz, Howard P. *Active and Passive Potency in Thomistic Angelology*. The Hague: Martinus Nijhoff, 1972.

——. *Natural Law: An Introduction and Re-Examination*. Chicago: Open Court, 2004.

Keck, David. *Angels and Angelology in the Middle Ages*. New York: Oxford University Press, 1998.

Kerr, Fergus. *After Aquinas: Versions of Thomism*. Malden, MA: Blackwell, 2002.

——, ed. *Contemplating Aquinas: On the Varieties of Interpretation*. London: SCM, 2003.

Kieninger, Josef. *Das Sein als Licht in den Schriften des Hl. Thomas von Aquin*. Vatican City: Libreria Editrice Vaticano, 1992.

Klubertanz, George Peter. *St. Thomas Aquinas on Analogy*. Chicago: Loyola University Press, 1960.

Kretzmann, Norman, and Eleonore Stump, eds. *The Cambridge Companion to Aquinas*. Cambridge and New York: Cambridge University Press, 1993.

Lambert, Malcolm. *The Cathars*. Oxford and Malden, MA: Blackwell, 1998.

Lindberg, David C. *Theories of Vision from al-Kindi to Kepler*. Chicago: University of Chicago Press, 1981.

Loring, William D. "Altar and Throne: A Study of Eucharistic Theology and the Vision of God in Saint Thomas Aquinas," *Anglican Theological Review* 52, no. 2 (1970): 91–102.

MacDonald, Scott, and Eleonore Stump, eds. *Aquinas' Moral Theory: Essays in Honor of Norman Kretzmann*. Ithaca, NY: Cornell University Press, 1999.

MacKenzie, Iain M. *The Obscurism of Light: A Theological Study into the Nature of Light*. Norwich, UK: Canterbury, 1996.

Mansini, Guy. "Are the Principles of *sacra doctrina per se nota*?" *The Thomist* 74, no. 3 (2010): 407–35.

Maritain, Jacques. *The Sin of the Angel: An Essay on a Re-Interpretation of Some Thomistic Positions*. Westminster, MD: Newman, 1959.

Marrone, Steven P. "Certitude or Knowledge of God? Thirteenth-Century Augustinians and the Doctrine of Divine Illumination." In *Medieval Philosophy and Modern Times*, edited by Ghita Holmström-Hintikka, 145–60. Dordt, Neth.: Springer Science & Business Media, 2000.

———. *The Light of Thy Countenance: Science and Knowledge of God in the Thirteenth Century; Volume One, A Doctrine of Divine Illumination*. Leiden and Boston: Brill, 2001.

———. *The Light of Thy Countenance: Science and Knowledge of God in the Thirteenth Century; Volume Two, God at the Core of Cognition*. Leiden and Boston: Brill, 2001.

Marshall, Bruce. "Christ the End of Analogy." In *The Analogy of Being: Invention of the Antichrist or the Wisdom of God?*, 280–313. Grand Rapids: Eerdmans, 2011.

Matthews, Gareth B. "Knowledge and Illumination." In *Cambridge Companion to Augustine*, 171–85. New York: Cambridge University Press, 2001.

McEvoy, James. "The Metaphysics of Light in the Middle Ages," *Philosophical Studies* 26 (1979): 126–45.

McInerny, Ralph M. *Aquinas and Analogy*. Washington, DC: Catholic University of America Press, 1996.

———. *Aquinas on Human Action: A Theory of Practice*. Washington, DC: Catholic University of America Press, 1992.

———. *Ethica Thomistica: The Moral Philosophy of Thomas Aquinas*. Washington, DC: Catholic University of America Press, 1982.

———. "Metaphor and Analogy." In *Inquiries into Medieval Philosophy: A Collection in Honor of Francis P. Clarke*, edited by James F Ross, 75–96. Westport, CT: Greenwood, 1971.

———. *The Logic of Analogy: An Interpretation of St. Thomas*. The Hague: Martinus Nijhoff, 1961.

Meehan, Francis. "Lux in Spiritualibus According to St. Thomas Aquinas." In *Philosophical Studies in Honor of the Very Reverend Ignatius Smith, O.P.*, 127–64. Westminster, MD: Newman, 1952.

Migne, Jacques-Paul. *Patrologia Latina*. 217 vols. Paris, 1844.

Milbank, John, and Catherine Pickstock. *Truth in Aquinas*. Radical Orthodoxy Series. London and New York: Routledge, 2001.

Montano, Edward J. *The Sin of the Angels: Some Aspects of the Teaching of St. Thomas*. Washington, DC: Catholic University of America Press, 1955.

Nash, Ronald H. *The Light of the Mind: St. Augustine's Theory of Knowledge*. Lima, OH: Academic Renewal, 2003.

Noone, Timothy. "Divine Illumination." In *The Cambridge History of Medieval Philosophy*, I:369–83. Cambridge and New York: Cambridge University Press, 2010.

O'Brien, Thomas C. "'Sacra Doctrina' Revisited: The Context of Medieval Education," *Thomist: A Speculative Quarterly Review* 41 (1977): 475–509.

O'Collins, S.J., Gerald, and Mary Ann Meyers, eds. *Light from Light: Scientists and Theologians in Dialogue*. Eerdmans, 2012.

O'Meara, Thomas F. *Thomas Aquinas, Theologian*. Notre Dame: University of Notre Dame Press, 1997.

O'Rourke, Fran. *Pseudo-Dionysius and the Metaphysics of Aquinas*. Studien und Texte zur Geistesgeschichte des Mittelalters Bd. 32. Leiden and New York: E. J. Brill, 1992.

Owens, Joseph. "Aquinas—'Darkness of Ignorance' in the Most Refined Notion of God." In *Bonaventure and Aquinas: Enduring Philosophers*, edited by Robert Shahan and Francis Kovach, 69–86. Norman: University of Oklahoma Press, 1976.

Park, David Allen. *The Fire Within the Eye: A Historical Essay on the Nature and Meaning of Light*. Princeton: Princeton University Press, 1997.

Pasnau, Robert. "Henry of Ghent and the Twilight of Divine Illumination," *Review of Metaphysics* 49, no. 1 (1995): 49–75.

———. *Theories of Cognition in the Later Middle Ages*. Cambridge and New York: Cambridge University Press, 1997.

———. *Thomas Aquinas on Human Nature: A Philosophical Study of Summa Theologiae 1a, 75-89*. New York: Cambridge University Press, 2002.

Pasnau, Robert, and Christopher John Shields. *The Philosophy of Aquinas*. Boulder, CO: Westview, 2004.

Pegis, A.C. "In Umbria Intelligentiae," *New Scholasticism* 14 (1940): 146–80.

Pieper, Josef. *Guide to Thomas Aquinas*. Notre Dame: University of Notre Dame Press, 1987.

——. *The Silence of St. Thomas: Three Essays*. South Bend, IN: St. Augustine's Press, 1999.

——. *Unaustrinkbares Licht: Das negative Element in der Weltansicht Thomas von Aquin*. Munich: Kösel-Verlag, 1963.

Pinckaers, O.P., Servais. *The Pinckaers Reader: Renewing Thomistic Moral Theology*. Edited by John Berkman and Craig Steven Titus. Translated by Mary Thomas Noble, O.P., Craig Steven Titus, Michael S. Sherwin, O.P., and Hugh Connolly. Washington, DC: Catholic University of America Press, 2005.

——. *The Sources of Christian Ethics*. Translated by Mary Thomas Noble, O.P. Washington, DC: Catholic University of America Press, 1995.

Plato. *Complete Works*. Edited by John M. Cooper and D. S. Hutchinson. Indianapolis: Hackett, 1997.

Pope, Stephen J., ed. *The Ethics of Aquinas*. Moral Traditions Series. Washington, DC: Georgetown University Press, 2002.

Porter, Jean. "Desire for God: Ground of the Moral Life in Aquinas," *Theological Studies* 47, no. 1 (1986): 48–68.

Poupin, Roland. *La Papauté, les Cathares et Thomas d'Aquin*. Portet-sur-Garonne: Loubatières, 2000.

Pseudo-Dionysius. *Pseudo-Dionysius: The Complete Works*. Translated by Colm Luibheid. The Classics of Western Spirituality. New York: Paulist, 1987.

Quinn, Patrick. "Aquinas's Views on Teaching," *New Blackfriars* 82, no. 961 (2001): 108–20.

Rahner, Karl. *Spirit in the World*. New York: Herder & Herder, 1968.

Raizman-Kedar, Yael. "Plotinus's Conception of Unity and Multiplicity as the Root to the Medieval Distinction Between *Lux* and *Lumen*," *Studies in History & Philosophy of Science Part A* 37, no. 3 (2006): 379–97.

Robb, James H. "St. Thomas on Intelligible Light." In *Conflict and Community: New Studies in Thomistic Thought*, edited by Michael B. Lukens, 35–49. New York: Peter Lang, 1992.

Robbins, Frank Egleston. *The Hexaemeral Literature: A Study of the Greek and Latin Commentaries on Genesis*. Chicago: University of Chicago Press, 1912.

Rocca, Gregory P. *Speaking the Incomprehensible God: Thomas Aquinas on the Interplay of Positive and Negative Theology*. Washington, DC: Catholic University of America Press, 2004.

Schmidt, James. *What Is Enlightenment?: Eighteenth-Century Answers and Twentieth-Century Questions*. Philosophical Traditions 7. Berkeley: University of California Press, 1996.

Schmidt, Robert William. *The Domain of Logic According to Saint Thomas Aquinas*. The Hague: Martinus Nijhoff, 1966.

Schumacher, Lydia. *Divine Illumination: The History and Future of Augustine's Theory of Knowledge*. Malden, MA: Wiley-Blackwell, 2011.

Soskice, Janet Martin. *Metaphor and Religious Language*. Oxford: Clarendon, 2002.

Stump, Eleonore. *Aquinas*. Arguments of the Philosophers. London and New York: Routledge, 2003.

Synave, Paul. *Prophecy and Inspiration: A Commentary on the Summa Theologica II-II, Questions 171-178*. New York: Desclée, 1961.

Tachau, Katherine H. *Vision and Certitude in the Age of Ockham: Optics, Epistemology, and the Foundations of Semantics, 1250–1345*. Studien und Texte zur Geistesgeschichte des Mittelalters Bd. 22. Leiden and New York: E. J. Brill, 1988.

Thomas Aquinas. *A Commentary on Aristotle's De Anima*. Translated by Robert Pasnau. Yale Library of Medieval Philosophy. New Haven: Yale University Press, 1999.

———. "Against the Errors of the Greeks." In *Ending the Byzantine Greek Schism*, translated by James Likoudis. New Rochelle, NY: Catholics United for the Faith, 1992.

———. *Commentaries on Aristotle's "On Sense and What Is Sensed" and "On Memory and Recollection."* Translated by E. M. Macierowski and Kevin White. Thomas Aquinas in Translation. Washington, DC: Catholic University of America Press, 2005.

———. *Commentaries on St. Paul's Epistles to Timothy, Titus, and Philemon*. Translated by Chrysostom Baer. South Bend, IN: St. Augustine's Press, 2007.

———. *Commentary on Aristotle's Physics*. Translated by Richard J. Blackwell. New Haven: Yale University Press, 1963.

———. *Commentary on Colossians*. Translated by Fabian R. Larcher and Daniel A. Keating. Naples, FL: Sapientia, 2006.

———. *Commentary on Saint Paul's Epistle to the Ephesians*. Translated by Matthew Lamb. Aquinas Scripture Series 2. Albany, NY: Magi Books, 1966.

———. *Commentary on Saint Paul's Epistle to the Galatians*. Translated by Fabian R. Larcher. Aquinas Scripture Series 1. Albany, NY: Magi Books, 1966.

———. *Commentary on Saint Paul's First Letter to the Thessalonians and the Letter to the Philippians*. Translated by Fabian R. Larcher. Aquinas Scripture Series 3. Albany, NY: Magi Books, 1969.

———. *Commentary on the Book of Causes*. Translated by Vincent A. Guagliardo, Charles R. Hess, and Richard C. Taylor. Washington, DC: Catholic University of America Press, 1996.

———. *Commentary on the Epistle to the Hebrews*. Translated by Chrysostom Baer. South Bend, IN: St. Augustine's Press, 2006.

———. *Commentary on the Gospel of John*. Edited by Daniel A. Keating and Matthew Levering. Translated by James A. Weisheipl and Fabian R. Larcher. 3 vols. Washington, DC: Catholic University of America Press, 2010.

———. *Commentary on the Letter of Saint Paul to the Hebrews*. Edited by J. Mortenson and E. Alarcón. Translated by Fabian R. Larcher. Latin/English Edition of the Works of Thomas Aquinas 41. Lander, WY: The Aquinas Institute for the Study of Sacred Doctrine, 2012.

———. *Commentary on the Letter of Saint Paul to the Romans*. Edited by J. Mortenson and E. Alarcón. Translated by Fabian R. Larcher. Latin/English Edition of the Works of Thomas Aquinas 37. Lander, WY: The Aquinas Institute for the Study of Sacred Doctrine, 2012.

———. *Commentary on the Letters of Saint Paul to the Corinthians*. Edited by J. Mortenson and E. Alarcón. Translated by Fabian R. Larcher, B. Mortensen, and D. Keating. Latin/English Edition of the Works of Thomas Aquinas 38. Lander, WY: The Aquinas Institute for the Study of Sacred Doctrine, 2012.

———. *Commentary on the Letters of Saint Paul to the Galatians and Ephesians*. Edited by J. Mortenson and E. Alarcón. Translated by Fabian R. Larcher and Matthew Lamb. Latin/English Edition of the Works of Thomas Aquinas 39. Lander, WY: The Aquinas Institute for the Study of Sacred Doctrine, 2012.

———. *Commentary on the Letters of Saint Paul to the Philippians, Colossians, Thessalonians, Timothy, Titus, and Philemon*. Edited by J. Mortenson and E. Alarcón. Translated by Fabian R. Larcher. Latin/English Edition of the Works of Thomas Aquinas 40. Lander, WY: The Aquinas Institute for the Study of Sacred Doctrine, 2012.

———. *Exposition of Aristotle's Treatise On the Heavens*. Translated by Fabian R. Larcher. Columbus, OH: College of St. Mary of the Springs, 1963.

———. *Exposition on the Divine Names of Dionysius*. Translated by Hannes Jarka-Sellers. Thomas Aquinas in Translation. Washington, DC: Catholic University of America Press, forthcoming.

———. *Faith, Reason and Theology: Questions I-IV of His Commentary on the De Trinitate of Boethius*. Translated by Armand A. Maurer. Medieval Sources in Translation 32. Toronto: Pontifical Institute of Mediaeval Studies, 1987.

———. *Lectura Romana in Primum Sententiarum Petri Lombardi*. Edited by John F. Boyle and Leonard E. Boyle. Toronto: Pontifical Institute of Mediaeval Studies, 2006.

———. *On Evil*. Translated by Richard J. Regan. Oxford and New York: Oxford University Press, 2003.

———. *On Love and Charity: Readings from the Commentary on the Sentences of Peter Lombard*. Translated by Peter Kwasniewski, Thomas Bolin, and Joseph Bolin. Thomas Aquinas in Translation. Washington, DC: Catholic University of America Press, 2008.

———. *On the Power of God*. Translated by Laurence Shapcote and English Dominican Fathers. Eugene, OR: Wipf & Stock, 2004.

———. *On the Unity of the Intellect Against the Averroists*. Translated by Beatrice H. Zedler. Mediaeval Philosophical Texts in Translation 19. Milwaukee: Marquette University Press, 1968.

———. *Selected Writings*. Translated by Ralph M. McInerny. London and New York: Penguin, 1998.

———. *Summa Contra Gentiles*. Translated by James F. Anderson, Vernon J. Bourke, Charles J. O'Neil, and Anton C. Pegis. 5 vols. Notre Dame: University of Notre Dame Press, 1975.

———. *Summa Theologiae*. Edited by Thomas Gilby. 60 vols. Blackfriars ed. New York: McGraw-Hill, 1964.

———. *Summa Theologica*. Translated by English Dominican Fathers. 5 vols. Complete English ed. Westminster, MD: Christian Classics, 1981.

———. *The Academic Sermons*. Translated by Mark-Robin Hoogland. The Fathers of the Church: Mediaeval Continuation. Washington, DC: Catholic University of America Press, 2010.

———. *The Aquinas Catechism: A Simple Explanation of the Catholic Faith by the Church's Greatest Theologian*. Translated by Laurence Shapcote. Manchester, NH: Sophia Institute, 2000.

———. *The Literal Exposition on Job: A Scriptural Commentary Concerning Providence*. Translated by Martin D. Yaffe and Anthony Damico. Classics in Religious Studies 7. Atlanta: Scholars, 1989.

———. *The Sermon-Conferences of St. Thomas Aquinas on the Apostles' Creed*. Translated by Nicholas Ayo. Notre Dame: University of Notre Dame Press, 1988.

———. *The Treatise on Human Nature: Summa Theologiae 1a, 75–89*. Translated by Robert Pasnau. Indianapolis: Hackett, 2002.

———. *The Treatise on the Divine Nature: Summa Theologiae I, 1–13*. Translated by Brian J. Shanley. Indianapolis: Hackett, 2006.

———. *Truth*. Translated by Robert Mulligan. 3 vols. Eugene, OR: Wipf & Stock, 2008.

Thomas Aquinas, and Albertus Magnus. *Albert & Thomas: Selected Writings*. Translated by Simon Tugwell. The Classics of Western Spirituality. New York: Paulist, 1988.

Thomas Aquinas, and Aristotle. *Commentary on Aristotle's Posterior Analytics*. Translated by Richard Berquist. Notre Dame, IN: Dumb Ox Books, 2007.

———. *Commentary on the Metaphysics of Aristotle*. Translated by John Patrick Rowan. 2 vols. Chicago: Regnery, 1961.

———. *Commentary on the Nicomachean Ethics*. Translated by C. I. Litzinger. Chicago: Regnery, 1964.

Thomas Aquinas, and Boethius. *An Exposition of the On the Hebdomads of Boethius*. Translated by Janice L. Schultz and Edward A. Synan. Thomas Aquinas in Translation. Washington, DC: Catholic University of America Press, 2001.

Torrell, O.P., Jean-Pierre. *Aquinas's Summa: Background, Structure, and Reception.* Translated by Benedict M. Guevin, O.S.B. Washington, DC: Catholic University of America Press, 2005.

———. *Saint Thomas Aquinas. Volume 1, The Person and His Work.* Translated by Robert Royal. Revised ed. Washington, DC: Catholic University of America Press, 2005.

———. *Saint Thomas Aquinas. Volume 2, Spiritual Master.* Translated by Robert Royal. Washington, DC: Catholic University of America Press, 2003.

Tugwell, Simon. *Albert & Thomas: Selected Writings.* The Classics of Western Spirituality. New York: Paulist, 1988.

Turner, Denys. *The Darkness of God: Negativity in Western Christian Mysticism.* Cambridge: Cambridge University Press, 1998.

Van Nieuwenhove, Rik, and Joseph Peter Wawrykow, eds. *The Theology of Thomas Aquinas.* Notre Dame: University of Notre Dame Press, 2005.

Vasiliu, Anca. *Du Diaphane: Image, Milieu, Lumière dans la Pensée Antique et Médiévale.* Études de Philosophie Médiévale 76. Paris: J. Vrin, 1997.

Velde, Rudi A. te. *Aquinas on God: The "Divine Science" of the Summa Theologiae.* Ashgate Studies in the History of Philosophical Theology. Aldershot, UK and Burlington, VT: Ashgate, 2006.

———. *Participation and Substantiality in Thomas Aquinas.* Studien und Texte zur Geistesgeschichte des Mittelalters Bd. 46. Leiden and New York: E. J. Brill, 1995.

Waddell, Michael M. "Aquinas on the Light of Glory," *Tópicos. Revista de Filosofía* no. 41 (July 2011): 105–32.

Wakefield, Walter L., and Austin P. Evans. *Heresies of the High Middle Ages: Selected Sources*. New York: Columbia University Press, 1991.

Weinandy, Thomas G., Daniel A. Keating, and John Yocum. *Aquinas on Doctrine: A Critical Introduction*. London and New York: T. & T. Clark International, 2004.

———. *Aquinas on Scripture: An Introduction to His Biblical Commentaries*. London and New York: T. & T. Clark International, 2005.

Weisheipl, James A. *Friar Thomas D'Aquino: His Life, Thought, and Work*. Garden City, NY: Doubleday, 1974.

———. *The Development of Physical Theory in the Middle Ages*. New York: Sheed & Ward, 1959.

Weisheipl, James A., and William E. Carroll. *Nature and Motion in the Middle Ages*. Studies in Philosophy and the History of Philosophy 11. Washington, DC: Catholic University of America Press, 1985.

White, Kevin. "Aquinas on Oral Teaching," *Thomist: A Speculative Quarterly Review* 71, no. 4 (2007): 505–28.

White, Victor. *Holy Teaching: The Idea of Theology According to St Thomas Aquinas*. London: Blackfriars, 1958.

Williams, A. N. "Is Aquinas a Foundationalist?" *New Blackfriars* 91, no. 1031 (2010): 20–45.

Wippel, John F. *Metaphysical Themes in Thomas Aquinas II*. Studies in Philosophy and the History of Philosophy 47. Washington, DC: Catholic University of America Press, 2007.

———. *Thomas Aquinas on the Divine Ideas*. Etienne Gilson Series 16. Toronto: Pontifical Institute of Mediaeval Studies, 1993.

Zajonc, Arthur. *Catching the Light: The Entwined History of Light and Mind*. New York: Oxford University Press, 1995.

Index